D1631222

ST. FRANCIS OF ASSISI
ESSAYS IN COMMEMORATION
1226—1926

vomū ıncı q̄ ur cēris
cri̅ ꝰ francıſco dıcıt
r̄ı mo ꝑuıt

THE SOLITUDE OF MOUNT ALVERNIA

By ANTONIO VIVARINI

In the collection of Viscount Lascelles

THE SOLITUDE OF MOUNT ALVERNIA
By Antonio Vivarini
In the collection of Viscount Lascelles

ST. Francis of Assisi: 1226–1926: Essays in Commemoration With a Preface by Professor Paul Sabatier ❦ ❦ ❦

WITH ELEVEN PLATES
and Frontispiece in Colour

LONDON
UNIVERSITY OF LONDON PRESS, LTD.
10 & 11 WARWICK LANE, E.C.4
1926

THIS VOLUME IS EDITED BY
WALTER SETON, M.A., D.LIT.
HON. SECRETARY OF THE BRITISH
SOCIETY OF FRANCISCAN STUDIES

23118

Printed in Great Britain for the UNIVERSITY OF LONDON PRESS, LTD.,
by HAZELL, WATSON AND VINEY LD., London and Aylesbury.

PRÉFACE

THOMAS D'ECCLESTON raconte[1] que la province franciscaine d'Angleterre était arrivée vers le milieu du XIIIᵉ
siècle à une telle perfection que lorsque Jean de Parme
s'y rendit, comme ministre général, il répétait souvent :
" Plût à Dieu qu'une pareille province fût placée au
centre du monde pour servir de modèle à toutes les
autres ! "

Le célèbre général, dont l'élection avait été pour
les zélateurs de la Règle comme l'avènement d'un
nouveau saint François, pourrait, s'il revenait sur la
terre, être plein du même enthousiasme et répéter les
mêmes paroles, en cette année du sept-centième anniversaire de la mort de saint François.

On est en effet tenté de se demander si du sol
britannique émane pour ceux qui y habitent une sorte
de prédisposition à comprendre mieux que les autres
peuples la pensée et la doctrine du Poverello.   Et ce
fait ne se vérifie pas seulement dans les milieux qui
sont franciscains de profession et se rattachent à l'une
des familles du premier ordre, à l'une ou l'autre des
institutions qui remontent à sainte Claire ou enfin à
une congrégation de Tertiaires, mais on peut le constater, à des degrés très divers naturellement, dans les
diverses régions britanniques et dans des milieux sociaux

[1] *De adventu Minorum in Angliam*, cap. xv, éd. A. G. Little (Paris, 1909),
p. 123.

▼

fort différents pour ne pas dire opposés ou contradictoires.

Dès les manifestations religieuses de 1924 qui ont eu lieu à Canterbury pour célébrer l'anniversaire de l'arrivée des disciples du Poverello dans la métropole ecclésiastique on a pu constater que le Saint d'Assise y était fêté d'un commun accord par l'Eglise Anglicane et les Catholiques Romains, comme aussi par les membres des églises non-conformistes. Mais ce qui fut encore plus caractéristique, c'est que cette union et cette unité n'étaient pas seulement extérieures ou constituées uniquement par la rencontre dans les mêmes églises de foules compactes qui d'ordinaire se réunissent dans des édifices différents : ce fut avant tout un rapprochement des cœurs et des âmes, une communion, très différente de la communion eucharistique, mais très réelle, très profonde, et qui fut à coup sûr pour beaucoup de ceux qui y participèrent une expérience bénie et qui restera une des dates principales de leur vie spirituelle.

On communia en saint François. Et la petite sœur française de Saint Vincent de Paul qui au sortir du service de la Cathédrale s'écriait : " Certainement saint François était là," résumait l'impression qui pendant toute cette journée fut celle de presque tous ceux qui ont eu le bonheur de la vivre.

Depuis lors bien d'autres célébrations franciscaines ont eu lieu sur tous les points de la Grande Bretagne et dans des milieux fort différents, mais elles paraissent avoir été influencées à peu près toutes par l'esprit de paix et de courtoisie cher au Patriarche Séraphique qui avait inspiré tout et tous à Canterbury.

Pourquoi ne pas le dire puisque c'est un fait : l'esprit franciscain est mieux compris en Angleterre que partout ailleurs. Parmi les innombrables biographies de saint François qui ont vu le jour depuis cinquante ans il y en a une qui vient se placer au tout premier rang, c'est celle du R. P. Cuthbert, capucin anglais. Peut-être même est-elle la meilleure de toutes, parce que l'auteur, sans trop se soucier des discussions critiques sur les sources, a été conduit par son intuition religieuse à reconstituer la pensée et l'activité du Saint, les yeux sans cesse fixés sur la simplicité et la pauvreté, les deux vertus qui ont caractérisé l'idéal franciscain.

Or voici qu'au moment où dans la cellule du moine Capucin s'élaborait ce livre où vibre de nouveau l'amour et l'admiration de frère Léon pour son Maître, se préparait l'œuvre d'un homme qui n'est ni capucin ni même catholique, qui a pourtant élevé à Celui qui aimait à se qualifier du titre de " *Giullare di Dio* " (Jongleur de Dieu), un monument à la fois tout différent et très analogue, où l'Epoux de la Pauvreté est compris et dépeint ainsi que tout son entourage avec une ardente sympathie qui pourtant ne diminue en rien ni la beauté, ni l'exactitude historique des tableaux franciscains que les " Little Plays of St. Francis " de Mr. Laurence Housman font passer sous les yeux des spectateurs.

Cette intuition de l'âme de François et de son histoire est donc un don particulièrement fréquent dans les pays Britanniques.

On en trouvera une nouvelle manifestation dans le volume que la British Society of Franciscan Studies offre aujourd'hui au public et pour lequel elle m'a fait le grand honneur de me demander une introduction.

Il m'aurait été doux de présenter aux lecteurs chacun des travaux qui constituent ce recueil, mais des circonstances indépendantes de ma volonté m'obligent à être très bref.

Je me bornerai donc à jeter un coup d'œil d'admiration et de reconnaissance sur la contribution du Professeur Edmund G. Gardner intitulée " Saint Francis and Dante."

Parmi les franciscanisants sérieux il n'en est probablement aucun qui n'ait pas été arrêté, dès le début de ses études, par la nécessité de rapprocher non seulement ces deux noms, mais surtout ces deux hommes, et de voir clair dans les rapports qu'il y a entre eux. La plupart des efforts qui ont été tentés dans cette direction ont eu pour résultat des publications qui satisfaisaient peut-être leurs auteurs, mais qui étaient loin de pouvoir s'imposer à l'attention générale comme des travaux, sinon définitifs, du moins d'une réelle valeur scientifique.

Parmi les innombrables écrivains qui ont évoqué Dante à propos de l'histoire du Poverello la plupart, préoccupés surtout d'édifier leurs lecteurs, n'ont songé à voir dans ce que dit l'Alighieri du Saint et de ses disciples qu'une glorification oratoire et n'en ont pas recherché les raisons profondes, l'origine et la valeur.

D'autres entraînés par l'excitation que créent dans certains cercles les discussions passionnées que soulève l'interprétation de presque chaque ligne de la *Divine Comédie* ont cru qu'il leur suffirait de se jeter dans ces joutes pour faire dans le monde figure d'exégètes dantesques.

Devant ces échecs on s'est vite aperçu que pour

commencer à étudier cette question ardue il faut d'abord avoir une connaissance étendue et familière de l'œuvre entière de Dante. Mais, parmi les franciscanisants, qui pouvait espérer arriver à bout d'une tâche si immense et si délicate ? Les conférenciers des chaires dantesques ont sondé le chant XI du *Paradis*, mais bien rares sont ceux qui ont songé à voir le problème dans son ensemble.

Aujourd'hui le Professeur Gardner offre au public franciscanisant une étude aussi alerte que savante, basée sur une connaissance approfondie des textes, où les qualités scientifiques se combinent avec le respect du lecteur et le désir de se mettre à sa portée, de lui rendre service, qualités qui deviennent de plus en plus rares dans la littérature historique contemporaine.

L'illustre Professeur nous ouvre ses trésors avec une générosité dont on ne saurait lui être trop reconnaissant. Et cependant ce sentiment prend des proportions qu'il serait difficile de décrire, lorsque nous voyons que ce grand seigneur de la science n'a pu si bien nous renseigner sur les rapports qui unissent les deux génies qui dominent tout le moyen-âge, que parce qu'avant d'étudier saint François scientifiquement il avait commencé par s'imprégner de son caractère et de ses enseignements spirituels.

PAUL SABATIER.

STRASBOURG.
19 *Novembre*, 1926.

CONTENTS

xi

LIST OF PLATES

xiii

SOME FRANCISCAN SUBJECTS IN ITALIAN ART

PROFESSOR TANCRED BORENIUS, PH.D.

B

ST. FRANCIS

I

SOME FRANCISCAN SUBJECTS IN ITALIAN ART

AFTER having been for the first time definitely and fully emphasized by the late Henry Thode,[1] the import-ance of St. Francis for the development of Italian Art has by now become one of the commonplaces of art history.   It is therefore not intended in this connection to re-traverse ground which must be familiar to anybody at all interested in the subject.   Again, to most of us nowadays the episodes of the life of St. Francis instinctively present themselves in our imagination as depicted in that incomparable series of frescoes with which the young Giotto and his assistants towards the end of the thirteenth century decorated the walls of the upper church of S. Francesco at Assisi.   For this very reason, those frescoes have not been drawn upon at all in selecting the illustrations of the present volume, which aim, on the contrary, at presenting material comparatively much less known.

Pre-Giottesque art is represented in our selection

[1] Henry Thode, *Franz von Assisi und die Anfänge der Kunst der Renaissance in Italien.*   First edition, 1884 ; second edition, 1904.

by three examples illustrating successive stages in the development of an early type of altarpiece, which combines a full-length figure of St. Francis with a series of subjects from his legend. First in order of time (Plate I) comes the altarpiece in the church of San Francesco at Pescia (near Lucca), a signed and dated work by Bonaventura Berlinghieri of 1235, and thus separated by but a very short space of time from the earliest portrait of St. Francis in existence, the fresco of 1228 in the Sacro Speco of Subiaco.[1] Bonaventura Berlinghieri was a leading master of the early school at Lucca—a city which afterwards was destined to play but an insignificant part in the history of Italian painting. The available records concerning this artist cover the period between 1228 and 1274, and in connection with the recent revival of interest in the painting of the Duecento, a good deal of attention has lately concentrated on him.[2] This is the only signed work by him at present known to survive[3] : and the noble, hieratic figure of St. Francis derives, of course, enormous interest from having been painted not even a decade after the saint's death. The six legendary subjects, depicted on each side of the central figure, three and three, are :

[1] Accessibly reproduced in *Apollo*, vol. iv. (Oct. 1926), p. 151.

[2] See Oswald Sirén, *Toskanische Maler im XIII. Jahrhundert* (Berlin, 1922), pp. 76 *sqq.*

[3] The reproductions of this picture and the altarpiece in San Francesco at Pisa (Plate III) are made from photographs, kindly supplied by the Italian Board of Education.

Left	Right
(i) St. Francis receiving the stigmata.	(iv) A group of cripples healed at the tomb of St. Francis, who appears himself.
(ii) The sermon to the birds.	
(iii) A crippled girl healed at the sarcophagus of St. Francis.	(v) St. Francis healing the lame leg of Bartolomeo da Narni.
	(vi) Two women and a youth exorcised by touching the altar of St. Francis.

It is, of course, impossible to claim that these are the very first pictures of the legend of St. Francis ever painted : but they are undoubtedly the earliest known to us, and this fact in itself invests the six compositions with exceptional interest. It will also be seen that the series of subjects includes several (iii-vi) which were to enjoy a great vogue later in the Duecento, but were not included in Giotto's selection. They reappear, for instance, in the *paliotto* (Plate II) which now hangs over the door of the sacristy of the lower church of S. Francesco at Assisi. The picture bears no signature or date : it is assigned by most critics to Giunta Pisano, an important early Pisan master mentioned in records between 1202 and 1258.[1] Two signed works by Giunta have come down to us, both crucifixes, one in S. Maria degli Angeli at Assisi, and the other in the church of SS. Raineri e Leonardo at Pisa ; he is, moreover, known to have painted a crucifix, now lost, but formerly in the upper church of S. Francesco at Assisi and inscribed with the date 1236, which may be regarded as being not very distant from that of the

[1] See Sirén, *op. cit.*, pp. 148 *sqq.*

present picture. The legendary subjects are here only four, viz. :

LEFT	RIGHT
(i) A crippled girl healed at the sarcophagus of St. Francis.	(iii) A woman exorcised by touching the altar of St. Francis.
(ii) St. Francis healing the lame leg of Bartolomeo da Narni.	(iv) A cripple healed at the altar of St. Francis.

Iconographically it will be noticed that there is a distinct connection between these compositions and the Pescia altarpiece : thus in the scene of the Healing of Bartolomeo da Narni there are two incidents depicted in ' continuous composition ' : first, St. Francis touching Bartolomeo's leg in the water, and then Bartolomeo walking off with the crutches on his shoulder.

Somewhat later in the thirteenth century comes the third of the cognate altarpieces devoted to St. Francis which we reproduce—a picture in the church of S. Francesco at Pisa (Plate III) which Vasari, obviously absurdly, assigns to Cimabue, but which Dr. Sirén claims for Ugolino di Tedice, a shadowy figure in the Pisan school of about 1270–80.[1] The number of legendary subjects is again six, as at Pescia, viz. :

LEFT	RIGHT
(i) A crippled girl healed at the sarcophagus of St. Francis.	(iv) A cripple healed at the altar of St. Francis.
(ii) A sick woman healed by St. Francis, who appears to her.	(v) St. Francis heals the lame leg of Bartolomeo da Narni.
(iii) A woman with a tumour is healed at the tomb of St. Francis.	(vi) A woman exorcised by touching the altar of St. Francis.

[1] See Sirén, *op. cit.*, pp. 195 *sqq.*

6

The treatment of the scenes which appear on the Assisi *paliotto* is closely echoed in the present picture : and it will be observed how in the early selection of subjects from the legend of St. Francis those which emphasize his power of healing physical ailments easily predominate.

Some twenty or thirty years after the picture in S. Francesco at Pisa was painted, Giotto undertook the decoration of the walls of the upper church at Assisi, returning to the same subject quite at the end of his career, in the frescoes of the Bardi chapel in the church of S. Croce at Florence. For the reasons stated above, no reproductions are here given of Giotto's Franciscan subjects ; and we turn instead for one of the most remarkable interpretations of the Franciscan spirit in art to a much later period. On September 15, 1437, Stefano di Giovanni, called Sassetta, of Siena (1392–1450), was commissioned to execute an altarpiece for the church of San Francesco in Borgo San Sepolcro. This altarpiece—which was completed by June 5, 1444 —is now dismembered.[1] The front, representing the Glorification of St. Francis, between St. John the Baptist and the Blessed Raineri Rasini, is now in the collection of Mr. Bernard Berenson at Settignano. At the back were seen eight panels depicting scenes from the legend of St. Francis, six of which were until

---

[1] Compare on this work B. Berenson, *A Sienese Painter of the Franciscan Legend* (London, 1909), reprinted from *The Burlington Magazine*, vol. iii, 1903.

lately in the collection of the late M. Chalandon of Paris, having subsequently been acquired by Messrs. Duveen. They are here reproduced by courtesy of Sir Joseph Duveen. The subjects of these pictures are : St. Francis clothing the Beggar and dreaming of the Church (Plate IV) ; St. Francis renouncing his Heritage (Plate V) ; St. Francis before the Sultan (Plate VI) ; St. Francis before the Pope (Plate VII) ; St. Francis receiving the Stigmata (Plate VIII) ; the Funeral of St. Francis (Plate IX). One picture of the same series (St. Francis and the Wolf of Gubbio) is in the collection of Comte de Martel, Château de Beaumont, Chéverny (Loir-et-Cher) ; and yet another[1] is the enchanting ' Mystic Marriage of St. Francis and the Lady Poverty ' in the Musée Condé at Chantilly (Plate X). Entirely independently of Giotto, and of course at ever so much greater a distance of time from St. Francis, Sassetta treats his subjects with a wonderful gift of sympathy and poetry.

Turning from the Sienese school of the Quattrocento to North Italian painting of the same century, the frontispiece of the present volume reproduces in colour, by kind permission of the owner, Viscount Lascelles, a very interesting fragment of a picture by Antonio Vivarini. This panel, of narrow upright shape ($31\frac{1}{2}$ by 14 inches) is cut out of a picture of St. Francis receiving the Stigmata on the desert of Mount Alvernia, a painting which must originally have been of consider-

---

[1] First identified by Langton Douglas, *History of Siena*, p. 386.

Plate I.

Church of San Francisco, Pescia

St. Francis and six scenes from his Legend.
By Bonaventura Berlinghieri (1235).

able dimensions. Along the left border of the panel we can still make out some portions of the figure of the kneeling St. Francis, who was seen turned to the right; while above these appears the lower part of the six-winged seraph containing the crucifix from which the stigmata were communicated to St. Francis. In the foreground, holding the end of the cord hanging from the saint's waist, is seen a small figure of a kneeling Franciscan friar, probably the donor of the picture, while the remainder of the scene is taken up by an elaborate representation of the country round the Mount Alvernia. A Franciscan friar—probably Brother Leo, who, against St. Francis's wishes, witnessed his communion with Heaven—is sitting on the ground reading a book; farther back are seen a church and a monastery surrounded by a wood; while in the distance a sequence of precipitous hills stand out against a sky of gold. The idyllic scene is enlivened by various animals sporting about—two bears meeting, two foxes, a stag at rest, and a small rabbit near the reading friar.

A scroll at the bottom of the panel contains a fragmentary inscription in Gothic characters; the last line, though mutilated, allows us however to read:

. . . de muriano pinxit.

This is the characteristic signature of Antonio Vivarini of Murano, the oldest member of a family of painters which achieved much distinction in Venice during the

fifteenth century. Neither the brother of Antonio
Vivarini, Bartolomeo, nor two contemporary artists,
Quiricio da Murano and Andrea da Murano, all of
whom on mere grounds of nomenclature might be
candidates for the authorship of this picture, can, for
reasons of style, be associated with it.

Antonio Vivarini is first heard of in 1446, when he
was already domiciled in Venice, where he continued to
live until his death, save for a sojourn in the neighbouring
Padua between 1447 and 1450. For some time he
worked in conjunction with his brother-in-law, Giovanni
d'Alemagna, who brought to Venice something of the
spirit and mannerisms of the late Gothic painters of
Cologne. Giovanni died in 1450, and after this
Antonio continued to work either on his own or in
conjunction with his younger brother, Bartolomeo.
The date of his death is unknown, but may with some
probability be placed about the year 1480.

The subject of the stigmatization offered a welcome
excuse for the elaborate rendering of landscape : and
the emphasis laid upon this as well as on the study of
animal life reflects in the present picture a characteristic
feature of late Gothic art, and reminds us more especially
of the work of such an exponent of its tendencies as
Antonio Pisano of Verona, known as Pisanello, himself,
as we may recall, active at Venice at the beginning of
the fifteenth century. The stag at rest in the background of Lord Lascelles' picture looks as if based on
one of Pisanello's exquisite drawings of animals ; and

on the whole conception of the idyllic scene there is much to remind us of the small picture of 'St. Jerome in the Wilderness' in the National Gallery, a signed work by Pisanello's pupil, Bono de Ferrara. The chief piece of evidence as regards the influence exercised by Pisanello upon Antonio Vivarini is supplied by the 'Adoration of the Magi,' by Antonio, now in the Berlin Gallery.[1] Lord Lascelles' picture amplifies the evidence as regards the artistic relations between Pisanello and Antonio Vivarini in the most interesting manner. As regards the history of the panel, one would have imagined that some record of an altarpiece of this magnitude and importance would exist. I can, however, trace no description of a picture corresponding to the present one in the early works on Venetian art and artistic topography. Lord Lascelles' panel was formerly in the collection of the late Lord Carmichael.

A later phase of North Italian art is represented by the engraving of St. Francis receiving the Stigmata (Plate XI) by Benedetto Montagna of Vicenza, the son and imitator of the well-known painter Bartolomeo Montagna, and working during the first half of the sixteenth century. The engraving, which from its severe simplicity of style probably belongs to an early period of the artist's career, is of extreme rarity. It was first described by Passavant,[2] and is also noted in

[1] Reproduced, e.g., in my edition of Crowe and Cavalcaselle, *History of Painting in North Italy*, 1912, vol. i, p. 32.

[2] Passavant, *Le Peintre-graveur* (Leipzig, 1860–4), vol. v, p. 147, No. 44.

the list of Benedetto Montagna's engravings which I published some time ago.[1] I have only been able to trace one impression of this engraving, in the Remondini collection in the Museo Civico at Bassano ; it has never been reproduced, so students of early Italian engraving will be glad of the accompanying illustration, which is reproduced from a photograph kindly supplied by Dr. Paolo M. Tua, Director of the Bassano Museum.

[1] Tancred Borenius, *The Painters of Vicenza* (London, 1909), p. 132, No. 3.

THE STUDY OF THE SOURCES OF THE LIFE OF ST. FRANCIS

Professor F. C. BURKITT, D.D.

II

THE STUDY OF THE SOURCES

ALL authentic history is based on the reports of eye-witnesses. This is, I venture to say, not quite such an universally accepted truism as it sounds when thus baldly formulated. But if King Alfred really burned the cakes, if Queen Eleanor really offered Fair Rosamund the alternative of the dagger or the poison, some one who was present must have told the tale to others or have written it down : however appropriately these tales may fit the persons concerned they were not automatically recorded. If therefore we are seriously to believe in any tale told of a historical personage such as S. Francis we must ask carefully through what channel it has been transmitted and, very often, who was the eye-witness on whose testimony the story ultimately depends.

The official biography of S. Francis is the Legend composed by Bonaventura in 1261. For five centuries this was the main source of information, though since 1504 a curious collection of anecdotes about S. Francis and his chief companions called the *Speculum Vitae*, the 'Mirror of a Brother Minor's Life,' had been available in print. This collection obviously included a good deal of later and quite legendary matter ; it was doubtless read by pious folk for edification, but was generally regarded as useless for serious students. The same might be said of the *Fioretti* or ' Little Flowers of S. Francis,' a collection of Franciscan tales written in charming old-fashioned Italian, which was very popular in North Italy as a book of religious reading.

A new era opened up in 1768, when the Bollandist Fathers gave to the world their study of S. Francis in the *Acta Sanctorum* (Oct., vol. ii). In this work were published for the first time 1 *Celano*, i.e. the Life written by Thomas of Celano in 1228 (or 1229), and 3 *Socii*, i.e. the Life which professes to have been written by Francis's three companions, Leo, Rufino and Angelo, in August, 1246.

In 1806 the second life by Thomas of Celano (2 *Celano*), written in 1247, was published by Rinaldi.[1]

With these publications the grave question of the relative value of our sources was already posed. The discussions that took place were not entirely unconnected with existing parties within the Franciscan body, and indeed it is necessary to have some idea of these parties, in order to estimate the weight of the historical evidence presented by the various documents. Almost from the first there were two main tendencies, which are still more or less represented by the Conventuals and the Observants. The official recognition of the Observant Franciscans in 1363 marks the end of a long struggle. It is not my purpose in these pages

[1] Republished by Amoni in 1879.

to follow the course of this struggle, still less to appraise the motives of those who waged it. It may suffice to say that the majority of the Franciscan friars, supported generally by the Popes and the leading officials in the Order, favoured a policy in which the extremely rigorous poverty and simplicity of the earlier days of the movement was more or less relaxed, while on the other hand there were never wanting earnest and sometimes very eloquent men who stood for the strict and literal observance of what S. Francis had enjoined. It must not be supposed that all the goodness and virtue were on one side. The community, represented by the Conventuals, might urge that the relaxations and modifications were necessary, if the work of a world-wide organization was to be carried on effectively. The protesting 'Spirituals' or *Zelanti*, on the other hand, might and did quote the words and exhortations of S. Francis himself as their justification for disobeying the new regulations of their ecclesiastical superiors. In any case the modern historical investigator has every reason to be grateful to the 'Spirituals,' for it is greatly to their insistence upon a literal obedience to what S. Francis desired that we owe the preservation of so many reminiscences of what he actually said and did.

The modern recognition of these 'Spirituals' is due in great measure to Cardinal Ehrle, who in the *Archiv für Literatur- und Kirchengeschichte* (1885–88) published many documents written by Ubertino da Casale and Angelo Clareno, the great leaders of the Spirituals, together with certain writings of their opponents about the time of the Council of Vienne (1311) and later at Avignon. The documents published by Ehrle bring out quite clearly the difference between the party of Ubertino and Angelo, who only wanted to obey literally the expressed wishes of S. Francis and based their case on documents and traditions handed down from S. Francis's companions, and on the other hand the people known as *Fraticelli*, bands of roving fanatics, who had inherited the freedom of the early Franciscans and some of their enthusiasm, but nothing else. These *Fraticelli* could not claim to be obeying the commands of Francis either in the spirit or in the letter, and are in fact quite distinct from the true *Zelanti*. But the two were confused at the time and came more or less under a common condemnation ; it was not till the contemporary documents were published by Ehrle that the distinction was fully admitted.

The Bollandists in 1768 gave the first place to Thomas of Celano, i.e. 1 *Celano*, the earliest in date, and they accepted the authenticity of 3 *Socii*, but they deliberately rejected the *Speculum Vitae* on the ground that some of that collection clearly belonged to the 14th century and that parts of it were obviously un-historical. The Franciscan historians of the century that followed held similar views. These men, of whom Papini is the type,[1] were persuaded that S. Francis was above all seemly and discreet, and that stories

---

[1] N. Papini (1751–1834), sometime General of the Conventuals.

about S. Francis were improbable in proportion as they represented him to be impulsive or undignified. They were not rationalists in the sense of disbelieving in 'miracles,' quite the contrary. But they were of the school of Brother Elias, and like him were not edified at the spectacle of a Saint who could make up rhymes about the Sun and Moon in the vulgar tongue almost on his death-bed, and who encumbered his Order with inconvenient last wishes enjoining an impracticable standard of poverty. Some of those who brought forward these impracticable and unconventional utterances had been in the past something very much like rebels against due ecclesiastical Authority : there was every temptation for Papini and his school to reject traditions chiefly alleged by those rebellious pens.

Some of the characteristics of Thomas of Celano will come up for consideration later on. But this must be said here at once. For about 30 years from S. Francis's death, i.e. till about 1260, Thomas of Celano was the more or less official historiographer of the Order. In 1228 and again in 1246 he was entrusted with the writing of S. Francis's Life, and after that with the collection of his Miracles. He was thus employed by Elias, by Crescentius, and by John of Parma, that is to say by General Ministers who were opposed to the zealous Spirituals and also by the one General Minister who whole-heartedly belonged to that party. We can surely gain from the writings of

Thomas of Celano a view of Francis and the Franciscan Movement which was that of the important body of men who were its leaders during the first generation of its existence. The question is, can we get behind the point of view that Brother Thomas puts before us ? Is there anything about Francis of historical value that has come down to us independent of Celano ? This is the decisive question in Franciscan research.

The best known, the deservedly best known, name in connexion with modern Franciscan studies is that of Monsieur Paul Sabatier. A good deal of what follows will be taken up with the criticism of some of his theories, so that the discussion of points in which I believe M. Sabatier to be more or less wrong will occupy more space than the enumeration of those where I believe him to be right. It is therefore just and proper to explain at the outset in what the great services he has performed for Franciscan studies do actually consist. There is first, of course, the charm of style and the instructed enthusiasm that have impelled so many of his readers to take an interest for themselves in Saint Francis and his age. But besides this his grand merit, if I may be allowed to say so, is that he has seen that the first task of the investigator of S. Francis and his ideas is to endeavour to get behind Thomas of Celano, to study with the utmost care every scrap of information which may be both genuine and non-Celanese, for it is only by the aid of such information that we are able to judge intelligently what Celano tells us. Again and again, so it seems to me, the expectation has been disappointed. Much of what Sabatier has brought forward is either non-historical or else turns out to have passed through the Celanese alembic after all. But, as I believe, there is a residue ; and that we have it and can appreciate its value is very much due to things that Sabatier was the first to put forward, or if not the first certainly the most impressive.

To understand the scope of what M. Sabatier's theories and discoveries have done for our understanding of S. Francis it is necessary to describe certain of them at some length. Which authorities, said he, should a modern historian go to in the first place for his materials ? Have we any external criterion by which we may test our authorities ? It is not enough that a historical source is early : strictly speaking, the one positive merit that an early work must have is that fables invented at a later date will be absent from it. Because a writer is contemporary we cannot therefore assume that he is intelligent or frank. He may be a party man, he may have an interest in concealing or modifying the naked truth. With these considerations in mind Sabatier started from S. Francis's own writings. They are not very extensive, but there is quite enough to form a decided impression. They were collected very soon after S. Francis's death, and there is little doubt about their authenticity or even their text. Since Sabatier wrote, what is practically an autograph of one of them has been discovered,[1] and the ancient pages of cod. 338 at Assisi which contain most of the certainly genuine writings (except the Rule of 1221) have been demonstrated on palaeographical grounds to have been penned in the middle of the 13th century, if not earlier.[2]

We have, then, in S. Francis's own writings a touchstone of authenticity. What is in harmony with their spirit is probably genuine. What is alien from their spirit is inadequate, if not actually false, however early it may have been written down.

Tried by these tests Sabatier, writing in 1893, found 1 *Celano* and 2 *Celano* both wanting ; on the other hand 3 *Socii* appeared to him to ring true, and so did much of what was contained in the *Speculum Vitae* of 1504. On these two documents, therefore, as principal authorities he based his famous biography, a work that has passed through many editions, and is indeed the starting-point of much of the modern interest in S. Francis. But each of these documents seemed to Sabatier gravely defective. The Legend of the Three Companions was good as far as it goes, but it is almost exclusively occupied with the early days, the days before either Leo, Angelo or Rufino had joined the Order and become themselves eye-witnesses. The Introductory Letter prefixed to the work promises a

---

[1] I refer to the Subiaco text of the *De Reuerentia* : see *A F H* vi 3–12 (1913).

[2] *Revue Bénédictine* for July, 1922.

select collection of anecdotes, not a regular narrative ; but what we have is a regular chronological narrative, which breaks off just where the most intimate anecdotes from these trusted Companions might be expected to begin.

Sabatier conjectured, therefore, that 3 *Socii,* as we have it, is only a fragment, that it is only the first quarter of a longer work, three-quarters of which have been suppressed. With this idea he began a search among MSS containing Franciscan documents, in the hope of finding one that should contain the missing chapters. That was thirty years ago : almost all the collections of mediaeval MSS have been ransacked, but the wished-for chapters have never appeared. On the other hand M. Sabatier's devotion was rewarded almost at once by a discovery of even greater importance. He had ventured to use the *Speculum Vitae* as a serious historical source because certain portions of it seemed to him excellent, instead of rejecting it altogether, as did most of his predecessors, because much of it was obviously late and inferior. These late and inferior parts he rejected, comprising chapters out of Bonaventura, chapters of the Fioretti, extracts from Chronicles and other extraneous matter, in all making up about three-quarters of the volume as printed in 1504. The remaining quarter he judged to be homogeneous and early : it was not, he saw, actually the conjectured missing portion of 3 *Socii,* but it seemed to him of the same quality and like it to be intimately connected with Brother Leo, the Companion of S. Francis.

It was therefore a grand confirmation of his views when he found in a MS at Paris (*Mazarine* 1743) just these chapters contained as a separate treatise called *Speculum Perfectionis*, " the Mirror of the perfection of a Brother Minor's state." Further search showed that this was no caprice of the scribe of the Mazarine MS. The *Speculum Perfectionis* is now known to be extant in ten or a dozen MSS, some of them written as early as the middle of the 14th century. M. Sabatier had claimed that his conjectural selection of chapters from the *Speculum Vitae* had " an energy of virile youth which the Fioretti suggest but never attain to." The tales told in these chapters were indeed for the most part the same tales that are told by Thomas of Celano, especially in 2 *Celano*. But he regarded 2 *Celano* not as the source, but as the copy. In 2 *Celano* the story of Francis is " abridged with all its freshness gone,— instead of a poem we have a catalogue."[1]

The publication of the full Latin text of the *Speculum Perfectionis* by Sabatier in 1898 is indeed a landmark in Franciscan studies.[2] It seemed to be a signal confirmation of Sabatier's theories, for here we are not dealing with a construction by a modern enthusiast, but the very words of Franciscan antiquity are speaking to us.

[1] The passages quoted are from the English translation of Sabatier's *Life of S. Francis*, published in 1894 before the discovery of the *Speculum Perfectionis*.

[2] *Speculum Perfectionis*, seu S. Francisci Assisiensis Legenda antiquissima, auctore fratre Leone, nunc primum edidit PAUL SABATIER, Paris, 1898.

Moreover Sabatier's leading MS, *Mazarine* 1743, gave a date to the work. This MS itself was only written in 1459, but the *Speculum Perfectionis* ended with the words " Done in the most holy place of S. Mary de Portiuncula and completed on the 5th of the Ides of May, A.D. 1228." [1] No wonder that Sabatier's Preface to his edition vibrates with excitement. I quote a few phrases here and there. " The biography of Saint Francis by Brother Leo : this work has been written at a single stretch, less than a year after the Saint's death. . . . It is not only the most ancient in date ; it is also that in which the likeness of the Poverello stands out with the greatest vigour, originality and poetry. Thomas of Celano wrote only a few months later, but his work, better as it is in Latinity, is that of a disciple, not of a companion. He is relating less from his reminiscences than from those of others, and is thinking above all of the Saint whom he salutes in glory. Brother Leo, on the contrary, is relating the life of a man whose existence he has shared, whose secretary, friend, confessor and nurse he was. . . . This Legend is like letters written just after the death of a dear friend. . . . We record his words, his looks, his smiles ; we try to fix them for ever. A few years roll by and our reminiscences are transformed. We see better the life of those whom we have loved, but the details of their final sufferings will have faded. . . .

---

[1] This means 11 May, 1227, according to our method of indicating dates (not 11 May, 1228).

This document makes us hear the sighs of Francis, his groans, while at the same time it brings us into the very heart of his spirit. The Letters and the Testament of Francis find their true setting. The work of the master and that of the disciple correspond and are henceforward inseparable " (*Spec. Perf.*, ed. of 1898, pp. xvii f.).

I do not quote these words to show how mistaken a great historian may be in his critical judgements. It is true that the view I hold is that the *Speculum Perfectionis* was compiled three generations after the death of Francis, not in the following year, and that the Legend of the Three Companions is later still. The problem before those who hold these views is why the *Speculum Perfectionis* produced, nay still produces, this impression of freshness, at least in parts. It is, in my opinion, a problem of very considerable interest, going far beyond the interests of merely Franciscan studies, for it seems to me that the full answer has a very real bearing upon an analogous case, the ever-fresh impression produced by the Gospels in general and the Gospel of Mark in particular. It is with this question in view that I venture to quote these expressions from a living scholar, expressions that he himself may now desire to phrase somewhat differently after the discoveries and discussions of the last thirty years.

I must now trace the steps by which Sabatier's view of the date and composition of his two chief sources has been called in question. The first was the study of 3 *Socii* by the Bollandist Father Van Ortroy, published in 1900.[1] Van Ortroy printed 3 *Socii* in parallel columns with 1 *Celano*, with the Life of Francis by Julian of Spires, and with 2 *Celano*. He declared that no further investigation was necessary : it was evident that 3 *Socii* was not a work of individual reminiscence but of scissors and paste, a mosaic made in the middle of the 14th century at earliest.

This revolutionary conclusion was not at once accepted by everybody, least of all by Sabatier, who replied in the *Revue historique* for 1901 (vol. lxxv). He claimed that the dependence upon 2 *Celano* was not made out, that in the parallel passages 3 *Socii* was the original and 2 *Celano* the copy. But he admits the use of 1 *Celano* and of Julian by 3 *Socii*, which indeed is impossible to deny after looking at Van Ortroy's parallels. The wonder is that this use was not formally recognised before.[2]

The effect of Van Ortroy's criticism was greatly to weaken the confidence felt in Sabatier's construction. Even those who held that the passages in 3 *Socii* sounded more fresh and ' Franciscan ' than the parallels in 2 *Celano* were more or less embarrassed. In the letter

---

[1] *Analecta Bollandiana* xix, pp. 119–197.

[2] The reason for this was, I think, that Julian's *Vita Francisci* was not published ; it was, in fact, not published in full till 1902, where Van Ortroy printed it in the *Analecta Bollandiana*. It was known to the Bollandists of 1768, who gave extracts, but they recognised that though an early work—it dates from 1235—it is wholly based upon 1 *Celano*, which it follows chapter by chapter.

prefixed to 3 *Socii* the Three Companions profess that they " write not after the manner of a Legend, seeing that for a long time have Legends been put together of his (Francis's) life. . . . But as it were from a pleasant meadow we pluck certain flowers that in our judgement are fairer than the rest, not following a continuous history." And of what they bring forward new they say " We believe that, had these things been known unto those venerable men that put together the said Legends, they would by no means have passed them by." These words are quite inappropriate to the existing 3 *Socii*, which is wholly made up of parallels to existing Legends, for the most part narrated in the very same words, including in the case of 1 *Celano* the very marked literary tricks characteristic of Brother Thomas.

As for the *Speculum Perfectionis*, not every one accepted the early date and authorship advocated by Sabatier. That it contained a very ancient element was indeed generally recognised.[1] But even Sabatier had been constrained to label the second part of § 71 as an Interpolation, though it is found in all the MSS, and there are other chapters, notably § 85, which seem in their present form to have been written after Leo's death. In this chapter the characteristics of a good Brother Minor according to the mind of Francis are enumerated, and amongst other things are mentioned " the simplicity and purity of Brother Leo who

[1] See e.g. E. d'Alençon's *Celano*, p. xxxv, last line.

28

really was of the most holy purity." But in another and shorter form of these characteristics, found in a set of tales given in the MS at San Antonio in Rome, all the clause about Leo disappears (*AFH* xii 377): this no doubt is the form as Leo wrote it, while that in the *Speculum Perfectionis* must be later than 1271 when Leo died.

These internal considerations were reinforced by the publication in 1901 and 1902 of *Documenta Antiqua Franciscana*, three little volumes edited by Fr. Leonard Lemmens, O.F.M. In the first of these are a couple of tracts, which actually profess to be the work of Leo himself ; in the second is a different recension of the *Speculum Perfectionis*, which Lemmens claims to be earlier than Sabatier's ; in the third is a description of the MSS used, from which it appears that these specially interesting documents all come from a single MS, no. 1/73 of the library of the Irish Franciscan Convent of Sant' Isidoro in Rome. It was some time before the publications of Fr. Lemmens made much way : many ignored them altogether, and others treated them with scant consideration. Lemmens' *Speculum* (*DAF* vol. ii) attracted most attention : it was clearly a work of less general charm than Sabatier's, though in certain respects it had a better text in detail. It is not too much to say that Franciscan investigators did not quite know what to make of it.

But it was really the *Scripta Leonis* in *DAF* vol. i that raised the most serious questions. There was nothing in them that was strictly new : the tract called *The Intention of the Rule* consisted of six or seven chapters of Sabatier's *Speculum*, that called *Words of Francis* consisted of five chapters followed by an appendix formed by three others. But those who have read Sabatier's Introduction to his edition of the *Speculum Perfectionis* will remember how much, very justly, he makes of the citations of Ubertino da Casale.[1] Ubertino quoted certain writings of Leo in his *Arbor Vite Crucifixe*, published in 1305, indicating where he does not quote in full and ending with *Huc usque uerba sancti Leonis*. These quotations were scattered over various chapters of Sabatier's *Speculum* in an irregular order, so that Ubertino seemed to have an acquaintance with the whole work. But the *Intentio Regule* published by Lemmens consisted of just these same chapters in the order that Ubertino quotes them, so it is evident that Ubertino in 1305 is quoting the *Intentio* and not the *Speculum*. Similarly almost the whole of the *Verba Francisci* is quoted in Angelo Clareno's Exposition of the Franciscan Rule as the work of Brother Leo ;[2] other quotations from the *Intentio* but not from the rest of the *Speculum* are scattered over this work, and further in his *History of the Seven Tribulations* he quotes the 4th section of the *Intentio* (§§ 13–15), which corresponds to the widely-separated sections 71 and 11 of Sabatier's *Speculum*.

Ubertino and Angelo, therefore, both writing soon

---

[1] *Sp. Perf.*, pp. cxlii ff.   [2] Ed. Oliger, pp. 126–129.

after 1300, do not quote from the *Speculum* but do quote from the short tracts ascribed to Leo in S. Isidoro 1/73, which are thereby proved to be more than extracts made by the scribe of that MS. Ubertino was the disciple of Conrad of Offida († 1306), a personal friend of Leo, so that he must have been well informed about Leo's writings. He does not speak about the *Speculum* or any regular Life of Francis by Leo, but he does appeal to *Rotuli* and *Cedule* of his, that is to Rolls and Notes, i.e. to tracts such as the *Intentio* and the *Verba*, and to short detached pieces such as are the single chapters of the *Speculum*.

The shorter recension of the *Speculum Perfectionis*, preserved in the same codex (*S. Isidoro* 1/73) as the *Intentio* and the *Verba Francisci*, was not at once accepted by all Franciscan scholars as the earlier form. It is certainly less impressive as a literary whole than Sabatier's, being almost without plan—a mere string of anecdotes,—while Sabatier's *Speculum* is grouped under headings and the tales concerned with the last days of Francis are all collected at the end. This gives a dramatic and biographical interest to the whole work, which is wanting in Lemmens' recension. But because it is less effective it is not therefore later; in fact the probability is the other way, and in a good many minor matters of text the shorter *Speculum* is actually superior. Moreover comparison of the two forms should not be made without taking into account the independent existence of the *Intentio* and the *Verba*. The tales told in these two tracts do not reappear in Lemmens' *Speculum*, which therefore must be regarded as a collection made to supplement them : Sabatier's *Speculum*, on the other hand, incorporates all three collections.

It may conveniently be mentioned here that the MS of the *Speculum Perfectionis* (longer recension) preserved in the Franciscan Convent of the Ognissanti at Florence, a MS written in the 14th century and one of the oldest and best yet found, has a similar colophon to Sabatier's MS, but in the Ognissanti codex the date is v°. yd'. Maij. M°.CCC.XVIIJ. (whereas Sabatier's MS has M.CC.XXVIIJ.). M. Sabatier is probably right in asserting that the reckoning employed at Assisi was the 'Pisan style,' according to which all dates after Lady Day are reckoned to one year *later* than our reckoning, so that the two dates given above are respectively the 11th of May, 1317 and 1227. But whether 1317 or 1318 be meant, the date given in the 14th century codex at Florence is more likely than that in the 15th century MS at Paris. Whether 1317 be in itself a probable date for the compilation may be left over for the present.

In addition to these documents four further discoveries of Franciscan MSS claim notice. (1) In 1899 was published Thomas of Celano's third work, the full collection of Miracles, collected during the Generalate of John of Parma (1247–57). It has been edited, together with 1 and 2 *Celano* in the admirable collection of Thomas's works made by Fr. E. d'Alençon

Plate II.

Assisi S. Francisco.

St. Francis, with four scenes from his Legend.
By Giunta Pisano.

(Rome, 1906). (2) In 1910 Prof. A. G. Little bought from the Phillipps Collection a MS (No. 12290) written in Italy about 1400 and containing some 230 Franciscan pieces of various interest and value. What gives special importance to the MS is that nos. 140–169 and 184–198, which form part of *Aliqua exempla de uita beati Patris nostri Francisci et sociorum eius*, seem to offer a better and often a more vivid text of the incidents which they relate.

(3) Somewhat similar in interest to the Phillipps MS (now usually quoted as *Little*) is the 14th century Codex of San Antonio at Rome, described in full by Fr. L. Oliger in *AFH* xii (1919). This MS contains the Life by Bonaventura and the Tracts known as ' Bartholi ' on the annual Indulgence of the Portiuncula, followed by a Third Part consisting of 95 Franciscan anecdotes, a few of which are not found elsewhere and several of which seem to have a better text than that of other MSS.[1]

(4) In *AFH* xv (1922) Fr. Ferdinand M. Delorme, O.F.M., published two papers called " *The Legenda Antiqua S. Francisci* from MS 1046 of the Communal Library of Perugia," in which he gives a full account of what he shows to be one of the most important Franciscan MSS yet studied. It contains (1) a large collection of Papal Bulls of Franciscan interest, (2) the Life by Bonaventura, (3) a collection of some 110 or 120 Franciscan anecdotes, arranged in five Chapters called by Delorme

---

[1] See above, p. 29, and Note 3 appended to this Paper.

A B C D and **E.** From the absence of Clement V's *Exiui de paradiso*[1] and from other indications Fr. Delorme concludes that the collection of Bulls dates from 1311, and as the handwriting of the MS belongs to the early years of the 14th century it seems likely that the collection was made by the scribe himself and that the MS was written in 1311. Owing to the loss of a quire the end of the *Legenda maior* by Bonaventura is missing, together with a small piece (6 columns only) at the beginning of the third part : the result has been that what followed the collection of Bulls had been catalogued only as ' Bonaventura,' and the precious third part containing what Fr. Delorme has called *Legenda antiqua* had been overlooked.

This *Legenda antiqua* of the Perugia MS has almost exactly the same contents as Sabatier's *Speculum Perfectionis*,[2] but it is fuller and in text more often agrees with the documents in S. Isidoro 1/73. Moreover the order of the several pieces agrees more closely with these than with that of Sabatier's *Speculum*. But the grand merit of the Perugia Legend is that the five sections in the MS differ in their relation to 2 *Celano*. This circumstance is so important for the evaluation of the matter in the *Speculum*, that it must be explained more particularly.

Most of the matter contained in Sabatier's *Speculum* is given in 2 *Celano*, sometimes almost word for word,

---

[1] 6 May, 1312.

[2] The chief omissions are the hexameters on the Portiuncula (Sp. S 84), the praise of the Ten Good Friars (Sp. S 85), and the *Canticum Solis* (Sp. S 120).

sometimes in totally different words. According to Sabatier's theory the *Speculum* is the original ; in certain cases Thomas of Celano saw no objection to copying out Brother Leo's words almost as they stood, in others he thought well entirely to modify Leo's language, whether for literary reasons or because it reflected too strongly the ideas of the party of strict observance. Other scholars regard 2 *Celano* itself as the most direct representation of the reminiscences of Leo and other old Companions of S. Francis : no doubt (they say) the literary style of Thomas is every-where felt, but we must accept his version as the most authentic we have. The *Speculum*, on the other hand, represents the way these tales were told by the more or less rebellious Spirituals, who have often freely modified them in the interest of the strict observance and to the discredit of the official leaders of the Order. Thus the criteria for the relative value and authenticity of the two sets of tales were essentially subjective.

A couple of contrasted parallels will make the state of things clearer :

Sp. *S* 27	2 *Cel* 22
Quodam tempore cum beatus Franciscus coepit habere fratres et maneret cum eis apud Rigum Tortum prope Assisium, accidit ut *quadam nocte, quiescentibus* omnibus fratribus, circa medium noctis ex*clama*ret *unus de* fratribus dicens : ' *Morior, morior !* ' Stupefacti autem et territi omnes fratres euigilauerunt.	*Clamat una de* ouibus *nocte quadam quiescentibus* ceteris : ' *Morior*, fratres, *morior* ecce *fame.'*

Sp. S 27

Et *exurgens* beatus Franciscus dixit : 'Surgite, fratres, et accendite lumen !' Et accenso lumine dixit : 'Quis est ille qui dixit, morior ?' Respondit frater ille : 'Ego sum.' Et ait illi : 'Quid habes, frater ? quomodo morieris ?' At ille ait : 'Morior *fame*.'

Tunc beatus Franciscus statim *parari* fecit *mensam* et sicut homo plenus *caritate* et discretione *comedit* cum illo ne uerecundaretur comedere solus ; et de uoluntate ipsius omnes alii *fratres* pariter comederunt.

2 Cel 22

Surgit protinus pastor egregius et ouicule morbide remedio debito subuenire festinat.

Mensam parari iubet licet rusticanis refertam deliciis, ubi uini defectum sicut et sepius aqua suppleuit. Incipit primus ipse *comede*re, et ad *charita*tis officium, ne tabescat frater ille rubore, reliquos *fratres* inuitat.

The natural inferences to be drawn from this parallel are : (1) The two tales cannot be wholly independent reminiscences of the same event. (2) That in the *Speculum* is much more original, and certainly cannot be derived from that in 2 *Celano*. (3) That in 2 *Celano* on the other hand may very well be a rewriting of the tale in the *Speculum* by an affected stylist.

Contrast on the other hand :

Sp. S 93

Ebrius amore et compassione
Christi quandoque *talia faciebat*,
nam *dulcissima melodia spiritus
intra* se *ipsum ebulliens* frequenter
*exterius gallice dabat sonum
et uena diuini susurrii quam
auris eius suscipiebat furtiue
gallicum erumpebat in iubilum.*
Lignum quandoque

colligebat de *terra, ipsumque*

2 Cel 127

Nonnumquam uero
talia faciebat.
*Dulcissima melodia spiritus
intra ipsum ebulliens
exterius gallic*um *dabat sonum
et uena diuini susurrii quam
auris eius suscipiebat furtiue
gallicum erumpebat in iubilum.*
Lignum quandoque,
ut oculis uidimus,
colligebat e *terra, ipsumque*

sinistro brachio superponens	*sinistro brachio superponens*
aliud lignum per modum *arc*us	*arc*ulum filo flexum
in manu *dextera* t*rahebat*	*tenebat in dextera*
super illud, *quasi super uiellam*	quem [*quasi*] *super uiellam*
uel aliud instrumentum,	trahens per lignum,
atque *gestus ad hoc idoneos*	et *ad hoc gestus* representans
faciens *gallice cantabat*	*idoneos gallice cantabat*
de Domino Iesu Christo.	*de Domino.*
Terminabatur denique *tota*	*Terminabatur tota*
*hec tripudia*tio *in lacrimas*	*hec tripudia* frequenter *in lacrimas*
et in compassionem passionis	*et in passionis Christi*
Christi hic iubilus soluebatur.	*compassionem hic iubilus soluebatur.*
In his *trahebat contin*ue	Inde hic sanctus *continu*a
suspiria et ingeminatis	*trahebat suspiria et ingeminatis*
gemitibus eorum *que* tenebat	*gemitibus* inferiorum *que*
*in man*ibus *oblitus*	*in manu* erant *oblitus*
suspendebatur ad celum.	*suspendebatur ad celum.*

For the first line of Sp. *S* 93 see 2 *Celano* 13, where we read that Francis *quasi spiritu ebrius lingua gallica petit oleum et acquirit.*

No one contests the charm and interest of the picture here conjured up : whoever first recorded it, it is evidently (as Thomas of Celano says) a picture drawn from life. But the language is the stilted jargon of Brother Thomas, not the unadorned style of the writer of the *Intentio.*[1]

---

[1] Here are some parallels : *Spiritu ebrius* (1 Cel 56 *post med.*) ; *tripudiant . . . in lacrimis* (1 Cel 124 *init.*), *tripudiat . . . suspiria trahens . . . ingeminans* (1 Cel 125 *fin.*) ; *defixis in terra oculis mente celo herebat* (1 Cel 41 *fin.*), *suspendebatur multitoties tanta contemplationis dulcedine ut . . .* (2 Cel 98 *init.*), *totos rapiebat auditores ad celica* (2 Cel. 107 *med.*) ; *ebulliebat foras* (1 Cel 115 *post init.*), *feruore spiritus bulliens . . . iam in celestis regni summa republica uersabatur* (2 Cel 95 *med.*). It is also worth note that the two *fratres Francigene* of Sp. *S* 34 are called *fratres Gallicos* in 2 Cel 181.

37

As long as it was only a question of the comparison of the *Speculum Perfectionis* with 2 *Celano* it seemed impossible to account for the double phenomena of literary difference and resemblance. It was indeed noteworthy that the second class, like that of Sp. *S* 93 = 2 *Cel* 127, had no parallels in the documents taken by Lemmens from *Isid* 1/73. But now we have in addition Delorme's text from Perugia. It falls into five long sections, distinguished partly by large initials, but chiefly by their relation to 2 *Celano*. The last three (**C D** and **E**) are not derived from 2 *Celano* : the parallel texts in 2 *Cel* are here inferior and derivative, and the language of **C D** and **E** contains none of the Celanese rhetoric. In the twenty stories grouped under **B**, on the other hand, the Celanese rhetoric is always present and the relative order of 2 *Cel* is almost uninterruptedly preserved : in other words, this section of the Perugia text (nos. 22–41) must be regarded as a set of extracts from 2 *Celano*. Section **A** is more mixed : §§ 8–19 of Lemmens' *Speculum* followed by the greater part of the *Verba* appear, but there are also three (or four) chapters, the ultimate origin of which seem to be 2 *Celano*.[1] Finally, while **C D** and **E** are all independent of 2 *Celano*, section **D** has a peculiar characteristic of its own. This section (nos. 59–91) has no parallels in *Isid* 1/73 ; its parallels in 2 *Celano* and Sp. *S* show both these documents to be, for this section, inferior and

[1] See Note 1 at the end of this Paper.

derivative ; and a notably large proportion of the stories contained in it has a connexion with the Valley of Rieti.

I have ventured elsewhere [1] to embody the historical and literary deductions which these bald bibliographical statements seem to me to imply. Let us turn our minds to 1246, to the situation indicated in the Letter of Leo, Rufino and Angelo prefixed to the Legend that bears their names. Even though 3 *Socii* be a later compilation, the situation in the Prefatory Letter is fully borne out by the Preface to 2 *Celano* : the only specific fact for which the Preface to 3 *Socii* is here being used is that Leo was at Greccio near Rieti in the summer of 1246 in close association with Angelo, i.e. Angelo Tancredi the Companion of S. Francis, himself a citizen of Rieti. It is a moment of great importance in the history of the Order. The Chapter-General has ordered that such of the wonderful deeds of Francis as have not yet been collected and written down in the existing Legend, i.e. in 1 *Celano*, shall be sent in to Headquarters at Assisi. Of those who really had first-hand reminiscences to contribute, who had more to write than Brother Leo ? Almost alone among the intimates of Francis he was a literary person. Caesarius of Speyer, who had helped Francis with the " First Rule " in 1221, was dead ; Brother Giles did not write, nor did Masseo, so far as we know. Rufino always had a difficulty in expressing himself, according

---

[1] *Revue d'Histoire franciscaine* for October, 1925.

to the tradition, and Angelo was a soldier rather than a clerk.

Leo, on the other hand, was a clerk in every sense of the word. He wrote a beautiful clerkly hand, which was no mean part of the stock-in-trade of a poor author in the days before printing. And he had already published the *Intentio Regule* and some form at least of the *Verba Francisci*.[1] We see from these writings that he was definitely of the party of the Strict Observance. Nevertheless it must always be borne in mind that he was not a rebel. He may indeed have protested in an insubordinate manner against the methods of Elias for collecting money to build the church of San Francesco, but he died in peace and honour at Assisi and *his* relic, the autograph Benediction written for him by Francis himself, is preserved still in the Sacro Convento, the citadel of the Conventuals.

Well, what has Leo to send to Crescentius? The Letter of the Three Companions talks about special narratives, not written down in the official Legend. This is indeed so probable in itself, that it does not need the Letter to make us believe it. I think it not unlikely that he sent a copy of the *Intentio*, neatly written out in his fine legible script, but even if he did not do so on this occasion it is likely that a copy was already to be found in the book-case of the Brothers at Assisi. Had Leo already written down and circulated other tales about S. Francis? Very likely; no

[1] See Note 1 at the end of this Paper.

doubt a good many are represented by those parts of Lemmens' *Speculum* which really do go back to Leo. These tales were also appropriate to send to Assisi in 1246, for they were not in 1 *Celano* : we may suppose, in other words, that Leo sent to Assisi a fair copy of what he had already written in separate Rolls and Notes. But these things did not exhaust his reminiscences or those of his old friends Angelo and Rufino. In Leo's packet for Crescentius there ought to have been something fresh, things that had not been written down before. If we are to identify this packet with anything that still survives, it must contain some things which do not appear to have been generally known even to those who appeal to Leo's testimony : in more concrete terms I mean some things which are not in *Isid* 1/73, or Ubertino, or Angelo Clareno.

It seems to me that Section **D** of the Perugia Legend published by Delorme is just such a collection of anecdotes as will satisfy these exacting conditions. Except to those who, as we shall see presently, may have actually seen the autograph of Leo these stories are unknown : in so far as they are known to-day they are known through what Leo sent to Assisi on this occasion. Moreover, as was stated just now, a large number of this set of tales are concerned with the Valley of Rieti, with Rieti itself, with Fonte Colombo, with Greccio. The first of them, *Per* 59, a tale which shows special acquaintance with the topography of Rieti, seems to be derived directly from Brother

Angelo.[1] How well all this fits in with the Letter prefixed to 3 *Socii* !

Brother Leo's packet arrived safely at Assisi : we know this, because Thomas of Celano made such extensive use of it in what we call 2 *Celano*. Thomas was chosen by Crescentius, as before he had been chosen by Elias, to be the historiographer of the Order, to arrange the mass of material sent to Headquarters into an orderly Legend.

A good deal must have been received besides Leo's packet, some of it good, some bad, much (no doubt) indifferent.[2] Many illiterate Friars must have sent in scrawls that required to be copied out by Celano (or his assistants, if he had any), before they could be fairly considered. Other Friars must have trudged to Assisi to testify by word of mouth. Their depositions had to be taken down. What outward form the depositions took we can only guess : in our days there would be a collection of filed Note-Books : Ubertino speaks of Leo's Rolls and Notes, but these may have been writings executed at different times under varying conditions. In the 13th century, in the work-room of so methodical a writer as Thomas of Celano, I think we may at least imagine a set of *uolumina*, of quires, which at some later time might be sewn together and bound, like the several parts of cod. 338, which consists of five distinct constituents.

[1] The same may be said of *Per* 91.
[2] See the separate Note on 2 *Cel* 117 at the end of this Paper.

The result of all that was sent in to Crescentius was the *Legenda Secunda* of Thomas of Celano. This is all that was ' published,' i.e. paraphrased by Thomas and copied out on vellum and multiplied. But to produce such a literary work from the material sent in, some such a collection of *uolumina* containing a good part of the material written out fair was almost necessary, and in any case that which Leo sent in would make several *uolumina*. Unless these were deliberately destroyed they would remain where Celano put them when he had done with them, i.e. *in armario fratrum de Assisio*, in the book-cupboard of the Sacro Convento, as indeed Ubertino says in his Declaration of 1311.[1]

In the same year as Ubertino was writing this Declaration at Avignon, the scribe of the Perugia Legend was making a great collection of Franciscan Bulls. He could not in those days consult Wadding or Sbaralea or Potthast as we do ; he would have to go to Headquarters, to the library of the Sacro Convento, to make up the set, even if some of the well-known ones had already been collected together.[2] We must therefore think of the scribe of Delorme's MS as working in the Library at Assisi. There he would doubtless find a copy of 2 *Celano*, a work which does not seem to me to have been very widely known in ancient times. It is certainly a work of great interest, and our scribe

[1] *Declaratio* of 1311 : to be found e.g. in Sabatier's ed. of the *Speculum*, p. cl.

[2] The original Bull of Honorius has always been kept there ever since S. Francis's death (Papini, *Storia de S. Francesco*, p. 123, note).

43

did well to copy out of it the 20 chapters that make up Delorme's **B**, i.e. *Per* 22–41. But besides the finished digest which Brother Thomas had made of the material sent to Assisi in 1246 our scribe interested himself in the *uolumina* that Leo had contributed. What he extracted from these make up Delorme's **C D** and **E**, of which **C** and **E** consist of tales which are known independently and so may be supposed to have been published or circulated by Leo independently of the circumstances of 1246. Section **D**, on the other hand, consists of tales which there is some reason to think were not written down before 1246; if they were known at all before Delorme's discovery of the Perugia MS it was through the use Celano made of Leo's tales (2 *Cel*), or through the use made of the Perugia MS itself (Sp. *S*). As for Delorme's Section **A** it is difficult to be certain, as Fr. Delorme himself avers:[1] my own conjecture would be that it represents an earlier smaller collection of anecdotes about S. Francis supplementary to the *Legenda Maior* of Bonaventura, perhaps already put together in a *uolumen* belonging to the Assisi Library.[2]

It is of course possible that what we read in the MS at Perugia was not first collected by the scribe of that MS in 1311. He must have gone to Assisi for his Bulls, but it is conceivable that the *Legenda antiqua* which he has transcribed was the copy of a volume in which these pieces had already been put together.

[1] Delorme in *A F H* xv, p. 98 f.   [2] See separate Note.

But what of the *Speculum Perfectionis*? What light does the MS at Perugia throw upon the way in which it was compiled? Here the essential fact is Delorme's Section **B**. This section is a set of extracts from 2 *Celano*, but they all are given in Sabatier's *Speculum*, though not one of them appears in Lemmens' *Speculum*. What is more, in *Per* these chapters form a compact group by themselves and they are given in the order that they come in 2 *Celano* (with a couple of exceptions); in Sp. *S*, on the other hand, they are scattered up and down the work, in inextricable mixture with chapters that are certainly not derived from 2 *Celano*. Why does Sp. *S* include these Celanese chapters and no others?[1] The answer must surely be that Sp. *S* is a rearrangement and reissue of *Per* itself, or else *Per* is a faithful copy of a volume of which Sp. *S* is a rearrangement and reissue.

Here the colophon of the Ognissanti MS becomes of fresh interest. If the Perugia Legend was made in 1311, the Ognissanti MS asserts that the *Speculum Perfectionis* was made in 1317 (or 1318). The contents of the two works are almost identical, but the arrangement is different. The outstanding characteristic of the order in *Per* is that the earlier works which are used remain grouped together, the *Intentio* and the *Verba* of Leo, the extracts from 2 *Celano*, are found in solid chunks; in Sp. *S*, on the other hand, everything is grouped according to its subject-matter, and the

---

[1] Except, of course, the four doubtful chapters from *Per* **A**.

Celanese chapters are found separately side by side with the Leonine ones. It seems to be impossible to avoid Fr. Delorme's conclusion that Sp. *S* is a literary work later than *Per* and formed from it by rearrangement and occasional rewriting of single words and phrases. This being so, the date 1317, given in the Ognissanti MS, seems to me the earliest we can place it, but I do not see why we should place it any later. The early years of the 14th century were just the very time when the zeal of the Spirituals was finding its outlet in literary work. Ubertino da Casale in 1305 had shown them the way and Angelo Clareno was following in his steps. While these great champions of the ideal of Evangelical Poverty were disputing at the Papal Court the cause could be served less controversially, and as effectively, by collecting and arranging what had been written down by the Companions of Francis, so that it could be displayed as the mirror of what a Brother Minor ought to be.

The *Speculum Perfectionis* as edited by Sabatier is an admirable work. One tale is told after another, some we may suppose well known to almost every Umbrian Friar, others not so widely spread though all are of the same spirit, until the Portrait of Francis moves and smiles and suffers before our eyes. For it tends to follow the natural order, the order of events. Enough is told us of the early days to make the reader feel their charm and *élan*, but in the main it is a Portrait of Francis from the time of the promulgation of the

Rule in 1223 to his death. Yet in the eyes of all the Friars it had two serious defects. There is, after all, very little about those early days, and there is very little about the Stigmata. For a mirror of Francis's perfection these two things surely were required in the 14th century. They were very soon supplied. I do not think the *Speculum Perfectionis* was compiled to complete 3 *Socii*, but it does seem to me likely that the Legend of the Three Companions was compiled to complete the *Speculum*. It is found in close connexion with the *Speculum* in several of the oldest MSS., e.g. *Isid* 1/25 in Rome and the Ognissanti MS at Florence. Together the two works form an almost complete *Vita Francisci*.

No doubt it was in the same circles and about the same time that the collection of documents and attestations dealing with the annual Indulgence of the Portiuncula on Aug. 2 was made. A little later comes the *Actus Francisci*, which is the Latin original of the Fioretti : this collection is evidently later than 1322, for it must have been made after the death of John of La Verna, who died in that year.

It was necessary to indicate the position of these works, because they were used in the compilation known as *Fac secundum exemplar*, which itself is the direct parent of the printed *Speculum Vitae*. Late as this compilation is, it nevertheless contains traces of the Perugia Legend. The chief MSS in which it is found are preceded by a preface which quotes Exod xxv 40

(*Fac secundum exemplar*) and goes on to say that what follows is a collection of things not contained in Bonaventura. The author says he had collected them when a student in Avignon, where also the Minister-General had had readings during meals *de legenda ueteri* to show that it was "true, useful, authentic and good,"[1] and he further explains that his tales are taken from (1) a book belonging to Frederick, a friar who was Archbishop of Riga from 1304–1341 but resided chiefly at Avignon, (2) an 'old legend' that was read at Avignon, (3) writings and lives of Companions of Francis, (4) some things about S. Antony and John of La Verna.

When we come to examine *Vat* 4354, which seems to be the most ancient MS of *Fac secundum*, we find that (3) with (4) means the *Actus* (i.e. practically the Fioretti), and that (1) seems to be the *Speculum Perfectionis*. About three-quarters of Sabatier's text is there, arranged in the peculiar order of Sp. *S*. The remainder therefore of *Fac secundum* we may suppose to have been extracted from the 'old legend' read at Avignon when the compiler was a student. Archbishop Frederick is not called 'of blessed memory,' so we may suppose this Preface to have been written before his death in 1341. But there is no reason to suppose that the compiler was still at Avignon, or that when he was writing matters were particularly favourable for militant Spirituals.

[1] It will not be forgotten that the Latin is ambiguous; it may mean '*the* old Legend' or '*an* old Legend.' At least this passage does not assert that there was only one old Legend, so called.

It has been too often assumed that documents of the 14th century which show zeal in recording tales of the early days of Franciscan poverty were all written or compiled by zealous *militant* Spirituals. The *Intentio*, no doubt, is written in the opposite sense to the policy of *Quo elongati* (1235), but it is not exactly militant. It says that strict poverty was the earnest desire of Francis for all his Friars, but that he yielded a little to the representations of the Ministers, though he was determined to practise it himself to the end of his days. It shows that the *Testament* was no mere afterthought of a dying man, but the expression of a life-long conviction. At the same time Leo does not incite his readers to disobey the Papal ruling. In any case the compiler of the Perugia Legend has a different standpoint from that of the *Intentio*. He transcribes Sp. *L* 44 (= Sp. *S* 50), in which Francis expresses his dislike of obtaining Papal privileges, but his book opens with a series of more than 160 Bulls, which take up considerably more than half the volume. The Perugia text cannot have been compiled by a practising Spiritual such as Angelo Clareno.

What is of direct interest to us here is that traces of the Perugia collection appear in *Vat* 4354 in the chapters that come neither from Sabatier's *Speculum* nor from the Fioretti-literature. Thus §§ 75–80 tell the story of the Novice, followed by the words about the devils being the *castaldi Domini*, followed by warning against idle words. This corresponds to sections 100,

101 and 102 of *Per*, but to Sp. *S* 4 + 71 + 11 + 82, or in Lemmens' documents to *Int* 7–16 followed by Sp. *L* 35.   It is obvious that *Vat* 4354 must have found these chapters put together as they are in the Perugia Legend.   Other sequences are *Vat* 4354 § 70, 71 = *Per* 78–9, § 72, 73, 74 = *Per* 51–3, § 85, 86 = *Per* 13, § 87, 88 = *Per* 21.   These sections come from all parts of the Perugia Legend except the extracts from 2 *Celano* : I venture to think the coincidences in arrangement here between it and the compilation found in *Vat* 4354 are useful *ad ostendendum eam esse ueram utilem et autenticam atque bonam.*[1]

If the final form of the *Speculum* be later than the text from Perugia and dependent on it, what of that found in *Isid* 1/73 and edited by Lemmens in *D A F* vol. ii, pp. 23–84 ?   Here we must make a distinction at the outset between the value of this text as a whole and its preservation in *Isid* 1/73.   The scribe of that MS is rather careless, he is capable of writing *gioia* for *gloria* and *forte* for *frate*, and he sometimes leaves out whole sentences by homoeoteleuton.   Consequently inferior texts sometimes preserve the true reading against *Isid* 1/73.   But such things are only on the surface. What is valuable in *Isid* 1/73 is the character of the sources used, both in the ' *Scripta Leonis* ' and the *Speculum* (Sp. *L*).

In the first place Sp. *L* contains no chapters taken from 2 *Celano*.   Nor is there in it anything corre-

---

[1] Preface to *Fac secundum*, quoted in Sabatier's ed. of the *Speculum*, p. clix.

sponding to *Per* **D**, i.e. the rather more intimate set of reminiscences, which we may suppose never to have been written down till 1246, and then not regularly published but sent in to Headquarters at Assisi for the official historiographer to use.   Of course Sp. *L* is not, as a collection, the work of Brother Leo.   It only claims to have been composed from certain things found in the writings of Leo and others.   Probably it was not used at all by the compiler of *Per*, but *Per* and Sp. *L* were independent compilations from Leo's *rotuli*.   The divisions or ' chunks ' of Sp. *L* which appear in *Per* will therefore indicate to us more or less the limits of these *rotuli*.

They are as follows :—

1. Sp. *L*	1–7.	Chiefly about the Franciscan view of begging for alms.
2. „	8–19.	Chiefly about the last days of Francis.
3. „	20–23.	Francis and his hard way of life.
4. „	24–33.	Miscellaneous.
5. „	34.	The last meal of Francis with the Brothers.
6. „	35–43.	Mainly about poverty and humility.
7. „	44.	No privileges for the Friars !

Of these No. 1 may be made of two separate tracts, but Nos. 2 and 3 seem to me homogeneous.   No. 4 comes in *Per* at the beginning of **C** and is marked by a specially large capital, as if it were the beginning of a document ; it also begins the extracts *De legenda*

ueteri beati Francisci which are found in the second
part of *Isid* 1/73 and printed in *D A F* ii 91–100.
In any case if we are to attempt to resolve Sp. *L* into
its constituents, the external witness of *Per* must be the
first thing to be taken into account.

To sum up the results of this long survey, we find
that a certain number of *prima facie* original authorities
for the Life of Francis are not originals and must be
used with caution. 1 *Celano* remains : we cannot
directly get behind it, though we may have reserves
based on our knowledge of the over-great discretion of
Brother Thomas and his subservience to those in
immediate authority over him. With 2 *Celano* it is
different ; for a large part of the work we possess his
materials, either directly as in the surviving writings of
Leo (*viz.* the *Intentio*, the *Verba* cc. 1–2, 4–5, and I
would add at least Sp. *L* 8–19), or indirectly from the
collection in the Perugia MS, sections **C D E.** Of
these last **D** appears to be nothing less than the special
and hitherto unpublished reminiscences which Leo sent
to Assisi in 1246, the very document to which the
Letter of the Three Companions refers.

From these writings of Leo we can have some idea
of how much Thomas of Celano alters his sources, and
that he may on the whole be trusted appears from the
fact that some things which were supposed to have
been written by his opponents turn out to be his own
composition. The historical value of what Celano tells

us depends almost entirely on the source he is using : where he is using material not derived from Leo there is at least one instance in which he appears to have been supplied with old hagiographical material in what professes to have been a direct reminiscence of Francis.

3 *Socii* is a late compilation, and the longer form of the *Speculum Perfectionis* is not an original composition but a mere rearrangement of the Perugia Legend. Yet each have their special uses. The *Speculum* is composed of such good material that the mere arrangement of the Perugia material in the new order, with the pathetic records of the last days at the end, sets Francis before our eyes more vividly than Celano does. 3 *Socii*, originally compiled to complete the picture of the Saint by giving the tale of the early days and of the Stigmata (both passed over almost completely in the *Speculum*), has still some historical value, for the tales in which 3 *Socii* is parallel to 2 *Celano* do not appear to be borrowed from 2 *Celano* direct, but to have been taken (like the Perugia Legend) from the sources of 2 *Celano*, i.e. the collection of reminiscences sent in to Assisi in 1246.

But these reminiscences were not those of Brother Leo only, and Leo's reminiscences are all of the nature of detached tales and sayings. Angelo Clareno was mistaken when he declared Leo to have written a *Vita Francisci* ; what he did was to leave us a wonderful series of tales, which supplement the tale told in 1 *Celano*, but do not supersede it.

53

THREE NOTES

1. *On Delorme's Section* **A** (= *Per* 1–21)

That Section **B** of the Perugia Legend (= *Per* 22–41) is, as Fr. Delorme maintains, a series of extracts from 2 *Celano* seems to be established beyond all doubt. The two texts agree almost word for word, the paragraphs of *Per* follow the order of 2 *Celano* with only a couple of exceptions at the end of the section, and finally most of the paragraphs are marked by the peculiar Celanese style. No doubt the material was originally supplied to Thomas from elsewhere, but in telling his stories he generally impresses upon them his own phraseology. Sometimes, of course, this is not very markedly the case : it might very well be that such-and-such a chapter of 2 *Celano* is told wholly in the words of Celano's source, but if there be such in this series it will have been from 2 *Celano* that the compiler of the Perugia Legend took it, along with all the others.

The case is rather different with Section **A**, where Fr. Delorme himself seems a little uncertain. **A** consists now of 21 divisions and perhaps five or six more have been lost at the beginning. Of those that remain, *Per* 4–13 corresponds to Sp. *L* 8–19 and *Per* 14 ff corresponds more or less to the *Verba Francisci*, i.e. to the second work ascribed to Leo in *Isid* 1/73. This work, collection, tract, or ' opuscule,' seems to have had a much less fixed content than the *Intentio Regule*. Lemmens divides it into six chapters. In all forms it contained 1. = Sp. *S* 12—' I was never a robber of alms ' ; 2. = Sp. *S* 13—' No property either in special or in common ' ; 4. = Sp. *S* 1—about Elias and the Ministers and the Voice from Heaven ; 5. = Sp. *S* 68—about Francis at the Chapter of the Mats. To this nucleus Angelo Clareno adds

6. = Sp. *S* 50, Sp. *L* 44—about Privileges, a section quoted also by Ubertino. *Isid.* 1/73, on the other hand, omits this but adds Sp. *S* 52, 79, 85, and inserts between 2. and 4. the Praise of the Rule, numbered by Lemmens as 3. In the Perugia Legend we have what corresponds to Sp. *S* 12, 13, 1, 68, 54, 50, 52, 88, i.e. Clareno's form of the *Verba* but with three more chapters of the *Speculum* added at the end. Is it not likely that the compiler took them all from the same source, that is, from an enlarged form of the *Verba* ?

But Sp. *S* 54 is not the source of *Per* 18, says Fr. Delorme ; the source is 2 *Cel* 146. I would plead for a suspension of judgement in this case. The Celanese style in 2 *Cel* is not very marked : it was a paragraph widely known, occurring in the San Antonio MS, no. 45, so that whoever first penned it, it may have been taken up by Celano without change. All I am suggesting is that the compiler of *Per* 18–20 took these chapters from an extended form of the *Verba*. Whether *Per* 21 (= Sp. *L* 34 = Sp. *S* 88) is from the same source, or to be regarded as an isolated fragment from elsewhere, is uncertain.

Of the rest of *Per* **A**, it is to be noted that the section corresponding to Sp. *L* 8–19 is all of a piece. It is all really concerned with the last days of S. Francis, though the consideration of the Saint's humility at the end of § 11 leads the writer to tell the tale of Francis's humility when preaching at Terni (§§ 12, 13) and of his resigning all his offices in the Order (§§ 14–16). But § 17 goes back to the Lady Jacoba and 'that dainty preparation,' i.e. the one referred to in § 11. Thus *Per* 4–13 (= Sp. *L* 8–19) is one whole : the text of § 10 is not quite perfect, as Delorme points out (p. 15), but must be supplemented from *Little* 158. Apart from this, these chapters seem to me to be another of Brother Leo's 'rolls,' probably written about 1235 soon after the death of

Bernard of Quintavalle. Such a Roll or *uolumen* might very well have been standing on the bookshelf side by side with the rest of Leo's ' dossier ' in the Library of the Sacro Convento when the compiler of the Perugia Legend was working there at his collecton of Franciscan Bulls.

It should be noted that Fr. Delorme in his *Legenda Antiqua S. Francisci* (Paris, 1926), p. xviii, continues to treat the *Intentio* and the *Verba* as mere extracts from the longer " Old Legend." I still agree with Fr. Lemmens that they are earlier independent works, which have been incorporated into the Perugia collection. My chief reason is the witness of Ubertino and of Angelo Clareno. These champions of the *Zelanti* appeal to what may be called the " Speculum-literature " and name Leo as the author, but *all* their quotations (enumerated by Delorme, p. xiii f.) come from the *Intentio* and the *Verba*, not from the rest of the tales. Further, Ubertino quotes the *Intentio* from beginning to end, indicating where he makes omissions, and at the end says *Hucusque uerba sancti Leonis* : it is difficult not to suppose that he, writing in 1305, knew the *Intentio* as a detached piece, one of Leo's Rolls.

The composition and contents of the *Verba* present a more difficult problem. It seems to me a sort of Appendix to the *Intentio*, and to consist of a fixed nucleus (§§ 1–2, 4–5), to which other pieces were added by Leo himself or by later transcribers. The form found in *Isid* 1/73 which adds Sp. S 52, 79, 85, is obviously later than Leo's death, but that cannot be said of the form used by Clareno and printed by Lemmens.

Most of the single paragraphs of *Per* **A C D** and **E** were penned by Leo, both according to Fr. Delorme's view and that advocated in these pages. Where we differ is that Fr. Delorme regards them as all strung together by Leo himself,

Plate III.

Church of San Francisco, Pisa.

St. Francis and six scenes from his Legend.
Attributed to Ugolino di Tedice (c. **1270-80**).

while I prefer to use Ubertino's language and speak of Leo's Rolls and Notes (two of which we know under the names *Intentio Regule* and *Verba Francisci*), and to regard the gathering of them into collections as a work of the generation after Leo's death in 1271.

2. *On 2 Celano* 117.

Obviously not all the material put before Thomas of Celano in 1246 came from one source, and that source Leo. Nor again is it likely that all that was sent in, even if sent in good faith, was historical. In such hagiographical collections one well-known form of historical error is the ascription to one Saint of something that properly belongs to a much earlier age, or at any rate to some one else. A good example is the story of the Harlot and the Saint who lay down in the burning hearth : this is told of S. Francis in Cod. San Antonio 87, and repeated in *Actus* 27, *Fioretti* 24, but according to Thomas of Chantimpré, writing in 1256, the story belongs to one John bishop of Pressburg who became a Dominican Friar.

The object of this Note is to suggest that the picturesque tale told in 2 *Cel* 117 is only another form of a much older story. Here are the tales.

The Devil having subjected Francis to the temptation of lust, and Francis finding that scourging himself was of no avail " he opened the door of his cell and went out into the garden and though it was covered with snow he bathed in it naked. So filling his hands with snow he made up seven heaps, and arranging them before him began to address them all, and said ' See, this big one is your wife, and these four—two are your sons and two your daughters, the other two are the servant and the maid that you must have to attend on them.

57

And make haste (said he) to clothe them all, for they are dying of cold. But if anxiety for their many wants annoys you be careful to serve One Master.' Thereupon the Devil departed in confusion and the Saint returned to his cell glorifying God." And Thomas of Celano adds that a certain spiritual brother who was then engaged in prayer saw the whole scene, it being a clear moonlight night, but the Saint having found out afterwards what he had observed was very grieved, and commanded him to reveal it to no one so long as he, Francis, lived in this world.

What this spiritual brother saw in the moonlight we can read in the tales of the Fathers of the Desert, where indeed there is no snow but only sand and mud. In Rosweyd 496-7 (= Migne, *Patrologia Latina* lxxiii 747) this story is told : " There was a certain Brother in the Desert who lived in the place called Cellia, and devils fought against him in the passion of fornication. So he thought within himself saying : ' It is because perchance I ought to work more with my hands, so that my carnal sense may be extinguished.' Now this Brother was a potter by trade. So he arose and fashioned in mud as it were the figure of a woman, and said to his thoughts : ' See, there is your wife ; so it is necessary for you to add beyond the ordinary to your daily work.' And after a few days he made a similar thing of mud and fashioned as it were a daughter for himself, and said to his thoughts : ' See, your wife has had a daughter ; so it is necessary for you to labour more and more still harder that you may be able to feed and clothe yourself and your wife and your daughter.' And so with overmuch labour he afflicted his body, so that he could not any more endure such labour. Then he said to his thoughts : ' If you cannot endure this overmuch labour neither do you need a wife.' But God seeing the fervent decision of his mind in the fight for chastity took away from him the annoyance of the devils' attacks, and he glorified God for the greatness of His grace."

The same tale is also to be found in the Syriac *Apophtheg-mata* (Budge, *Paradise*, p. 772, no. 553).

The story as given in 2 *Celano* 117 has a charm and vividness which recalls the Fioretti, but it is not told elsewhere of S. Francis. Nor do I think the moral that working for a wife and family involved more trouble than it was worth is truly Franciscan.

3. On the Codex of S. Antonio at Rome.

This MS has been fully described by the competent pen of Fr. Livarius Oliger in *Archivum Franciscanum Historicum*, vol. xii, pp. 321–400. It is a 14th cent. text, containing Bonaventura (adorned with very curious miniatures), the Portiuncula Indulgence documents, and a Collection of Franciscan anecdotes. Most of these are well known, but the special merit of the S. Antonio codex is that it contains a few quite unknown from other sources. Thus § 59*b* is, so far as I know, our only ancient surviving authority for the very interesting tale of Brother Stephen [1] when he was cook to S. Francis.

The Praise of the Good Nine Friars will be found in § 47 : " Blessed Francis used to say, He would be a good Brother Minor who had the faith of Brother *Bernard* with his love of poverty, the charity of Brother *Angelo*, the devout feeling and speech of Brother *Masseo*, the lofty mind of Brother *Giles*, the continuous prayer of Brother *Rufino*, the patience of Brother *Juniper*, the bodily and spiritual strength of

---

[1] Quoted and annotated by G. G. Coulton in *The Beginnings of Christianity*, vol. ii, p. 441, from Wadding's Annals, but it is possible that Wadding got his information from the Codex. The story is also preserved in an old Italian version (See Minocchi, *Leggenda antica*, Florence, 1905).

Brother *John de Laudibus*, who at that time was the strongest of men, the charity of Brother *Roger*, the carefulness of Brother *Lucido*, who would not stay in any place more than about a month, but as soon as a place pleased him went away to another, saying 'We have not here an abiding city or dwellings, but in heaven.' "

Very likely 'charity' as applied to Angelo Tancredi should rather be 'courtesy (*curialitatem*), but otherwise this seems to me to be the original, from which Chap. 85 of Sabatier's Speculum has been expanded to include Brother Leo.

Two other tales from the Cod. S. Antonio seem worth quoting here for their intrinsic merits. In § 72 we read :— " Brother Theobald said he saw, when once S. Francis was preaching to the people at Trevi, a certain donkey, very strong and untamed, frightened every one by running among the people in the market-place. And when he saw it could not be captured by any one and held S. Francis said : ' Brother donkey, stand quiet and let me preach to the people.' On hearing this immediately the donkey put its head between its legs and to every one's astonishment stood in great silence. And blessed Francis, in order that men might not take notice of a miracle so stupendous began to say comic things to make them laugh."

There is plenty of testimony to the fact that Francis was one of those who have a strange power over animals, but what makes this story so noteworthy is the detail at the end about his making jokes to prevent the crowd making too much of the occurrence.

The other story, a most picturesque example of Francis's manner of speech, is as follows (§ 54) :—" Brother Leo, the companion of blessed Francis, said that there was a certain Brother whose holiness was such that he seemed like a new

Apostle, but at last he was tempted and left the Order. In the world also, after he had left the Order he showed such ripeness of character that even then he seemed to approach apostolical excellence. And when one day Brother Leo and some other Brethren were going on a certain way with blessed Francis the question was proposed by the Brethren in the Saint's presence why the aforesaid Brother had left the Order. And he answered : ' I will give a lecture and ask myself some questions, answering them, I mean, and solving them ; let no one speak to me till I finish.' And he began to say ' Humility !' two or three times—' Chastity !'—' Abstinence !'— ' Poverty !' And thus he named many virtues one by one, each one several times. And with each he would say to himself ' Do you know this one well ? ' and answer ' I do.' But at the end of the lecture he said several times ' Fear !' And when he said ' Do you know this one ? ' he answered ' No.' And again he called ' Fear !' repeating it several times. And when he asked himself ' Do you know this one ? ' he answered ' No.' And he called again ' Fear !' And in the end he managed to answer ' I do !' And he added : ' It's no use for a man to heap up virtues without Fear, which few have, so that it is learned with difficulty,' and he ended by saying ' For want of Fear that virtuous Brother fell and has left the Order.' "

ST. FRANCIS AND DANTE

PROFESSOR EDMUND G. GARDNER, LITT.D., F.B.A.

III

SAINT FRANCIS AND DANTE

I

I FEEL that I cannot more fittingly open this course of lectures in commemoration of the seventh centenary of St. Francis of Assisi than by quoting a passage from the message which the head of the Italian National Government, Benito Mussolini, has addressed to the representatives of Italy abroad :

"Il più alto genio alla poesia, con Dante ; il più audace navigatore agli oceani, con Colombo ; la mente più profonda alle arti e alla scienza, con Leonardo ; ma l'Italia, con San Francesco, ha dato anche il più santo dei santi al Cristianesimo e all'umanità."

It is well perhaps, even during this centenary, to remember the words of one who was likewise a lover of the *poverello* of Assisi, Thomas à Kempis : " Do not question or dispute concerning the merits of the Saints, as to who is more holy than another, or who greater in the kingdom of heaven."[1] Yet we may assuredly claim that, among the Saints, St. Francis is the most perfect and characteristic fruit of the religious genius of mediæval Italy, as St. Louis and St. Joan of mediæval

---

[1] *De Imitatione Christi*, iii. 58.

France, St. Ignatius Loyola and St. Teresa of sixteenth-century Spain. And with St. Francis, the national saint, stands Dante, the national poet, who so profoundly felt his influence, and so wonderfully interpreted his spirit :

> " Degno è che, dov'è l'un, l'altro s'induca ;
> sì che, com'elli ad una militaro,
> così la gloria loro insieme luca." [1]

Their names and their work are indissolubly linked ; the *verus paupertatis amator*, the *vir praedicans iustitiam.*

Dante himself—in the noblest of those lyrical poems of his which preceded the *Divina Commedia*—adapts a spiritual experience allegorically reported of St. Francis to a moment of his own inner life : the moment, perhaps, in which he realised his mission. It is the legend or allegory—told by Thomas of Celano, somewhat elaborated by St. Bonaventura, and painted by Sassetta in the most beautiful of all Franciscan pictures—of how the Saint, on his way to Siena, in the plain between Campiglia and San Quirico, was met by three poor women, " mulieres pauperculae," who offered a new salutation : " Bene veniat domina paupertas." " And, when he heard this, the true lover of poverty was filled with unspeakable joy, for no salutation from men would he have received so gladly as that which these gave him." When they disappeared, the friars, his companions, deemed that some mystical thing was signified

---

[1] *Par.* xii. 34–36.

concerning the holy man, and that they represented
Chastity, Obedience, and Poverty, " which shone out in
equal form in the man of God, albeit he chose rather to
glory in the privilege of Poverty, whom he was wont
to call now his Mother, now his Bride, now his
Lady."[1]

Such allegorical picturings, and there are many in
mediæval literature, in which a mystery is played by
three figures, probably hark back to the passage in
Genesis (xviii. 1–2), where the Lord appeared unto
Abraham as " he sat in the tent-door in the heat of the
day ; and he looked, and, lo, three men stood by him ;
and when he saw them, he ran to meet them from the
tent-door." Richard of St. Victor interprets the tent
as " the habitation of the human mind," and the running
out to meet the Lord " the excess of the human mind,
through which it is rapt above itself into the mysteries
of divine contemplation."[2] In composing his canzone,
Tre donne intorno al cor mi son venute, Dante may well
have had as model also a *romanza* of Giraut de Borneil,
but the influence of the Franciscan allegory is unmistakable.[3] Here, too, three women appear around
Dante's heart ; that is, to his inner sight ; and they

---

[1] Bonaventura, *Legenda maior*, vii. § 6. Cf. Thomas of Celano, *Legenda
secunda* (ed. P. Edouard d'Alençon), (ii) lx. § 93.

[2] *Benjamin maior*, v. 8.

[3] *Rime*, ed. M. Barbi (*Testo critico*), civ ; Oxford Dante, ed. P. Toynbee,
Canz. xx. Cf. F. Torraca, *La canzone delle tre donne*, in his *Nuovi studi danteschi*
(Naples, 1921) ; E. G. Gardner, *Notes on the Lyrical Poetry of Dante*, in *Modern
Language Review*, vol. xix. pp. 310–312.

are poorer of aspect than the "mulieres pauperculae" who had been the visitants of St. Francis :

> " Ciascuna par dolente e sbigottita,
> come persona discacciata e stanca,
> cui tutta gente manca
> e cui vertute nè beltà non vale.
> Tempo fu già nel quale,
> secondo il lor parlar, furon dilette ;
> or sono a tutti in ira ed in non cale." [1]

Their leader is " discinta e scalza " ; " povera, vedi, a panni ed a cintura." But they are no longer Poverty with Chastity and Obedience, for the times require more active virtues from him who would be their reformer : " ut utiliter mundo pervigilem." [2] The Franciscan visitants are transformed into Justice (*Drittura*), and her spiritual offspring, Natural Justice and Legal Justice ; and, when Love who is lord of Dante's heart takes up the word and announces the ultimate triumph of right, the same joy fills the poet's mind as had filled that of St. Francis at the salutation of Lady Poverty :

> " E io, che ascolto nel parlar divino
> consolarsi e dolersi
> così alti dispersi,
> l'essilio che m'è dato, onor mi tegno."

The apparition of Drittura before the heart of which

---

[1] Cf. the words about Lady Poverty in Thomas of Celano, *Legenda secunda*, (ii) xxv. § 55 : " Hanc Filio Dei familiarem attendens, iam iamque *toto orbe repulsam* studet charitate perpetua desponsare." Also *Sacrum Commercium* (ed. E. Alvisi, p. 20) : " Cunctis viventibus odiosa non modicum existebas et omnes te fugiebant, et prout poterant effugabant."

[2] *Monarchia*, i. I.

Love is lord will lead naturally to the claim to be " vir praedicans iustitiam," in the letter to the friend at Florence refusing to return to the city under dishonouring conditions. Justice becomes for Dante what Poverty had been for Francis of Assisi.

II

It was nearly thirty-nine years after the death of St. Francis when Dante was born in 1265. The last survivor of the original group of twelve companions, Egidio, the blessed Giles of Assisi, had died three years before (1262). St. Bonaventura was minister-general of the Order, the seventh in succession from the death of St. Francis, his immediate predecessor, the blessed John of Parma, having been compelled to abdicate in 1257 ; he was engaged in his hopeless task of imposing a *via media* upon the brethren which should at once recall the one faction to the observance of the rule and check the dangerous zeal of the other. With the same reconciliatory purpose he had written his own life of St. Francis, the *Legenda maior*, in 1260, and in 1266— the year after Dante's birth—the chapter-general at Paris had decreed the destruction of the earlier lives or legends. Two of the earliest followers and closest associates of St. Francis were still living : Ruffino, the kinsman perhaps of St. Clare, he of whom the Seraphic Father used to say that he had been canonised in this life by Christ, and Leone, " Brother Leo," the " pecorella di Dio," the Saint's secretary, special confidant,

69

and most loved spiritual son. They died in 1270 and 1271 respectively. Bonaventura himself died in 1274, the year in which Dante first saw Beatrice. There still lived—if the generally accepted identification is right— another of those who had been with Francis from the earliest days of the Order, one whom Dante was to see by the side of Bonaventura in the *Paradiso* : Illuminato of Rieti.

In a famous passage of the *Inferno*, Dante represents himself as following Virgil in Franciscan fashion through one of the circles of Hell :

> " Taciti, soli, sanza compagnia
> n'andavam l'un dinanzi e l'altro dopo,
> come frati minor vanno per via." [1]

He has previously spoken of wearing the cord, with which he had once thought to subdue the leopard of sensuality :

> " Io avea una corda intorno cinta,
> e con essa pensai alcuna volta
> prender la lonza a la pelle dipinta." [2]

Nevertheless, there is no reliable evidence of any direct connection between Dante and the Franciscan Order. The statement of his fourteenth-century commentator, Francesco da Buti, that the poet became a Franciscan novice in his youth, but returned to the world before making his profession, is probably no more than an attempt to explain the wearing of this cord, which is presently taken off and given to Virgil

---

[1] *Inf.* xxiii. 1–3. [2] *Inf.* xvi. 106–108.

to cast into the abyss.[1]   The tradition that he was in later life a Franciscan tertiary, and was buried in the Franciscan habit, seems to date at the earliest only from the end of the fifteenth century, and must be regarded as unproved, though not in any way impossible.[2]   But the Franciscan influence upon Dante is none the less deep and penetrating. He tells us in the *Convivio* that, in his quest of philosophy after the death of Beatrice, he frequented " le scuole de li religiosi." [3] Though, on the theological and philosophical side, he unquestionably drew more from Aquinas, his " buono frate Tommaso d'Aquino," than from Bonaventura, the latter's contribution was not small, while the spirit of St. Francis himself has inspired many a motive and episode in the sacred poem.

Two motives—not, indeed, exclusively Franciscan, but supremely exemplified in the teaching and practice of St. Francis—run from the *Vita Nuova* to the *Paradiso* : the conception of the courtesy of God, on the one hand, and, on the other, of humility as the supreme and crowning virtue, after love, of the spiritual life.

We read, in the *Fioretti*, that St. Francis on one occasion was profoundly moved by the courtesy of a certain nobleman, and said to his companion : " Know, dearest brother, that courtesy is one of the attributes of God, who gives His sun and His rain to the just and

---

[1] *Inf.* xvi. 109–114.

[2] Cf. the present writer, *Dante and the Mystics*, pp. 199–201.

[3] *Conv.* ii. 12 (13).

71

to the unjust for courtesy ; and courtesy is sister of
charity, and she quenches hatred and preserves love.
And because I have recognised so great a divine virtue
in this good man, I would gladly have him as companion." The story may or may not be precise
history, but we can scarcely doubt that the phrase—
la cortesia è una delle proprietà di Dio, or, in its Latin
form, *curialitas est una de proprietatibus Dei*—must be
taken as an authentic saying of St. Francis.[1] And the
Franciscan legend is full of this virtue of " curialitas "
or " cortesia." Thomas of Celano says of the Saint
himself that he was " curialissimus," and, in the
Legend of the Three Companions, we read : " Erat
tamen quasi naturaliter curialis in moribus et in verbis."
When St. Francis compels Bernardo da Quintavalle in
the name of holy obedience to tread three times upon
him, his faithful follower fulfils the command " as
courteously as he could " : " quanto potè il più cortesemente." Among the many faults that Fra Salimbene
imputes to Brother Elias is lack of " curialitas" in dealing
with those under him : " A curialitate humana etiam

---

[1] *Fioretti di San Francesco,* cap. xxxvii. " Les paroles si originales de saint
François sur la courtoisie de Dieu," as M. Sabatier well says. The Latin
original of this chapter of the *Fioretti,* which was lacking in M. Sabatier's
edition of the *Actus beati Francisci et Sociorum eius* (Paris, 1902), has been
found and published by A. G. Little, *Description of a Franciscan Manuscript
formerly in the Phillipps Library,* in *Collectanea Franciscana* (Aberdeen, 1914),
pp. 41–43. " Curialitas enim, frater karissime, est una de proprietatibus Dei,
qui solem suum et pluviam suam et omnia super iustos et iniustos curialiter
administrat. Est enim curialitas ordinata soror caritatis et extinctrix odii et
conservatrix amoris."

habetur, quod proximus diligi debet. Caritas enim et curialitas sorores sunt." [1]

And with this we cannot but associate Dante's own emphasis upon *cortesia*. In the *Vita Nuova*, not only do we hear of the "ineffabile cortesia" of Beatrice (where, perhaps, the poet is merely following the troubadours and his own lyrical predecessors), but the Blessed Virgin is "la donna della cortesia," and God Himself "Sire della cortesia." [2] There is a passage in the *Convivio* where Dante says "cortesia e onestade è tutt'uno," and we know that for him, as for Augustine and Aquinas, *onestade*, *honestas*, has frequently the sense of spiritual beauty. [3] In the *Divina Commedia*, God—the "avversario d'ogni male"—was "cortese" to Æneas, in allowing his descent into the lower world for the foundation of Rome and her Empire ; Cacciaguida blesses the Holy Trinity for the grace vouchsafed to Dante, "che nel mio seme se' tanto cortese" ; and Beatrice speaks of God forgiving sin "per sua cortesia." Virgil is "anima cortese mantovana." Indeed, "cortesia" is the note of all that second canto of the *Inferno*, which is the preparation for the poet's spiritual pilgrimage ; a note that is repeated throughout the *Purgatorio*, where the Angels utter "cortesi inviti," and

---

[1] Thomas of Celano, *Legenda prima*, (i) vii. § 17 ; *Legenda trium Sociorum*, ed. P. P. Marcellino da Civezza e Teofilo Domenichelli, p. 8 ; *Fioretti* iii ; Salimbene, *Cronica fratris Salimbene de Adam Ord. Min.*, ed. O. Holder-Egger, pp. 113–115.   [2] *V.N.* iii, xii, xlii.

[3] *Conv.* ii. 10 (11). Cf. *Conv.* iii. 15 ; *De Vulgari Eloquentia*, i. 18, ii. 2 ; Aquinas, *Summa Theologica*, II. ii., q. 145, a. 2 ; *Liber Sapientiae*, vii. 11.

the souls—who are reforming the image of God within themselves—imitate the divine attribute of courtesy. And, in the *Paradiso*, it is "l'infiammata cortesia" of St. Thomas Aquinas, in his panegyric of St. Francis, that moves St. Bonaventura to utter the corresponding praises of St. Dominic.[1] Students of English mystical literature will remember how the Franciscan conception of the courtesy of God, how God is our courteous Lord and would have His blessed creatures like to Himself in this, is elaborated by Mother Julian of Norwich.

Again, Dante says of St. Francis that he " cominciò umilmente il suo convento." [2] " Strive after humility," said St. Bernard, " for it is the foundation and guardian of the virtues." The biographers of St. Francis— indeed every legend that has come down to us—lay stress upon his basing, not merely his Order, but his whole life, on the virtue of humility. Thus Thomas of Celano : " On this he sought to build himself, that he might lay the foundation which he had learned from Christ." [3] And it is on the note of humility that the Saint himself closes his *Laudes creaturarum*, his *Canticum fratris Solis* :

" Laudate e benedicete lu mi signore e rengratiate e servite a lui cum grande humilitate." [4]

[1] *Inf.* ii. 17, 58, 134 ; *Purg.* ix. 92, xiii. 27 ; *Par.* vii. 91, xii. 143, xv. 48. Notice, too, the terrible effect of the ironical application of the epithet to the treacherous bishop of Feltre, " questo prete cortese " (*Par.* ix. 58).

[2] *Par.* xxii. 90.

[3] *Legenda secunda*, (ii) cii. § 140. Cf. Bonaventura, vi. § 1.

[4] I quote the Canticle in the text given by I. Della Giovanna.

Dante confesses himself as particularly tempted to pride, but no true student of the poet can doubt for a moment that humility in his eyes was indeed " the foundation and guardian of the virtues." We see, in the *Vita Nuova*, how constantly he associates it with Beatrice. He sees her " benignamente d'umiltà vestuta " ; in his dream of her death, " avea seco umilità verace " ; the light of her humility passes the heavens, and, when she leaves the world, she is placed by the Lord " nel ciel de l'umiltate, ov'è Maria." And humility is the fruit in others of her salutation : " E sì l'umilia, ch'ogni offesa oblia." It is wrought by the sound of her voice :

> " Ogne dolcezza, ogne pensero umile
> nasce nel core a chi parlar la sente " ;

her very aspect transforms all things to its likeness : " La vista sua fa onne cosa umile." The unfinished canzone, to show " come operava in me la sua vertude," closes the story of her life on earth on the note of humility, the crowning effect of her influence upon Dante : " E sì è cosa umil, che nol si crede."[1] In the *Purgatorio*, among those Angels who preside over the seven terraces, the most beautiful is surely the Angel of Humility :

> " A noi venia la creatura bella,
> bianco vestito e ne la faccia quale
> par tremolando mattutina stella." [2]

---

[1] *V.N.*, Son. xv. 6, Canz. ii. 69, Canz. iii. 21, Son. xviii. 4, Canz. i. 40, Son. xi. 9-10, Son. xvi. 9, § xxvii.

[2] *Purg.* xii. 88-90.

And those cantos which deal with the purification of the once proud are in effect a hymn to humility. We notice the singular delight with which Dante gazes upon the images of that virtue sculptured upon the mountain wall : " l'imagini di tante umilitadi " ; humility in them of low degree exemplified in Mary herself, she who is " umile e alta più che creatura " ; humility in the mighty represented in David and Trajan. The story of Trajan and the poor widow, told by mediæval writers as an example of justice, is characteristically transformed by the poet into one of humility.[1] The motive of thus taking the Blessed Virgin as the first example in each terrace, of the virtue contrary to the capital vice which is to be purged away, came to Dante from a Franciscan book : the *Speculum beatæ Mariæ Virginis* of Friar Conrad of Saxony. And, among the stories of the souls in this terrace, is one that has taken shape with words borrowed from the life of St. Francis himself. Provenzano Salvani—the great burgher politician and faction leader of Siena, who in his pride thought to become master of his native city—has been allowed to enter Purgatory in virtue of an act of humility when he begged the money for his friend's ransom in the Campo :

> " Quando vivea più glorioso (disse),
>   liberamente nel Campo di Siena,
>   ogni vergogna diposta, s'affisse ;
> e lì, per trar l'amico suo di pena
>   che sostenea ne la prigion di Carlo,
>   si condusse a tremar per ogni vena." [2]

[1] *Purg.* x. 28–99 ; *Par.* xxxiii. 2.   [2] *Purg.* xi. 133–138.

So, in St. Bonaventura's *Legenda*, we read how Francis, "founded in the humility of Christ," begged alms for the restoration of the church of San Damiano : "Laying aside all shame, for the love of the poor Crucified, he begged from those among whom he had used to be rich."[1]

That is the terrace where the roots of pride are removed from the soul, but even more numerous are the Franciscan echoes in the terrace where avarice is purged away. It is true that the opposing virtue, represented by the Angel at the steps, is not Voluntary Poverty, but Justice—for that is demanded by Dante's ethical scheme. But, in the examples that the souls themselves recite of Voluntary Poverty and Liberality, the emphasis is laid upon the former in the proportion of two to one, and the first, that of the Blessed Virgin, recalls another passage in Bonaventura's *Legenda* :

> "E per ventura udi' ' Dolce Maria '
>   dinanzi a noi chiamar così nel pianto
>   come fa donna che in parturir sia ;
> e seguitar : ' Povera fosti tanto,
>   quanto veder si può per quello ospizio
>   dove sponesti il tuo portato santo."[2]

St. Francis, says St. Bonaventura, "would often with tears recall to mind the poverty of Jesus Christ and of His Mother, and declare that this was the queen of

---

[1] *Legenda maior*, ii. § 7. Note the verbal echoes : "Depositaque omni verecundia propter amorem pauperis Crucifixi, mendicabat apud eos inter quos abundare solebat." Dante's indebtedness to Bonaventura in this passage was first indicated by A. Bertoldi, *Il canto XI. del Paradiso* (Florence, 1904).

[2] *Purg.* xx. 19–24.

virtues, because she shone forth so pre-eminently in the King of Kings and in the Queen His Mother." [1] In this terrace, too, Dante and Virgil receive from Statius the Franciscan greeting : " Frati miei, Dio vi dea pace " ; even as St. Francis himself had said in his *Testament* : " The Lord revealed to me this salutation, that we should say : *The Lord give thee peace.*" [2] And the poet, among the penitent souls in this circle, has already spoken with Pope Adrian V, who—as Cardinal Ottobono de' Fieschi—had protected John of Parma from persecution, and after his brief pontificate, " un mese e poco più," had chosen as his burial-place the church of the Friars Minor in Viterbo. " In that same place," writes Salimbene, " was buried the lord pope Adrian, who, because of his great love for them, wished to have his sepulchre with the brethren." [3]

It is a striking fact (such things with Dante are never mere coincidences) that the Pope whose figure is contrasted with that of Adrian, in the numerically corresponding canto of the *Inferno*, was likewise associated with John of Parma and a friend of the Franciscan Order : Nicholas III. [4] He had as a child even seen St. Francis himself. Salimbene says : " Concerning him, when he was a boy and offered to blessed Francis by his father, who was of the third order, the Saint

[1] *Legenda maior*, vii. § 1. Cf. St. Francis in his Letter to all the Faithful, *Opuscula S. Patris Francisci*, Quaracchi edition, p. 88.

[2] *Purg.* xxi. 13 ; *Opuscula S. Francisci*, p. 80. Cf. Bonaventura, iii. § 2.

[3] *Cronica, ed. cit.*, p. 666 ; *Purg.* xix. 97–114.

[4] *Inf.* xix.

foretold that he was not to be a friar in habit, but the defender of his Order and the lord of the world."[1] The fate of Pope Nicholas and that of Guido da Montefeltro, the only friar in the *Inferno*, are, for Dante, Franciscan tragedies which even the intervention of the Saint himself was powerless to avert :

> " Francesco venne poi, com'io fu' morto,
>   per me ; ma un de' neri cherubini
>   li disse : ' Non portar : non mi far torto.
>   Venir se ne dee giù tra ' miei meschini'." [2]

Two Franciscans are named in the *Purgatorio*, but presumably already in Paradise : " lo buon Marzucco," Marzucco degli Scornigiani, the powerful nobleman of Pisa who, become a friar in later life, stayed for a while the factions of his citizens over the body of his slain son ; Piero Pettinagno, the Sienese combseller and Franciscan tertiary, that " great practiser of seraphic wisdom," who instructed Ubertino da Casale " in the whole process of the higher contemplation of the life of Christ." [3] In the *Paradiso*, Dante learns from a Franciscan nun, Piccarda Donati, the doctrine of the Mansions of Beatitude, and the " perfetta vita e alto merto " of St. Clare.[4] In the fourth heaven he finds the great Franciscan doctor, St. Bonaventura, presiding with St. Thomas Aquinas over the two garlands of

---

[1] *Cronica, ed. cit.*, p. 667, and cf. his pathetic story of the visit of John of Parma to the Pope, p. 302.

[2] *Inf.* xxvii. 112–115.

[3] *Purg.* vi. 18, xiii. 128 ; Ubertino da Casale, *Arbor Vitae Crucifixae Jesu*, Prologus I.

[4] *Par.* iii. 97–108.

79

doctors and teachers, and hears from the latter the story of St. Francis himself.

III

There were no doubt various reasons, connected with the mystical structure of the *Paradiso*, for which Dante selected the fourth heaven as that in which to receive the legend of St. Francis from the mouth of Aquinas, but one at least was that no sphere was so fitting as that of the Sun for the praise of him who had hailed the Sun as his brother in the *Canticum fratris Solis*:

" Laudato si', mi signore, cum tucte le tue creature spetialmente messer lu frate sole, lu quale lu iorno allumeni per nui ; e ellu è bellu e radiante cum grande splendore ; de te, altissimu, porta significatione."

It is possible to find something missing in this sublime hymn of praise from the greatest of mediæval poets to the greatest of mediæval saints : the touching familiarity and simplicity of word and deed, the apostleship of love among men, the fellowship with birds and beasts, all the tender personality which is revealed in the *Fioretti* and the *Speculum Perfectionis*. It was not Dante's purpose to dwell upon this aspect of St. Francis, but to present him as the creator of a new religious order based upon humility and poverty, the instrument of Divine Providence on behalf of Rome to restore the primitive life of Christ in the Church by his perfect imitation of her Divine Founder.[1] He is the " padre "

[1] Cf. F. Novati, *Dante e S. Francesco d'Assisi*, in his *Freschi e minii del dugento* (Milan, 1908), p. 213.

and " maestro " of the Franciscan family, its " archi-
mandrita," and the reception of the Stigmata itself is
the *ultimo sigillo*, the third and final confirmation of his
Order—after the approbation of Popes Innocent and
Honorius—by Christ Himself.

Bonaventura's *Legenda* is unquestionably Dante's
chief source for the actual events of the Saint's life,
though he apparently knew something of the earlier,
equally official in its own day, *Legenda prima*, of Thomas
of Celano. But the poet was also acquainted with
another, unofficial and—from the ecclesiastical standpoint—decidedly unorthodox source : the *Arbor Vitae
Crucifixae Jesu* of Ubertino da Casale, composed on
La Verna itself in 1305, and representing the standpoint of the persecuted spiritual party in the Order.[1]
From Ubertino comes in part the conception of what
we may call Dante's prelude to the legend ; the purpose
of Divine Providence in the raising up simultaneously
of Francis and Dominic :

> " La provedenza, che governa il mondo
>   con quel consiglio nel quale ogni aspetto
>   creato è vinto pria che vada al fondo,
> però ch'andasse ver lo suo diletto
>   la sposa di colui ch'ad alte grida
>   disposò lei col sangue benedetto,
> in sè sicura e anche a lui più fida,
>   due principi ordinò in suo favore,
>   che quinci e quindi le fosser per guida.

---

[1] This was first indicated by U. Cosmo, *Le mistiche nozze di frate Francesco
con madonna Povertà*, in *Giornale Dantesco*, anno vi (1898).

L'un fu tutto serafico in ardore ;
l'altro per sapienza in terra fue
di cherubica luce uno splendore.
De l'un dirò, però che d'amendue
si dice l'un pregiando, quale uom prende,
perch' ad un fine fuor l'opere sue." [1]

Similarly, Ubertino speaks of the rising of St. Francis and St. Dominic as the succouring of the fallen Church by a new offspring of the spirit of poverty, the last summons of the Bridegroom to the Spouse of Christ, through men " who both by the example of their life strenuously rebuked the deformed Church, and by the word of the preacher excited the people to repentance ; and by the argument of defence confuted the pravity of heresy, and by the pleading of prayer appeased the divine wrath. Among whom, typifying Elias and Enoch, Francis and Dominic singularly shone out ; of whom the first was purged by the Seraph's coal, and, inflamed with heavenly ardour, seemed to enkindle the whole world ; but the second, like a Cherub, stretching out and covering, glowing with the light of wisdom, and fruitful with the word of preaching, shone the brighter above the world's darkness . . . albeit, in each, splendour and ardour were united in abundance of spirit." [2]

[1] *Par.* xi. 28-42.
[2] *Arbor Vitae Crucifixae,* lib. v. cap. 3. Ubertino has the respective images of seraphical ardour and cherubical light, but, for Francis, Dante's " tutto serafico in ardore " is a literal rendering of Bonaventura's " incendio seraphico totus ignitus " (*Legenda maior*, prologus, § 1). So Celano, *Legenda prima*, (ii) ix. § 115 : " Seraphim imaginem tenuit atque formam."

In the beautiful lines describing Assisi, and the birth of Francis as the rising of a new spiritual sun upon the world, the imagery was traditional with the Franciscans. Thus Thomas of Celano, on the Saint's death : " O vere mundi lucerna, sole splendidius lucens in Christi Ecclesia," and Pope Gregory IX, in the exordium of his sermon when canonising him : " Quasi sol refulgens, sic iste effulsit in templo Dei " : [1]

> " Intra Tupino e l'acqua che discende
>   del colle eletto dal beato Ubaldo,
>   fertile costa d'alto monte pende,
> onde Perugia sente freddo e caldo
>   da Porta Sole ; e di rietro le piange
>   per grave giogo Nocera con Gualdo.
> Di questa costa, là dov'ella frange
>   più sua rattezza, nacque al mondo un sole,
>   come fa questo tal volta di Gange.
> Però chi d'esso loco fa parole,
>   non dica Ascesi, chè direbbe corto,
>   ma Oriente, se proprio dir vuole." [2]

From this point onwards, Dante closely follows Bonaventura for the story of the " mirabil vita del poverel di Dio," even occasionally in the actual phraseology, with apparently here and there an echo of Thomas of Celano, but transforms the tale, giving it a colour which is less Bonaventura's than that of the spiritual party in the Order, by making the mystical espousals with Lady Poverty the centre of the whole.

In the *Legenda prima* of Thomas of Celano, Francis —when asked by his friends whether he is going to

---

[1] *Legenda prima*, (ii) viii. § 111, § 125.   [2] *Par.* xi. 43–54.

take a wife—answers : " I am going to take a nobler
and fairer bride than you ever saw, who excels all
others in beauty and surpasses all in wisdom." [1] Thomas
—writing (about 1228) under the influence of Brother
Elias who was then Vicar-General—represents the chosen
Bride as True Religion, *vera religio*. But who can
doubt that it was Lady Poverty whom Francis himself
meant ?   And indeed, in the *Legenda secunda*, composed
nearly twenty years later, and now under the influence
of the party of the strict observance, we are left with
no uncertainty on the subject :

" Placed in the valley of tears this blessed father
scorns as penury the common riches of the sons of
men, since, seeking a higher degree, he longs with all
his heart for Poverty. Considering her as the familiar
friend of the Son of God, he strives to espouse with
perpetual love her who was now cast out by all the
world. Having thus become a lover of her beauty,
that he might cleave more strongly to his bride, and
that they two might be one in spirit, he not only left
his father and mother, but even put all things from
him. Therefore he draws her to himself with chaste
embraces, nor for a moment does he endure not to be
her husband." [2]

But, before Thomas of Celano, in the *Sacrum
Commercium*—questionably attributed by some to Gio-

[1] *Legenda prima*, (i) iii. § 7.

[2] Thomas of Celano, *Legenda secunda*, (ii) xxv. § 55. See Father Cuthbert,
St. Francis and Poverty, in *Franciscan Essays*, by Paul Sabatier and others
(Aberdeen, 1912), pp. 18, 19. Cf. Bonaventura, *Legenda maior*, vii. § 1.

vanni Parenti and by others to John of Parma, and written, according to the former, in 1227, the year after the Saint's death—we read how " the blessed Francis, like a true imitator and disciple of the Saviour, from the beginning of his conversion, gave himself up to seek, to find, and to hold Holy Poverty, that he might come unto her to whom the Lord had given the keys of the kingdom of heaven," and how at last he and his brethren attained to her embrace on the topmost pinnacle of the mountain of light. Here, too, we read that Poverty suffered with Christ upon the Cross, " so that nothing did seem more glorious in Him than her."

It is in this spirit that Dante transforms the whole scene, which he had read in Bonaventura, of Francis renouncing all things in the presence of his father and the Bishop of Assisi, into the wedding solemnity of the Saint and Lady Poverty :

> " Non era ancor molto lontan da l'orto,
> ch'el cominciò a far sentir la terra
> de la sua gran virtute alcun conforto ;
> chè per tal donna, giovinetto, in guerra
> del padre corse, a cui, come a la morte,
> la porta del piacer nessun diserra ;
> e dinanzi a la sua spirital corte
> et coram patre le si fece unito ;
> poscia di dì in dì l'amò più forte.
> Questa, privata del primo marito,
> millecent' anni e più dispetta e scura
> fino a costui si stette sanza invito ;
> nè valse udir che la trovò sicura
> con Amiclate, al suon de la sua voce,
> colui ch'a tutto 'l mondo fè paura ;

85

nè valse esser costante nè feroce,
  sì che, dove Maria rimase giuso,
  ella con Cristo salse in su la croce.
Ma perch'io non proceda troppo chiuso,
  Francesco e Povertà per questi amanti
  prendi oramai nel mio parlar diffuso." [1]

Most probably Dante had no direct knowledge of the *Sacrum Commercium*, much less of the *Legenda secunda* of Thomas of Celano. It may be that the conception of the mystical espousals had become so well known that a literary source need not be assumed (Giotto's fresco at Assisi, whenever painted, is almost certainly earlier than the *Paradiso*); but there can be no doubt that the poet was directly influenced by the *Arbor Vitae Crucifixae*, into which Ubertino had incorporated certain portions of the *Sacrum Commercium* as of other writings of the spiritual party. The famous image of Poverty with Christ upon the Cross, found already—though without the further image of Mary remaining below—in the *Sacrum Commercium*, came to Dante from the prayer to obtain Poverty (" O domine Jesu, ostende mihi semitas tuae dilectissimae paupertatis ") which Ubertino places on the lips of St. Francis himself : " When, by reason of the height of the Cross, even Thine own Mother (who, nevertheless, alone did then faithfully worship Thee, and was joined by agonised love to Thy passion), even she, I say, and such a Mother, could not reach up to Thee ; Lady Poverty, with all her penury, as Thy most dear servitor, held

[1] *Par.* xi. 55–75.

Thee more than ever closely embraced, and was joined most intimately to Thy sufferings." [1]

Upon these mystical espousals the whole narrative that follows is made to depend :

> " La lor concordia e i lor lieti sembianti,
>   amore e maraviglia e dolce sguardo
>   facieno esser cagion di pensier santi ;
> tanto che 'l venerabile Bernardo
>   si scalzò prima, e dietro a tanta pace
>   corse e, correndo, li parve esser tardo.
> Oh ignota ricchezza, oh ben ferace !
>   Scalzasi Egidio, scalzasi Silvestro,
>   dietro a lo sposo, sì la sposa piace.
> Indi sen va quel padre e quel maestro
>   con la sua donna e con quella famiglia
>   che già legava l'umile capestro." [2]

The description of Bernardo da Qu ntavalle, though the epithet " venerabile " is Bonaventura's, seems to contain a reminiscence of Thomas of Celano : " Brother Bernard, embracing the embassy of peace, ran swiftly after the holy man of God to purchase the kingdom of Heaven." [3]

---

[1] *Arbor Vitae Crucifixae*, lib. v. cap. iii. Cf. *Fioretti*, cap. xiii. In Dante's line, *Par.* xi. 72, the two earliest dated MSS and the first four editions all read : " Ella con Cristo *pianse* in su la croce," which is the reading accepted in the *testo critico* by Vandelli as also by Casella. The alternative *salse* is given by Benvenuto da Imola, and retained by Dr. Toynbee in the Oxford Dante. While *salse* seems required by the passage, *pianse* is hardly less supported by the words in Ubertino : " Immo ipsa matre propter altitudinem crucis, que tamen te sola tunc fideliter coluit et affectu anxio tuis passionibus iuncta fuit, ipsa inquam tali matre te non valente contingere, domina Paupertas cum omnibus suis penuriis tamquam tibi gratissimus domicellus te plus quam unquam fuit strictius amplexata et tuo cruciatu precordalius iuncta."

[2] *Par.* xi. 76–87.   [3] *Legenda prima*, (i) x. § 24.

So the sublime lyric continues, from the first approbation by Innocent to the final confirmation by Christ Himself on La Verna, with now and then a phrase of Bonaventura's almost literally rendered :

> " Nè li gravò viltà di cor le ciglia
>   per esser fi' di Pietro Bernardone,
>   nè per parer dispetto a maraviglia ;
> ma regalmente sua dura intenzione
>   ad Innocenzio aperse, e da lui ebbe
>   primo sigillo a sua religione.
> Poi che la gente poverella crebbe
>   dietro a costui, la cui mirabil vita
>   meglio in gloria del ciel si canterebbe,
> di seconda corona redimita
>   fu per Onorio da l'etterno Spiro
>   la santa voglia d'esto archimandrita.
> E poi che, per la sete del martiro,
>   ne la presenza del Soldan superba
>   predicò Cristo e gli altri che'l seguiro,
> e per trovare a conversione acerba
>   troppo la gente, per non stare indarno,
>   reddissi al frutto de l'italica erba,
> nel crudo sasso intra Tevero e Arno
>   da Cristo prese l'ultimo sigillo,
>   che le sue membra due anni portarno." [1]

Bonaventura, too, speaks of the Saint as " desiderio martyrii flagrans " in his mission to the Soldan, and of the Stigmata as " sigillum summi pontificis Christi." [2] The wonderful lines on the death of the " poverello " in the embraces of Lady Poverty give the mystical essence of Bonaventura's picture of him dying on the bare ground, when " the holy man rejoiced in gladness

[1] *Par.* xi. 88–108.   [2] *Legenda maior*, ix. § 5, xiii. § 9.

Plate IV.

St. Francis clothing the Beggar and Dreaming of the Church.
By Sassetta (1444).

of heart, for he saw that he had kept faith with Lady Poverty even unto the end." [1]

> " Quando a colui ch'a tanto ben sortillo
> piacque di trarlo suso a la mercede
> ch'el meritò nel suo farsi pusillo,
> a' frati suoi, sì com'a giuste rede,
> raccomandò la donna sua più cara,
> e comandò che l'amassero a fede ;
> e del suo grembo l'anima preclara
> mover si volse, tornando al suo regno,
> e al suo corpo non volse altra bara." [2]

We have heard Aquinas name for Dante three as the first companions of Francis : Bernardo, Egidio, Silvestro. Here Dante follows Bonaventura, who similarly associates these three [3]—although in reality Silvestro, " columbinae simplicitatis vir," seems to have been one of the last of the original twelve who travelled to Rome with the Saint in 1210 for the approbation of Pope Innocent. But in the next canto, where Bonaventura is the spokesman, and, after reciting the praises of St. Dominic, laments the dissensions of the Order in the poet's own day, two others of the early followers of St. Francis, though not of the original twelve, are by his side, as models of that primitive fervour and discipline which the speaker himself, as minister-general, had attempted to restore :

> " Illuminato e Augustin son quici,
> che fuor de' primi scalzi poverelli
> che nel capestro a Dio si fero amici." [4]

---

[1] *Legenda maior*, xiv. § 4.
[2] *Par.* xi. 109–117.
[3] *Legenda maior*, iii. §§ 3–5.
[4] *Par.* xii. 130–132.

Dante had read of these two friars in Bonaventura's pages. Agostino is the " vir utique sanctus et iustus," who, when minister of the friars in Terra di Lavoro at the time of the death of Francis, saw a vision of him going up into heaven, and, recovering his speech (for he was dying), cried : " Wait for me, Father, wait for me, I am coming with thee " ; and died the same hour.[1] Again, in Bonaventura, Illuminato—" vir utique luminis et virtutis "—is the socius of St. Francis on his mission to convert the Soldan, and, a little later, " gratia illuminatus et nomine," bids the Saint not to conceal the reception of the Stigmata : " Brother, know that, not only for thine own sake, but for that of others, divine mysteries are sometimes shown thee. Therefore it may rightly be feared lest, if thou concealest what thou hast received for the profit of many, thou mayest be judged guilty of the hidden talent." [2] This is, perhaps, all that Dante knew about him. But, in 1244, eighteen years after the death of the Saint, we have the letter of the three companions—Leo, Angelo, Ruffino—to the minister-general of the Order, Crescentius, in which " frater Illuminatus de Reate " (or " de Arce " in another text) is one of the holy friars from whom they have learned things about St. Francis in addition to those which they saw with their own eyes.[3]

So far we understand the position Illuminato holds in the *Paradiso*, but there are perplexing documents

---

[1] *Legenda maior*, xiv. § 6.   [2] *Ibid.*, ix. § 8, xiii. § 4.
[3] *Legenda trium Sociorum, ed. cit.*, p. 2.

and records. In 1238 a friar who describes himself as "frater Alluminatus, qui olim in seculo vocabar Accarinus de Rocha Accarini," cedes to the commune of Spoleto a part of the Rocca Accarina, between Spoleto and Rieti, which has lapsed to him on the death of his son—Elias, then minister-general, having given him permission to dispose of it as he pleases.[1] In that same year, 1238, Salimbene of Parma was received into the Order by Elias. He tells us that Illuminato was then the secretary of Elias, and that he—Salimbene—was afterwards with him in the convent at Siena : " This Frate Illuminato was afterwards minister in the province of St. Francis (i.e. Umbria), but later on was made Bishop of Assisi, where he closed his days." [2] And there is documentary evidence that a friar minor Illuminatus—he is called " de Theate " (that is, of Chieti, which may be a mistake for Rieti, in the document)—was elected Bishop of Assisi in 1273 (the same year in which Bonaventura became Cardinal and Bishop of Albano), the election being confirmed by Gregory X in the following year. He was still living in 1280, but a bull of Martin IV, March 10, 1282, speaks of him as dead : " bonae memoriae Illuminatus." [3]

Is the " Illuminatus," or " Alluminatus," of the documents the Illuminato of Bonaventura's *Legenda* and of the *Paradiso* ? If, as Accarino, he was old

[1] See *Miscellanea francescana*, xii (Foligno, 1910), p. 103.
[2] *Cronica, ed. cit.,* p. 39.
[3] Cf. Sbaralea, *Bullarium Franciscanum,* iii. pp. 206, 215, 483 ; Sabatier, *Speculum Perfectionis,* pp. 220 n 2, 306 n 3.

enough to have had a son before he entered the Order, and if he accompanied St. Francis to the east in 1219, it is clear that he must have been a very old man when he became Bishop of Assisi. We may note, too, that several friars minor in the thirteenth century bore the name of Illuminato,[1] and that Bartolommeo of Pisa, in his *De Conformitate vitae beati Francisci* (finished in 1390), knows only of Illuminato as the socius of St. Francis in the mission to the Soldan and in the episode of the Stigmata, citing him as one of those holy men of whom the friars have kept no record of their end or place of burial : " ubi jaceat, non habetur." [2]

Nevertheless, I am not prepared to reject the generally accepted identification of the Illuminato of Bonaventura, and therefore of Dante, with Accarino of Rocca Accarina, the secretary of Elias, the Bishop of Assisi. It has some significance for us in that, if Illuminato was so closely associated with Elias, if he thus disposed of his own property and ended as a bishop, he was, perhaps, not quite that ideal type of Friar Minor that Dante meant to represent. But it is an attractive picture : the last of the immediate followers of the Saint ending in this way as the bishop of his native city. We may hope that he received his elevation to the episcopate in the same spirit as that in which Bonaventura greeted the papal envoy who brought him the

---

[1] Celano, *Tractatus de Miraculis*, ed. E. d'Alençon, p. 407 ; Salimbene, *Cronica*, p. 612.

[2] *Analecta Franciscana*, iv (Quaracchi, 1906), p. 245.

red hat : " Hang it on a peg until I have finished washing up the convent platters."

Dante has thus heard the legend of St. Francis, seen the glorified spirits of two of his friars with that of his chief successor and biographer, before he looks upon the face of the *poverello* himself, enthroned in the Empyrean Heaven in the descending line in the Celestial Rose which begins with St. John the Baptist :

> " E sotto lui così cerner sortiro
> Francesco, Benedetto e Augustino,
> e altri fin qua giù di giro in giro." [1]

His place is significant ; representing the renovation of the evangelical life of perfection, he is opposite to Eve restored to the beauty that was hers before the fall ; higher even than St. Benedict and St. Augustine, he is next in order, in post-Apostolic days, to John the Baptist, than whom " among men that are born of women there hath not risen a greater." Thus, for Dante too, " l'Italia, con San Francesco, ha dato anche il più santo dei santi al Cristianesimo e all'umanità."

[1] *Par.* xxxii. 34–36.

THE "LITTLE FLOWERS" OF ST. FRANCIS

Professor EDMUND G. GARDNER, LITT.D., F.B.A.

THE "LITTLE FLOWERS" OF
ST. FRANCIS

I<small>T</small> is, perhaps, inevitable that the literal English equivalent of the title of the best known and best loved Franciscan book, *I Fioretti di San Francesco*, should have a
somewhat sentimental sound. But—in Italian literature
of the thirteenth and fourteenth century—such words as
" fiore," " fiori," " fioretto," " fioretti," or collectively
" fiorita," were used to denote a selection or compilation. Thus we have *Il fiore di rettorica* of Fra Guidotto
da Bologna, a compendium of the pseudo-Ciceronian
treatise on Rhetoric ; the *Fiori e vita di filosafi ed altri
savi ed imperatori* ; the *Fiore di parlare* or *Somma
d'arengare*, a collection of models for vernacular
speeches in various contingencies ; the *Fiorita* of
Armannino da Bologna, and the *Fiore d'Italia* of the
Carmelite, Guido da Pisa, summaries of universal and
Roman history ; the *Fioretto di croniche degli imperatori* ;
the *Fioretti della Bibbia* ; the *Fioretti delle Morali di
Santo Gregorio* ; and so on. The delightful *Cento
novelle antiche*—an earlier counterpart to our Franciscan anthology in the secular field—relates " alquanti
fiori di parlare, di belle cortesie," and the like, of
noble men in the past. But the title " Little Flowers "
is best justified and explained by a passage in the

H 97

letter prefixed to another, somewhat problematical Franciscan work, the *Legenda trium Sociorum* : " These things we write not in the manner of a legend, since for a long time legends have been composed of his life and of the miracles that God wrought through him. But as from a pleasant meadow we pluck certain flowers which in our judgment are fairer, not following a continuous history, but leaving out many things as they befell, which in the foresaid legends have been set down in truthful and clear speech." [1] Thus, in the introductory rubric of some texts of the *Fioretti* : " In questo libro si contengono certi fioretti, miracoli ed esempli divoti del glorioso poverello di Cristo, messer santo Francesco, e d'alquanti suoi santi compagni."

To the student of Italian literature, the *Fioretti* is a work of inestimable value. For, in a Tuscan removed only by some half century from Dante's own, it supplements and completes the Francis of the *Divina Commedia*, giving us all those human and legendary features in his personality which the poet omitted while presenting the general course of Franciscan history, the struggle between the two parties in the Order which had already begun in the Saint's lifetime and came to a head in Dante's own days, from a different standpoint.

But the *Fioretti* is not, in the more usual sense of the word, an original work. The friar who here and there speaks of himself in the first person is never the actual

---

[1] *Legenda trium Sociorum, ed. cit.,* p. 4.

writer of the Italian book, nor perhaps always one and the same man. In chapter XLV, the story of Fra Giovanni della Penna, we read : " E tutte queste cose recitò a me, frate Ugolino, lo stesso frate Giovanni." The seventeenth century annalist of the Franciscan order, Luke Wadding, first stated that the author of the *Fioretti* was a friar of the Marches, Ugolino da Santa Maria in Monte, and that the title of his original Latin work was the *Floretum.* In 1902, M. Paul Sabatier published the *Actus beati Francisci et Sociorum eius,* a Latin compilation of which various manuscripts exist, and which—as supplemented twelve years later by Mr. A. G. Little from a manuscript in his possession— consists of 76 chapters, of which 52 or 53 (according to the division or absence of division of the first chapter) reappear in an Italian garb as the *Fioretti.*[1] There are scholars who still hold that both the Latin *Actus* and the Italian *Fioretti* are derived independently from the (at present undiscovered) *Floretum* ; but the more probable view remains that of Sabatier : that the *Fioretti* are directly extracted from the *Actus* which

---

[1] *Actus beati Francisci et Sociorum eius,* ed. P. Sabatier (Paris, 1902) ; A. G. Little, *Description of a Franciscan Manuscript preserved formerly in the Phillipps Library now in the possession of A. G. L.,* in *Collectanea Franciscana,* I (Aberdeen, 1914). Six of the *Fioretti* chapters—XXXVII, XXXVIII, XLI, XLIV, XLVI, XLVIII—were lacking in M. Sabatier's text, and (with the exception of XXXVII, of which no Latin original was known) were supplied by him from other sources ; all these six are included in Mr. Little's manuscript and (excepting XLVIII) printed by him in extenso (*op. cit.,* pp. 33–47). I refer to the *Fioretti* throughout as in 53 chapters.

is itself, to all intents and purposes, the *Floretum* of Ugolino.[1]

The name of Fra Ugolino occurs three times in the *Actus*. In the story of the reception of the Stigmata as seen by Brother Leo upon La Verna : " This history Fra Jacopo da Massa had from the mouth of Fra Leone, and Fra Ugolino da Monte Santa Maria from the mouth of the said Fra Jacopo, and I who wrote from the mouth of Fra Ugolino, a man in all respects worthy of faith." [2] Again, in the chapter on Fra Giovanni della Penna : " All these things the said Fra Giovanni related to me, Fra Ugolino " ; where, however, in Mr. Little's manuscript, it runs : " And all these things Fra Giovanni himself related to Fra Ugolino." [3] Yet again, in Mr. Little's text of the tale of how Fra Simone of Assisi—in what was surely not quite the spirit of St. Francis—drove away the crows that disturbed his prayers in the wood of Brunforte so that they were never more heard or seen in that region : " And I,

[1] Sabatier reprinted the *Fioretti* chapters of his text of the *Actus* in the order in which they occur in the Italian: *Floretum S. Francisci Assisiensis. Liber aureus qui italice dicitur I Fioretti di San Francesco* (Paris, 1902) See his preface to this and to the *Actus*. Cf. G. Garavani, *Il Floretum di Ugolino da Montegiorgio e i Fioretti di S. Francesco*, in *Atti e Memorie della R. Deputazione di Storia Patria per le provincie delle Marche*, N.S., Vols. I–II (Ancona, 1904–1905) ; A. della Torre, introduction to his edition *I Fioretti di San Francesco* (Turin, 1909), pp. xii–xxxiv ; F. van Ortroy, in *Analecta Bollandiana*, XXVII (1908), pp. 488–492, XXXIII (1914), pp. 455–457. Note the phrase, quoted by Mr. Little (*op. cit.*, p. 47), written in another hand on his manuscript of the *Actus*: " principium flosculorum."

[2] *Actus*, ed. Sabatier, IX.

[3] *Actus*, LXIX, *Fioretti*, XLV.

Fra Ugolino da Monte Santa Maria, stayed there three years, and saw with certainty that the said miracle was known both to laymen and to the friars of the whole custody." [1] Further, the writer speaks of himself anonymously in the first person four times as the intimate associate of Fra Giovanni della Verna,[2] and once in the same way—though here the " I " is generally believed to be another person—in connection with the famous vision of Fra Jacopo da Massa.[3]

With the exception of that one chapter, it seems the most plausible theory that Fra Ugolino is the original author of the *Actus*, and that he had a collaborator, or perhaps an editor after his death, in the unnamed friar—" ego qui scripsi "—who says that he took down the story of the Stigmata from his lips. Sabatier would identify this Ugolino da Monte Santa Maria or da Montegiorgio, so called from the convent in the March of Ancona near Ascoli Piceno where he passed part of his life, with Ugolino da Brunforte, a friar minor of the spiritual party, who had been appointed bishop of Teramo by Celestine V and whose election was annulled by Boniface VIII : " ex certis causis iustitia exigente," as the latter Pontiff's bull of December 12, 1295, puts it.[4] This Ugolino seems to have lived many years, if he is the same who was minister provincial of the Marches in 1340 and died in

1 Little, *op. cit.*, pp. 34–36; *Fioretti*, XLI.
2 *Actus*, LI, LII, LIV, LVIII.
3 *Actus*, LXXVI, *Fioretti*, XLVIII.
4 Sbaralea, *Bullarium Franciscanum*, IV. p. 376.

1348, and the identification—which is unsupported
by external evidence—presents almost insuperable
chronological difficulties.[1] In the *Fioretti* there is express mention of the death of Giovanni della Verna.
This is said (though not proved by documentary
evidence) to have taken place in August, 1322. The
passage does not occur in the Latin text of the *Actus*,
where, nevertheless, the friar is spoken of as though
he were no longer living. It seems therefore fairly
clear that the *Actus* took their present shape after 1322,
and Sabatier has shown grounds for holding that they
were written between that date and 1328.[2] The book
originated in the Franciscan convents of a small district
in the March of Ancona, where the spirit of St. Francis
had very early taken strong root, and where the friars
adhered zealously to the party of the strict observance,
not only holding the memory of Brother Elias in ab-
horrence as that of an apostate, but regarding even the
great St. Bonaventura—with his reconciliatory *via
media*—as a persecutor, one who had drunk but a
portion of the chalice of life which the Seraphic Father
proffered to the lips of his followers.

The date and author of the Italian text are not

[1] Cf. A. della Torre, *op. cit.*, pp. xxvii–xxviii. If this is the Ugolino of
the *Actus*, he must have been little more than a child when he received the
confidence of Giovanni della Penna and spoke with Jacopo da Massa. On the
other hand, the references to Brunforte in the *Actus* are noteworthy.

[2] An alternative theory would regard the *Actus* as originally composed
in the latter part of the thirteenth century, but with later additions
after 1322.

known, though the name of a certain Fra Giovanni of Florence has, on inadequate grounds, been put forward. The earliest dated manuscript is 1396, and the work probably took shape shortly after the middle of the fourteenth century. In its earliest and primitive form, the *Fioretti* consists of two parts : fifty-three chapters, the *Floretum* or *Fioretti* proper, derived with considerable modification from the *Actus*, and the five *Considerazioni delle gloriose Stimmate di santo Francesco*, a compilation from various sources which is probably the original work of the translator who was a Tuscan, most likely a Florentine, and perhaps actually writing in the convent at La Verna. To these, slightly later, various other translations from the Latin were added : the *Vita di frate Ginepro*, the life of Brother Juniper, which is included in its Latin form in the *Chronicle of the Twenty-four Generals* (completed about 1379), and the *Vita del beato frate Egidio*, the life of Blessed Giles, together with his *detti notabili* translated from his well-known *Aurea verba*. This life of Giles, again, corresponds with portions of the " Long Life " in the *Chronicle of the Twenty-four Generals*, which—like the " Short Life," of which it is probably an expansion— is ultimately derived from the (no longer extant) original life by Brother Leo.[1] As a further appendix to the

---

[1] The Short Life has been edited by Dr. Walter W. Seton, *Blessed Giles of Assisi* (Manchester, 1918). The *Chronica XXIV Generalium*, attributed to Arnold of Sarano, is published in *Analecta Franciscana*, III. (Quaracchi, 1897). A good deal of the matter of the *Actus* and *Fioretti* proper is likewise included in the *Chronica*.

Fioretti, some manuscripts and editions have a series, varying in number, of " esempi e miracoli di messer santo Francesco," of small interest or significance compared with those of the *Fioretti* proper, including one decidedly unpleasing legend about the fate of the abbot who refused to receive the first band of friars under Agnello of Pisa whom St. Francis sent to England.[1]

Each of the *Fioretti* is complete in itself, and there is no attempt to make the book a chronological history. But they fall naturally into two groups. The first —chapters I to XXXVIII—consists of stories concerning St. Francis and his first companions and followers ; the second—from XLII to LIII—treats of the lives of certain friars, mostly of a later date, in the province of the March of Ancona, the contemporaries of the original compiler of the *Actus,* whether Fra Ugolino or another. Between the two groups, as a kind of *intermezzo,* are the two stories of St. Antony of Padua (XXXIX, XL) and that of Fra Simone of Assisi (XLI).

In the first group of stories there is, no doubt, a

[1] To mention a few of the more recent editions : that of A. della Torre includes only the *Fioretti* proper and the *Considerazioni,* as does also that of L. Manzoni (Rome, 1900), which presents the text of the MS. of 1396 (the Amaretto Manelli MS. of the Biblioteca Nazionale of Florence). The edition of G. L. Passerini (2nd ed. Florence, 1919), based upon the early fifteenth century MS. 1670 of the Riccardiana, contains also all the supplementary matter, as does the latest edition of Mario Casella (Florence, 1926), which offers a critically constructed text. Casella's promised critical edition with a commentary has not, I think, yet appeared.

purely fantastical element, illustrating the growth or later elaboration of legends of miracles and the like (sometimes of no spiritual significance) ; but much is of genuine historical value, representing—even though the Latin original may not date from less than a century after the death of St. Francis—a most primitive and authentic tradition. As Sabatier well puts it : " For the first Franciscan generation, Ugolino made use of pre-existing documents, which he rehandled and transformed, but without entirely destroying the primitive character." [1] He has behind him, not only written sources, but an oral tradition coming straight from the Saint's first followers. One of his chief informants is the somewhat mysterious Fra Jacopo da Massa—who had been a friend of Blessed Giles and clearly a light among the spiritual party in the days of Bonaventura's generalship [2]—and Fra Jacopo had received these matters from Brother Leo. Here, as in so much of the literature of the strict observance, like the *Speculum Perfectionis* and even the *Arbor Vitae Crucifixae*, the tradition comes from the memories, and perhaps the actual writing, of Francis's beloved secretary, his " pecorella di Dio." Hence the singular beauty, the convincing Franciscan simplicity, of some of the stories in which Francis and Leo alone appear together upon

[1] *Actus*, preface.

[2] Cf. Garavani, *op. cit.*, i. pp. 285–288. There seems no secure evidence for the statement sometimes made that Jacopo da Massa died about 1260. If he is the same as the " laico santo " of *Fioretti*, Cap. LI, he must have lived into the next century.

the scene ; the one where the Saint instructs his companion upon the Friar Minor finding perfect joy when rejected even by his own brethren : " O frate Leone, scrivi che ivi è perfetta letizia " ; and the following, where the two contend lovingly in speech, Francis bidding Leo repeat the words of rebuke which he utters, while the faithful " pecorella " can only obey by transforming them into words of praise : " And so in this humble contention, with many tears and with much spiritual consolation, they kept vigil until day." [1]

The same primitive Franciscan character appears in one of the most beautiful of all the chapters : the story of how the mysterious pilgrim came to visit Egidio, Blessed Giles, at Perugia, and how, though neither spoke a word to the other, the friar knew him to be St. Louis, the king of France.[2] The story occurs again in Latin, about half a century after the *Actus*, in the life of Giles included in the *Chronica XXIV Generalium*, though not in the " Short Life." But, as Dr. Seton observes, " Granted that evidence cannot be produced to show that St. Louis ever was in Italy or ever visited Blessed Giles at Perugia, that does not of itself prove that the story is not a genuine and integral part of the Legend of Blessed Giles." [3] We may, then, be allowed to believe that Brother Leo is again the source of this story, and that, whoever that silent pilgrim from beyond the Alps may have been, Egidio had told his friend that he believed that he had held

[1] Capp. VIII–IX.   [2] Cap. XXXIV.   [3] *Op. cit.*, p. 43.

in his embrace that great king, who, in Walter Pater's words, " because his whole being was full of heavenly wisdom, in self-banishment from it for a while, led and ruled the French people so magnanimously alike in peace and war."

There are few more familiar Franciscan stories than that of how St. Francis converted the ferocious wolf of Gubbio into that delightful " frate Lupo," who went from house to house as a domestic friend and whom the citizens fed *cortesemente* (note the true Franciscan word), and after whom no dog ever barked.[1] We are told that it is a symbol of the Church assuaging the ferocity of the Middle Ages, or merely a poetical version of St. Francis himself converting the bandit Lupo into Frate Agnello. However that may be, the tales of the Saint's familiar relations with the birds of the air assuredly stand in no need of such explaining away : his taming of the turtle doves, his bidding the swallows keep silence while he preached, the falcon which nested near his cell and woke him at the hour of matins. There is a whole chapter of such episodes with birds and beasts in Bonaventura.[2] The preaching to the birds, " alle mie sirocchie uccelli," already in Thomas of Celano, is nowhere told so fully or so beautifully as in the *Fioretti* ; and notice that here it is not borrowed from any literary source, but comes

[1] Cap. XXI.

[2] *Legenda maior*, cap. VIII: " Quomodo ratione carentia videbantur ad ipsum affici."

again from Fra Jacopo da Massa, who had it by word
of mouth from Fra Masseo, who was one of the companions of the Saint on that occasion :

"Passing on with that fervour, he raised his eyes,
and saw some trees by the side of the way, upon which
were a vast multitude of birds ; whereat St. Francis
wondered and said to his companions : 'Do you await
me here in the road, and I will go and preach to my
sister birds.' And, having entered the field, he began
to preach to the birds who were on the ground ; and
straightway those who were on the trees came to him,
and all together stayed motionless until St. Francis
had finished preaching ; and even then they did not
depart, until he had given them his blessing. And, as
Fra Masseo afterwards related to Fra Jacopo da Massa,
while St. Francis went among them, though he touched
them with his cloak, not one of them moved. The
substance of the sermon of St. Francis was this : 'My
sister birds, you are greatly beholden to God your
Creator, and always and in every place you should
praise Him, for He has given you the liberty of flying
everywhere, and also double and threefold raiment
has He given you ; next, because He preserved your
seed in the ark of Noah, in order that your kind might
not come to an end in the world ; also you are beholden
to Him for the element of the air which He has assigned
to you. Besides this, you neither sow nor reap ; and
God feeds you, and gives you the rivers and the springs
for your drink, and He gives you the mountains and the

alleys for your shelter, and the high trees for you to make your nests ; and, since you can neither spin nor sew, God clothes you and your little ones. Thus the Creator loves you much, since He gives you so many benefits, and therefore beware, my sisters, of the sin of ingratitude, but strive always to praise God.' When St. Francis said these words, all those birds began to open their beaks, to stretch out their necks, to spread out their wings, and reverently to bow their heads even to the ground, and with their movements and their songs to show that the words of the holy father gave them very great delight. And St. Francis rejoiced and delighted with them, and marvelled much at so great a multitude of birds and their beauty and variety and their attention and tameness ; for which thing he with them devoutly praised the Creator." [1]

It is a noteworthy testimony to the wide diffusion of this episode in the life of St. Francis that we find it already painted in 1235, in the altarpiece by Bonaventura Berlinghieri at Pescia, and also related by the English chronicler, Roger of Wendover, who wrote before 1236. Roger of Wendover lays the scene outside Rome (instead of near Bevagna on the road from Assisi to Montefalco), and represents the Saint as leaving the city and going to the birds because the Romans refused to hear him. There is a note of bitterness in his discourse : " I bid you in the name of Jesus Christ, whom the Jews crucified and whose

[1] Cap. XVI. Cf. Thomas of Celano, *Legenda prima*, (i) xxi. § 58.

preaching the miserable Romans have despised, t
come to me and hear the word of God, in the name o
Him who created you and delivered you in the ark o
Noah from the waters of the flood." He preaches t
them for three days, until the Roman clergy and peopl
come to fetch him back with honour into the city
We see that this is a sadly perverted form of the story
In the *Fioretti*, it is sheer love of the birds that move
Francis to address them, and the whole spirit of th
scene is one of pure joy in nature as the handiwork o
God. But, even in the *Fioretti*, there is the manifestl
later attempt to improve the occasion and point a moral

"Finally, having finished his sermon, St. Franc
made the sign of the Cross over them, and gave ther
leave to depart; and then all those birds in a floc
rose up into the air with marvellous songs; and afte
wards, according to the cross which St. Francis had mad
upon them, they divided into four parts; one pa
flew towards the east and another towards the wes
the third towards the south, the fourth towards th
north, and each flock sang marvellously as it went
signifying in this that, as St. Francis, the standard
bearer of the Cross of Christ, had preached to them, an
had made the sign of the cross over them, according t
which they went off singing into the four quarters o
the world; so the preaching of the Cross of Chris
renewed by St. Francis, should be carried by him an
by his friars through all the world; and these friars, i

[1] *Flores Historiarum*, ed. H. G. Hewlett, II. pp. 330–331.

the fashion of birds, possessing nothing of their own in this world, committed their life to the providence of God alone." [1]

There is a singular charm about all the chapters connected with St. Clare. The one relating how she ate with St. Francis and his companions at Santa Maria degli Angeli is surely primitive and authentic. The scene is simple: " In the meanwhile St. Francis had the table prepared on the ground, as he was wont to do. And, when the hour for dining was come, St. Francis and St. Clare sat down together, and one of the companions of St. Francis with the companion of St. Clare, and then all the other companions took their places at the table humbly. And, for the first course, St. Francis began to speak of God so sweetly, so loftily and so wondrously that, the abundance of divine grace descending upon them, all were rapt in God." But the writer will not leave it at that. " And, while they stayed thus rapt, with eyes and hands raised to heaven, the men of Assisi and Bettona and those of the country round saw that Santa Maria degli Angeli and all the place, and the wood that was then beside it, burned mightily ; and it seemed that it was a great fire that was taking hold of the church and the place and the wood together. For which thing the folk of Assisi with great haste sped down there to extinguish the fire, believing firmly

[1] Thomas of Celano (*loc. cit.*) has merely: " Benedixit denique ipsis et signo crucis facto licentiam tribuit ut ad locum alium transvolarent. Beatus autem pater ibat cum sociis suis per viam suam gaudens, et gratias agebat Deo, quem omnes creaturae confessione supplici venerantur."

that every thing was burning." ¹ The underlying mystical conception is beautiful and significant—we find it again in the account of the reception of the Stigmata—but the writer has materialised the symbolism somewhat as later Italian poets, like Tebaldeo, were to materialise the imagery of Petrarca. The story of how St. Clare was miraculously conveyed on Christmas night to hear the office in the church of San Francesco, and received Holy Communion there, is clearly a later elaboration of the episode in her Legend where she hears all the music and the singing, but with no hint of her having been materially transported to the building. ² Yet I do not think that there are many cases in the *Fioretti* of pure literary elaboration. One unquestionably is the long story of the " nobilissima visione " of the robber whom St. Francis converted to become a most holy friar. It is obviously modelled upon the earlier mediæval visions of the other world, like those in the Dialogues of St. Gregory and the Vision of Tundal, with the motive of the " Bridge of Dread " which had already become antiquated by the time that Dante wrote the *Divina Commedia*.³

The great chapter on Holy Poverty, where St. Francis and Fra Masseo beg bread for the love of God and finally make their way to Rome, has that most noteworthy discourse, placed on the lips of the Saint, which

¹ Cap. XV.

² Cap. XXXV. Cf. *Legenda Sanctae Clarae Virginis* (attributed to Thomas of Celano), ed. F. Pennacchi (Assisi, 1910), pp. 40–42.

³ Cap. XXVI.

Plate V.

St. Francis renouncing his heritage
By Sassetta (1444).

invites comparison with the prayer given by Ubertino da Casale which, as we saw, is echoed in the *Paradiso* :

" Dearest companion, let us go to St. Peter and St. Paul, and pray them to teach and help us to possess the immeasurable treasure of most holy Poverty ; for she is a treasure so all worthy and so divine, that we are not worthy to possess in our most lowly vessels ; inasmuch as she is that heavenly virtue through which all things earthly and transitory are trampled under foot, and every obstacle is removed from before the soul, in order that it may freely unite itself with God eternal. This is that virtue which makes the soul, while still placed on earth, converse in heaven with the Angels. This is she who accompanied Christ upon the Cross ; with Christ she was buried, with Christ she rose again, with Christ she mounted into Heaven ; and it is she who, even in this life, gives to the souls who are enamoured of her the means of flying to Heaven ; inasmuch as she guards the weapons of true humility and charity. And, therefore, let us pray the most holy Apostles of Christ, who were perfect lovers of this evangelical pearl, that they beg for us this grace from Our Lord Jesus Christ, that, by His most holy mercy, He may grant us to merit to be true lovers and observers and humble disciples of the most precious and most beloved evangelical Poverty." [1]

It is inevitable that Brother Elias should fare badly

[1] Cap. XIII. Cf. above. *St. Francis and Dante*, p. 86.

in the *Fioretti*. Almost at the beginning of the book, he is studiously contrasted with Fra Bernardo, the "figliuolo primogenito" of St. Francis. It is the somewhat comic story of the impatient Angel who knocks at the door of the convent, asks an awkward question of Elias, and has the door shut in his face; whereas he is presently saluted kindly by Bernardo. The point of the question, "if the observers of the holy Gospel are permitted to eat whatever is put before them as Christ bade His disciples," is a reflection upon the modifications of the original Franciscan constitution which Elias had attempted to introduce during the lifetime of St. Francis.[1] The Saint rebukes him: "You do ill, proud Brother Elias, to drive from us the holy Angels who come to teach us. I tell thee that I fear mightily lest thy pride make thee end outside of this Order." The story is obviously sheer fiction, as also its sequel where St. Francis knows in spirit that Elias is damned and will die out of the Order, but nevertheless, at his entreaties, by his prayers obtains his final salvation. It is a striking story, finely and pathetically told, but utterly perverting the relations that actually existed between the two men, the one historical element in it being the reception of the sacraments by the fallen and excommunicated minister-general on his deathbed, here put forth as the crowning effect of the prayers of St. Francis that could save even his apostate son from the

---

[1] Cap. IV. Cf. Father Cuthbert, *Life of St. Francis of Assisi* (London, 1912), pp. 240, 241.

sentence of damnation.[1] Probably St. Francis trusted
Elias to the last, even though the *Fioretti* tells us " how
St. Francis blessed the holy Brother Bernard, and
left him his vicar when he was about to pass from this
life." The account of the blessing is of singular
historical importance and interest :

" When St. Francis drew near to death like that holy
patriarch Jacob, and his devoted sons were around him,
full of sorrow and weeping at the passing of so beloved a father, he asked : ' Where is my first-begotten ?
Come to me, son, that my soul may bless thee before I
die.' Then Brother Bernard said in secret to Brother
Elias, who was vicar of the Order : ' Father, go on the
right hand of the Saint, that he may bless thee.' And,
when Brother Elias placed himself at the right hand,
St. Francis, who had lost his sight through excess of
tears, placed his right hand on the head of Brother
Elias, and said : ' This is not the head of my first-
begotten Brother Bernard.' Then Brother Bernard went
to him on the left hand ; and St. Francis then crossed
his arms in the fashion of a cross, and placed his right
hand on the head of Brother Bernard and his left on
the head of Brother Elias, and said to Brother Bernard : ' The Father of Our Lord Jesus Christ bless
thee in every spiritual and heavenly blessing in Christ.
Even as thou art the first chosen in this holy Order to
give the evangelical example of following Christ in
evangelical poverty, for not only didst thou give what

[1] Cap. XXXVIII.

thou hadst, and distribute it entirely and freely to the poor for the love of Christ, but didst also offer thyself to God in this Order in sacrifice of sweetness ; blessed be thou then by Our Lord Jesus Christ and by me, His poor little servant, with eternal blessings in thy going and staying, waking and sleeping, living and dying. May he who blesses thee be full of blessings, and he who curses thee not remain without punishment. Be thou the chief of thy brethren, and let all the friars obey thy command ; have thou power to receive into this Order and to expel from it whomso thou shalt wish ; and let no friar have rule over thee, and be it lawful to thee to go and to stay wherever thou shalt please." [1]

The pathetic beauty of the scene, the overflowing love of the dying Saint, the touching humility of Bernardo's attempt not to usurp the rights of Elias, speak for themselves. But Thomas of Celano—in the account he gives in the *Legenda prima*—makes no mention of Bernardo. St. Francis calls to himself certain of the friars (they are not named) and blesses each ; then, crossing his hands, he lays the right on the head of Elias, and gives him a special blessing. This is before he is transported to the Portiuncula. Afterwards, a brother " whom the Saint loved with exceeding great love " (evidently Bernardo) is bidden bless the whole Order in his name.[2] Later, in the *Legenda secunda*, Celano says that the Saint stretched out his right hand over all the friars present, and, " beginning with his

[1] Cap. VI.   [2] *Legenda prima,* (ii) vii. § 108, viii. § 109.

vicar, placed it upon the head of each "—the writer insisting that it was a general blessing upon the whol : Order and not to be usurped by an individual.[1] St. Bonaventura, who puts the event when the Saint was at the point of death, has simply : " While all the brethren sat around, he stretched out his hands over them, crossing his arms in the form of a cross, because he always loved this sign, and, in the virtue and name of the Cross, blessed all the friars both present and absent." [2] In the *Speculum Perfectionis*, Bernardo asks for the blessing. The Saint lays his right hand upon the head of Egidio, and then, saying : " This is not the head of my brother Bernard," transfers it to the latter, and gives him the blessing, ending with the words : " Whence I will and enjoin as far as I am able, that whoever shall be minister-general shall love and honour him as myself. Let the ministers, also, and all the brethren of the whole Order hold him in my stead." [3] It would then seem clear that the two factions in the Order disputed as to which had been thus specially chosen, the first follower or the vicar-general, to represent Francis after his death. The compiler of the *Actus* has, perhaps, combined two different events, and, unable to deny the presence of Elias, has either transferred his blessing to Bernardo or given to the latter's blessing a significance which the Saint himself never intended.[4]

[1] *Legenda secunda*, (ii) clxii. § 216.   [2] *Legenda maior*, xiv. § 5.
[3] *Speculum Perfectionis*, ed. Sabatier, cap. cvii.
[4] Cf. E. Lempp, *Frère Élie de Cortone* (Paris, 1901), pp. 65–68 ; Father Cuthbert, *op. cit.*, pp. 375, 388 *n*.

The deathbed repentance of Elias ends the first group of stories.   It is followed, as a kind of supplement, by the two chapters about St. Antony of Padua, probably here introduced as one of the chief opponents of the work of Elias,[1] and the first Franciscan canonised after St. Francis himself.   The two miracles here attributed to him—the sermon preached before the Pope and Cardinals in consistory, when each heard him in his own tongue, and the preaching to the fishes at Rimini—are not found in either of the two earliest lives of the Saint.[2]   As in Roger of Wendover's version of St. Francis' preaching to the birds, Antony preaches to the fishes of the sea because the heretics of Rimini will not hear his words, and these heretics are, of course, converted by the miracle.   The *Legenda prima*—written a few years after his death—speaks of his preaching to the people of Rimini and converting heretics there, but with no hint of the fishes.   The story appears—probably slightly earlier than the compilation of the *Actus (Fioretti)*—in the life of St. Antony by Jean Rigauld, a French friar who died at Rome in 1323 ; but, instead of Rimini, the scene is laid by him near Padua on the Brenta.[3]   It is natural to suppose

[1] Capp. XXIX-XL. Cf. *Legenda secunda*, in *Acta Sanctorum* for June 13, pp. 203-4.

[2] *Legenda prima*, ed. L. de Kerval (*Sancti Antonii de Padua vitae duae*, Paris, 1904), written between 1232 and 1245 ; *Legenda secunda*, by Julian of Speyer (the *Vita auctore anonymo* in *Acta Sanctorum*, June 13).   Both miracles are in the *Liber Miraculorum* of the Bollandists (*loc. cit.*), which is simply from the *Chronica XXIV Generalium*, in the same form as in the *Actus (Fioretti)*.

[3] *Vita beati Antonii de ordine Fratrum Minorum a fratre Joanne Rigaldi de eodem ordine ordinata* (*La vie de Saint Antoine de Padoue par Jean Rigauld*, ed. P. F.-M. d'Araules. Bordeaux, 1899).

that the legend is a later replica of the story of St. Francis ; but the sermon, as given in the *Fioretti*, though closely modelled upon that to the birds, is a beautiful thing in itself, with a touch of that true Franciscan spirit which made Antony one of the worthiest followers of the Seraphic Father.

Then follows the story of Fra Simone of Assisi, which is a kind of link between the two groups of *Fioretti*. Chronologically he is one of the friars who entered the Order while St. Francis still lived, but his own life was for the most part passed in the March of Ancona. Of him, too, Ugolino—if he is the writer— has learned from Fra Jacopo da Massa : " One evening, when he had gone into the wood with Fra Jacopo da Massa to speak of God, and he was speaking most sweetly of the Divine Love, they stayed all night in that talk, and, when morning came, it seemed to them that they had been a very brief space of time, as the said Fra Jacopo told me." [1] Simone anticipates what Sabatier regards as the characteristic feature of the friars in the second group of *Fioretti* : the emphasis being no longer laid upon the glory of Poverty, but upon the joys of mystical contemplation. This, however, has already appeared, to some extent, from the outset in the person of Fra Bernardo.[2]

The second group deals with the lives of the friars of the province of the March of Ancona, Ugolino's own region. " The province of the March of Ancona

[1] Cap. XLI.   [2] Cf. Cap. XXVIII.

was of old, even as the sky with stars, adorned with
holy and exemplary friars, who—like the luminaries
of heaven — have illumined and adorned the Order of
St. Francis and the world with examples and with
teaching." [1] Some belong to the earliest Franciscan
generation ; like Fra Pacifico, in that beautiful story of
the love of the two brothers in the Order, if he indeed
be the same as that chief of minstrels who in the world
had been called " rex versuum " and had been " in-
ventor saecularium cantionum," and had been crowned
by the Emperor ; he whom Francis had converted at
San Severino.[2] Others, notably Currado da Offida,
" mirabile zelatore della evangelica povertà e della
regola di santo Francesco " (which means that he was
a leader of the spirituals),[3] and Giovanni della Verna,
are the contemporaries of Fra Ugolino himself and of
Dante. They illustrate the words that Bonaventura
utters to Dante, from the standpoint of 1300, when he
admits that the true Franciscan spirit is still to be found
in a few here and there :

> " Ben dico, chi cercasse a foglio a foglio
>   nostro volume, ancor troveria carta
>   u' leggerebbe : ' I' mi son quel ch'i'soglio ' " ; [4]

even though the spiritual colour of their lives, absorbed

[1] Cap. XLII.

[2] Cf. Celano, *Legenda secunda*, (ii) lxxii, § 106 ; U. Cosmo, in *Giornale
Storico della Letteratura Italiana*, XXVIII ; F. Torraca, *Studi di Storia Letteraria*
(Florence, 1923), pp. 43, 44. Torraca shows that the Emperor who crowned
Pacifico was probably, not Henry VI, but Otto IV.

[3] Cap. XLIII.   [4] *Par.* XII. 121–123.

for the most part in contemplation and visions away from the world in lonely convents, is not, in all respects, that of the first band of followers.

Indeed, Dante's own chief guide in Franciscan matters, St. Bonaventura himself, is severely handled, in the famous chapter : " How Fra Jacopo da Massa saw all the friars minor of the world in the vision of a tree, and knew the virtue and the merits and the vices of each." It is an allegorical representation of the deposition of John of Parma, the leader of the spiritual party, and the succession of Bonaventura to the minister-generalship. John of Parma has drunk fully of the chalice of life which St. Francis has offered to his followers, and, having thereby " profoundly contemplated the abyss of the infinite divine light," has descended from the summit of the tree. Fra Bonaventura, " who had taken part of the chalice and had poured out part," mounts up into the place which he has left ; and straightway the nails of his hands become iron claws sharp as razors, and he hurls himself upon John to do him hurt. But John calls upon Christ, who gives St. Francis a flint with which he cuts the nails of Fra Bonaventura so as to render him harmless. A great tempest smites the tree and it falls, but " from the root of this tree, which was of gold, there came forth another tree which was all of gold, which produced leaves and flowers and golden fruit." We are to understand that the *via media* of Bonaventura will lead to the destruction of the Order, but from the pure Franciscan stock it will arise again in the perfect spirit of its founder. Now this chapter is not included in the majority of manuscripts of the *Actus*, though it is in Mr. Little's manuscript ; it occurs, in a very similar form, in the *Historia septem tribulationum*, written about 1325 by Angelo da Clareno, the leader of the Fraticelli who formed a separate body in the Order. It is usually regarded as an interpolation into the body of the *Actus* ; the narrator, who had such great desire to speak with Fra Jacopo and who narrates the vision as delivered to him, being not Ugolino, but Angelo da Clareno.[1] But it is still possible to take the view that the chapter does form part of the *Actus*, and was borrowed by Angelo da Clareno, the " I " being again Ugolino. We should, in this case, have to suppose that this was Ugolino's first introduction to Fra Jacopo da Massa, whose vision would have given him that general conception of Franciscan ideals which the *Actus–Fioretti* reveal.[2] It may be observed that elsewhere, for the Italian writer of the *Fioretti*, Bonaventura is " il santo frate Bonaventura." [3]

But the great figure in the closing chapters of the *Fioretti* is Giovanni da Fermo, known as blessed Gio-

[1] Cap. XLVIII. Cf. F. Ehrle, *Die " historia septem tribulationum ordinis minorum " des fr. Angelus de Clarino*, in *Archiv für Litteratur- und Kirchengeschichte des Mittelalters*, II (Berlin, 1886), pp. 279–281 ; A. G. Little, *op. cit.*, pp. 46–47. The Italian version is somewhat confused.

[2] Cf. Garavani, *op. cit.*, i. pp. 292–297.

[3] In the *Considerazioni*.

vanni della Verna from his long residence in that convent, " nel crudo sasso intra Tevero e Arno," on the
spot that had witnessed the supreme mystery in the
life of St. Francis. Dante may well have known him,
for, when the poet was in the Casentino in 1311 during
the Italian expedition of Henry of Luxemburg, the
friar was guardian of the convent. Like his friend
Jacopone da Todi (to whom, according to the latter's
legend, he administered the last sacraments), Giovanni
della Verna is one of the purest types of later Franciscan
mysticism ; not entirely in the very spirit of St. Francis,
who would most certainly not have approved of the
youthful austerities attributed to him.[1] I will not
quote the wonderful chapter, " How Christ appeared
to Fra Giovanni della Verna," for it must be read in
its entirety ; it is unmistakably a genuine document
of mystical experience, setting forth how Fra Giovanni
on the sacred mountain was all enkindled with the love
of Christ, how after three years he was deprived of this
ray and flame of divine love, and plunged into that
state of spiritual dryness which mystics call the Dark
Night of the Soul, how he sought Christ through the
wood and pursued the Divine Vision until it turned
to him, and how, when the vision passed away, its fruits
abode with him. It is the counterpart of Francis
Thompson's *Hound of Heaven* ; the soul's quest of
adored Reality instead of that Reality's quest of the
soul. These are but two sides of the whole mystical

[1] Cf. the beginning of Cap. XLIX with the end of Cap. XVIII.

experience ; for the soul is solicited and sustained by the Reality which it seeks.[1]

Another vision of Giovanni della Verna, described with less detail, has singular interest for the student of Dante :

" One night he was so uplifted and caught up into God, that he saw in Him, the Creator, all created things both of heaven and earth, and all their perfections and grades and orders distinct. And then he knew clearly how every created thing represented its Creator, and how God is above and within and without and beside all created things. Straightway he knew one God in three Persons and three Persons in one God, and the infinite Charity that made the Son of God take flesh in obedience to the Father." [2]

It is the same as that in which Dante actualises all potentialities of spiritual vision in the last canto of the *Paradiso* : the vision of all Being in the vision of the First Cause which becomes revealed as the Mystery of the Blessed Trinity. Such is the form in which the experience of ultimate Reality took shape for the mystics of the fourteenth century in the *momentum intelligentiae*, after which St. Augustine and St. Monica sighed, the half-hour during which there is silence in Heaven.

The five *Considerazioni* on the Stigmata stand on

[1] Cap. XLIX. Cf. Walter Hilton, *Scale of Perfection* (ed. Evelyn Underhill), Bk. II, ch. 41.
[2] Cap. LII.

a somewhat different footing from that of the *Fioretti* proper. It would seem that the translator did not consider this subject treated with sufficient fullness in the *Actus*, and therefore, instead of simply translating the relevant chapters, took them as the basis for an entirely new work. He accordingly removed three chapters, " Of the invention of Monte La Verna and the vision of Brother Leo," " How the death of St. Francis was revealed to Madonna Jacopa di Settesoli," " Of Brother Leo who saw St. Francis lifted from the earth, and saw and touched his Stigmata,"[1] wove them in with episodes from other sources, written and oral, and thus composed the most beautiful and convincing piece of Franciscan literature that we possess. It is true that there are incidents introduced, usually with admirable dramatic effect, which probably occurred at other epochs in the Saint's life. That wonderfully vivid scene at the beginning—Francis coming with Brother Leo to the festivities at the castle of the counts of Montefeltro, and there meeting Messer Orlando da Chiusi who offers him his " monte divotissimo," La Verna itself—in reality took place ten years before the reception of the Stigmata. Then, as they make their way to the mountain, there is the countryman in charge of the ass : " And, when they had gone on a little way, the rustic said to St. Francis : ' Tell me, art thou Brother Francis of Assisi ? ' St. Francis answered that he was. ' Now take heed then,' said the rustic, ' to be as good

[1] *Actus*, IX, XVIII, XXXIX.

as thou art held by all folk, for many have great faith in thee ; and, therefore, I admonish thee that there be not in thee aught else than what folk hope.' When St. Francis heard these words, he did not disdain to be admonished by a rustic, but straightway cast himself to earth from the ass, and knelt before the man and kissed his feet, and thanked him humbly for that he had deigned to admonish him so charitably." The story comes from Thomas of Celano,[1] where it is referred to another occasion, and where it is not the driver of the ass, but a labourer working in the fields who sees the Saint pass and runs to question him. Again, we are told that it was because of the reception of the Stigmata that Francis summoned the Chapter General at which, feeling himself unable any longer to continue as minister-general, he appointed Pietro Cattaneo as his vicar ;[2] whereas, in reality, this happened some years previously, and Pietro was dead before the Saint received the " ultimo sigillo." But such details are of minor importance. In all essentials we are on sure ground in turning to the writer of the *Fioretti* for the fullest and most spiritually significant version of the crowning experience in the life of the Saint, of whom, in the Encyclical Letter of Pope Pius XI, it is said : " Men have rightly hailed him as ' another Christ,' because to his contemporaries, and to all future ages, he presented Christ living once again."

[1] *Legenda secunda,* (ii) ciii. § 142.   [2] *Considerazioni,* IV.

THE DILEMMA OF ST. FRANCIS AND THE TWO TRADITIONS

Mr. HAROLD E. GOAD, o.b.e., m.a.

THE DILEMMA OF ST. FRANCIS AND THE TWO TRADITIONS

St Bonaventure, the greatest and wisest saint of the second generation of the Sons of St. Francis, opens the twelfth chapter of his " Legenda Major " with the following account of a most significant episode in the Founder's life. We quote the text in full from the translation by Miss Salter.

" The truly faithful servant and minister of Christ, Francis, that he might faithfully and perfectly fulfil all things, strove most chiefly to exercise those virtues that he knew, by the guidance of the Holy Spirit, were most pleasing unto his God. Wherefore it came to pass that he fell into great striving with himself by reason of a doubt, the which that he might end—on his return after many days of prayer—he set before the Brethren that were his intimates. 'What,' saith he, ' do ye counsel, Brethren, what do ye commend ? Shall I devote myself unto prayer, or shall I go about preaching ? Of a truth, I that am little, and simple, and rude in speech, have received more grace of prayer than of speaking. Now in prayer, there seemeth to be the gain and heaping up of grace, in preaching, a certain giving out of the gifts received from Heaven ;

in prayer, again, a cleansing of the inward feelings, and an union with the one, true, and highest good, together with a strengthening of virtue ; in preaching, the spiritual feet wax dusty, and many things distract a man, and discipline is relaxed.   Finally, in prayer, we speak with God and hear Him, and live the life of angels, while we converse with angels ; in preaching, we must needs practise much condescension toward men and, living among them as fellow-men, must think, see, say, and hear such things as pertain unto men.   Yet one thing is there to set against these, the which in God's sight would seem to weigh more than they all, to wit, that the only-begotten Son of God, Who is the highest wisdom, left His Father's bosom for the salvation of souls, that, instructing the world by His ensample, He might preach the word of salvation unto men, whom He both redeemed at the cost of His sacred Blood, and cleansed in a laver and gave them to drink, keeping back nothing of Himself, but for our salvation freely bestowing all.   And forasmuch as we ought to do all things after the pattern of those things that was shown us in Him as on a lofty mount, it seemeth that it might be more acceptable unto God that, laying aside leisure, I should go forth unto the work ! '   And albeit for many days he pondered over such sayings with the Brethren, he could not of a surety discern whether of the twain he should choose as more truly pleasing unto Christ.   For albeit he had known many wondrous things through the spirit of prophecy, he was not able thereby to resolve this question clearly, the providence of God better ordaining, so that the merit of preaching might be made evident by an heavenly oracle, and the humility of Christ's servant be kept intact.

" He, true Brother Minor, was not ashamed to ask little things from those less than himself, albeit he had learnt great things from the greatest Teacher. For with an especial zeal he was wont to enquire after what way and manner of life he might most perfectly serve God according to His will. This was his highest philosophy, this his highest desire, so long as he lived, so that he would enquire of wise and simple, of perfect and imperfect, of young and old, in what way he might with most holiness attain unto the summit of perfection. Therefore, calling unto him twain of the Brethren, he sent them unto Brother Silvester—he that had seen the Cross proceeding from his mouth, and was at that time giving himself up unto continuous prayer in the mountain above Assisi—that he might seek an answer from God concerning this doubt, and announce it unto him from the Lord. This same bidding he laid upon the holy virgin Clare, that through some of the purer and simpler of the virgins that were living under her rule, yea, and through her own private prayers united with those of the other Sisters, she might ascertain the will of the Lord touching this matter. The reverend priest and the virgin vowed to God were marvellously in agreement concerning this, the Holy Spirit revealing it unto them, to wit, that it was the divine will that the herald of Christ should go forth to preach. When, therefore, the Brethren returned, and according unto what they had learned, pointed out the will of God, Francis forthwith rose and girded himself, and without delay set forth upon his journey. And with such fervour did he go, to fulfil the divine behest, and with such speed did he hasten on his way, that he seemed—the hand of the Lord being upon him—to have put on new power from Heaven."

Such is the account of this all-important crisis and its solution, as given by that great Minister-General, St Bonaventure, in his " Greater Legend," which was written at the request of the Chapter-General of Narbonne in the year 1260.

The narrations of mediæval religious writers, however saintly, are not always guiltless of that reproach of many latter-day historians, namely of reading into past events contemporary prejudices and not infrequently emphasizing or even inventing episodes tending to support their point of view. Thus the First Life of St Francis by Thomas of Celano, written at the command of Gregory IX and under the influence of his agent, Ex-Vicar-General Elias, undoubtedly reflects the official view of the Saint's ideal at the moment of writing, that is, about two years after his death. The point for us is whether it did not also represent, as we believe, the opinion of the vast majority of the Friars, including those who knew St Francis best. The Second Life by the same author gives the same view some seventeen years later, as modified by the fall and apostasy of Elias and enlarged by memoirs of the First Companions, compiled by order of Crescentius. The " Greater Legend " of St Bonaventure is the view of a great scholar, based on all these and other material, that his travels as Minister-General enabled him to collect at a period when most of the first Brothers were still living. This also, we believe, reflects the opinion of the whole Order, except that of a small minority of hermits.

But in the early fourteenth century, when for divers reasons the hermit section in the Order had placed itself in definite opposition to the Hierarchy and to the larger or apostolic section, a number of books appeared, the best-known being the " Speculum Perfectionis," and the " Actus Beati Francisci et Sociorum Ejus " (translated as the " Fioretti " or " Little Flowers of St Francis "), which embodied a different point of view, a tradition of St Francis the Hermit, which will not fit with the older portrait, the tradition of St Francis the Apostle. We desire briefly to consider the respective claims of these two traditions upon our credence.

It is, of course, in the last resort conceivable that St Bonaventure may have invented this particular episode, for many such episodes in Franciscan books were invented with a purpose—such as, we suggest, that repulsive miracle with which the " Speculum Perfectionis " opens, the story of Christ's audible Voice from Heaven, speaking in anger to the discontented Ministers in answer to a question addressed to Him by St Francis, and declaring with emphatic repetitions that the Rule, which St Francis had just drawn up, was written by God only and must be followed to the letter without gloss, on pain of expulsion from the Order. Scarcely historical seems the story of the Angel, who according to the " Fioretti " knocked at the door of the hermitage at Farneto, demanding to see Elias, in order to ask him why he had forbidden the Brethren to eat flesh and made certain other ordinances contrary to evangelical liberty ; while the tale of how St Clare ate with St. Francis at the Portiuncula, and the people of Assisi and Bevagna hurried down, thinking the friary and the wood was burning on account of the great radiance that shone out from them, seems—in view of our knowledge from the Bull of her Canonisation and her biography by Thomas of Celano that the Seraphic Mother never left St. Damiano from the moment she was first taken there by St Francis—to be no more than an argument to prove that the " Poor Ladies " might on occasion go out and beg, not be for ever dependent on the Friars. Many other similar stories might be quoted from those most beautiful books.

But this episode in St Bonaventure's Legend sounds authentic. In the first place, it is characteristically Franciscan both in substance and in detail. Secondly, it is told also in the " Fioretti " with some added points, as that Masseo was the messenger. Moreover, we feel that St Francis with his love of nature, his humility and the example of many saintly hermits would certainly have preferred his " life of angels," but for an inward sense that his mission was to men. We must remember that he had begun his religious life as a solitary, dwelling alone in the ruins of the old Benedictine house at St Mary of the Angels in the midst of the far-stretching forest. Here, however, he had been commanded to go forth to preach by an inspiration received from the Gospel of St Matthew : " Go ye to the lost sheep of the House of Israel, and as ye go, preach, saying, The Kingdom of Heaven is at hand. Heal the sick, raise the dead, cleanse the lepers, cast out devils. Freely ye have received, freely give." There is no question of a life of solitary prayer. Poverty is enjoined, but for a reason. " Provide neither gold, nor silver, nor brass in your purses ; nor scrip for your journey ; neither two coats, neither shoes, nor yet staves ; for the workman is worthy of his meat." The workman was to be provided for in return for special service. St Francis had carried out these orders literally ; cast away shoes and staff, girt himself with a cord, gone into cities and villages, preached and converted. How was it that he now began to hesitate ?

The more recent experience of his life was such as to cause him to believe that God wished him after all to devote himself to a life of contemplation. On the one hand, his first attempt to preach to the heathen had been discouraging. Setting out for Syria, he had been shipwrecked off Dalmatia and forced to return to Ancona. On the other, while travelling homewards through the Marches, he had attended a festival at the Castle of Montefeltro and there won the friendship of Count Orlando of Chiusi, who had given him the mountain of Alvernia, a place which by reason of its seclusion and its beauty would seem almost unique as a sanctuary for prayer. Nevertheless the doubts persisted, with what results we have just seen.

We merely note in passing one significant discrepancy between the two accounts of the same incident, that whereas St Bonaventure emphasizes the Founder's obedience and attributes his hesitation to the desire of God to make the merit of preaching the more evident by a heavenly oracle, the hermit author of the " Fioretti " lays stress on the Saint's humility and limits his doubt as to " whether he ought to be wholly intent upon prayer or sometimes ought to preach."

But for Francis the immediate success of his new mission must have been proof that his decision was God's will. At Cannara, we are told, the entire population came out into the fields to meet him and after his sermon asked to a man to be admitted to his Order. He was obliged to send them back to their homes with a promise to devise a means for their salvation, a promise wherein, it is claimed, lay the first seed of his Third Order.

From St Bonaventure and Thomas of Celano's

" Legends " it is not difficult to reconstruct these missionary journeys. Wherever he went crowds followed.
When he was seen approaching a village, church-
bells sounded, the peasants left their fields and went
forth to meet him with boughs of olive in their hands.
Conducted to an open space within or without the
walls, with a flat stone for pulpit, this ill-favoured,
eager, little friar in his torn, worn, dirty habit
would pour forth streams of ardent and unlettered
eloquence, illustrated, one would suppose, by homely
parables and pointed by passionate appeals for repentance. If we may judge from his letters, one of his
most frequent themes must have been a plea for reverence for the secular priests and devotion to the Sacra-
ment ; indeed some of his later journeys must almost
have resembled Eucharistic missions. At other times
he appealed for peace between warring factions, as
when Thomas of Spalato heard him at Bologna and
when he expelled the devils of discord from Arezzo.
In all this his preaching must have vividly contrasted
with the railings of the heretics, with their fantastic
doctrines, their denunciations of the prelates and the
older Orders, and their frequent attacks upon secular
authority, as well as with the doctrinal and doubtless
somewhat arid homilies of the Bishops, delivered in the
conventional Latin of the period. New to men must
have been this ex tempore appeal in its obvious sincerity,
its single-hearted passion for peace and the saving of
souls. Yet, apparently, his words were most difficult

to remember, as witness the report of a doctor, un-
learned and most eloquent man, to Thomas of Celano :
" the sermons of others I can remember word for word,
but not those of St Francis, and if so be that I do recall
some little, it never seems to be that which issued from
his lips." It was in his depth and ardour that lay his
peculiar power.

Everywhere the citizens besought the Saint to
remain with them, to have a little hut for his friars
beside the gate. He accepted such gifts, provided
they were poor enough ; and thus hostels or " places "
to dwell in with a tiny oratory sprang up in every
city. But such fruits were by no means the meed of
St Francis only ; the other Brethren, his imitators, met
with like success. Bernard, the noble and once rich
Assisan magistrate, at first received with contumely at
Bologna, gradually by his patience won general admiration, until a rich man offered him " a place, wherein
he could serve God conveniently," and he fled back to
St Francis in fear for his humility, having founded the
first Franciscan house in the famous University city.
Thus " places " were established all over Italy and as
the missions went farther afield, all over Catholic
Europe.

Next, these " places " in their turn became centres
of conversion, to which men would apply for spiritual
counsel and often to be vested with habit and cord.
For some years there was not even a novitiate ; the
Order grew rapidly, even dangerously, without due

organisation. Who was to protect Society from the unworthy, the sturdy tramp, the mere impostor, who sheltered himself under Francis's name in order to live by begging? Is it unnatural that authorities, both ecclesiastical and secular, began to see dangers in the growing movement, the one fearing a new source of heresy in these untrained and ignorant preachers, the other a vehicle of conspiracy and rebellion? It soon became evident that the Order must be organised, if it were not to become a peril to the world.

The crisis was precipitated by St Francis's absence in the East. A rumour went about that he was dead. The efforts of his vicars to impose some sort of order only added to the confusion. The more independent Brothers refused to obey, forming themselves into new sects, schismatical, even heretical; others threw off their vows and returned to their work in the world; while a remnant retired into distant hermitages to watch events and pray for the Founder's return. Jordan of Giano, the chronicler for Germany, tells that St Francis first heard from a Syrian Pythoness that his Order was in confusion. Soon afterwards arrived a lay Brother with a copy of certain new impolitic regulations. Together with Peter of Cataneo, Elias of Beviglie and Cæsar of Spires, the Saint returned to Italy, saw Cardinal Ugolino at Bologna and Pope Honorius at Orvieto and asked the latter to appoint the Cardinal as Protector of the Order. Peter was made Vicar-General, and on his death, Elias, who promptly took strong measures to stem the ruin, and, despite his many faults, must in the circumstances be regarded as the second founder of the Order. He gave each province a definite organisation under a Minister, who should supervise all the communities, each to be ruled by a guardian, responsible for the friars. The latter were not to wander about without permission or to preach without licence from the Bishops. Meanwhile St Francis set himself to draw up the Rule, which apostolic act he accomplished after one unsuccessful effort and repeated consultation with his ministers and with Cardinal Ugolino at Rome.

But having in the East contracted malaria, besides a disease of the eyes which eventually cost him his sight, he was naturally henceforth less able to stand the strain of preaching, with the pressure of crowds that it entailed for him, and was therefore more and more obliged to withdraw himself into the hermitages. But such periods of spiritual recollection and repose were always subsidiary to the performance of his great apostolacy. His long fast on Alvernia led to the greatest apostolic act of the whole of his amazing life, that consummation whereby the whole of his frail body became a proof and a tongue to proclaim the truth of the Gospel of Divine Redemption. But even after his stigmatisation had rendered him physically helpless, he was constantly filled with desire to renew his efforts to convert mankind. " Let us begin to serve God better," he would cry. " All we have done so far is nothing!" He caused himself to be carried about the little towns and villages upon an ass, exhorting and blessing the crowds as far as he was able, sometimes even visiting as many as five places in one day. The enthusiasm of the populace approached fanaticism; everywhere miracles bore witness to God's will.

Nothing is more certain than that St Francis never intended his Order to be an order of hermits, like those of St Romuald at Camaldoli or St John Gualberto at Vallombrosa. A careful examination of the sequence of his life reveals a certain inner rhythm, wherein periods of solitary prayer lead up to vivid flashes of illumination, followed by periods of intense apostolic activity, thus proving that the first of the series are preparatory and subsidiary to the last. At times the flash is so vivid as to dazzle us even to-day and to be in itself a supreme apostolic act. For symbols and parables embody for all mankind doctrines or spiritual lessons in strongly dramatic or imaginative form. What could be more apostolic than the scene of the Renunciation of the World, the parable of the Marriage with Lady Poverty, the preaching to the birds, the Christmas crib at Greccio, the miracle of the Stigmatisation, and indeed all the chief actions of the last years of the marvellous life? The appeal of these symbolic *gestes* is to all the world and to all times; they are not the deeds of a contemplative, but of an apostle. The earliest account of his life by Thomas of Celano is a record of apostolacy — of preaching, travel, miracles of healing,—ceaseless and indefatigable service for the conversion and consolation of his fellow-men. To underestimate the supreme importance of this transcendent factor is to upset the balance of St Francis's whole career and to destroy the conformity of his life with Christ's.

It was in this apostolic sense that Elias ruled for him during the last five and a half years of his earthly mission. On his deathbed the blind Saint blessed his Vicar with a grateful benediction, praying that the Lord, Who had so multiplied the Brethren under his direction, would especially remember his great labours. And truly these must have been very great indeed,—for besides the many missions into distant and even Moslem countries, there were now " places " in almost every city and countless hermitages on mountain sides, not to speak of the care of all the houses of " Poor Ladies."

The first natural result of the restrictions upon wandering was a great increase in the number of stationary friars in the larger houses with a consequent Labour Crisis. Hundreds or thousands of young men found themselves tethered to the little " places," without employment, except begging. There was nothing that St Francis hated more than sloth. " I worked with my hands," he wrote in his will, " and I desire that all the Brethren work at some honest trade. Let those who know not one learn, not desiring wages, but for example's sake and to drive out idleness." Hundreds of unlettered novices had to be taught some useful handicraft, for the exercise of which spacious rooms were needed. Another result was a great stimulus to study, involving libraries, and theological schools for priests and preachers. Thenceforth the Order inevitably became more clerical. Again, St Francis himself inaugurated a school of music, and soon after his death Friars were appointed as choir-masters at half the courts of Europe.

Thus quite inevitably the little " places " grew to convents, the name " conventual " being given to those friars who dwelt in communities of over twelve and necessarily had certain dispensations with regard to laying in stores of provisions at each convenient season. Apparently it was the English Minister-General, Aymon of Faversham, who introduced kitchen-gardens, admirable fields of employment for the rough lay-brother and of recreation for the over-worked student,—as St Bonaventure observes. But long before this, even during the life-time of St Francis, the provision of the means of livelihood for the larger communities, and especially for the sick, necessitated the transaction of business, involving even the holding of property, on behalf of the Brothers, by " nuncii " or agents,—a custom that in 1230 was sanctioned by Pope Gregory in his Bull *Quo Elongati*, which gave much offence to the Rigourists. Furthermore, as regards dwellings, clusters of wooden sheds or wattle huts beside the city gates were no longer fit for the

housing of scores or even hundreds of men, and the
cities, which were now rapidly overflowing their old
circuits into new suburbs or " Borghi," soon to be
incorporated also and surrounded by new walls, naturally insisted on replacing the first hovels by larger,
more solid and sanitary constructions. It was precisely in these rapidly increasing, overpopulated and
squalid " Borghi " that the Order found its most fruitful field of apostolic work. It was here especially that
their great bare barnlike churches proved so valuable
for the evangelisation of the children of new social
conditions, a new industrial class. It is idle to repeat
that St Francis desired that his friars should preach in
the secular churches ; the answer to that argument
can usually be found in a reconstruction of the plan
of the cities of his day and a comparison with the
plan of the same cities fifty or a hundred years later.
In the former you find a small compact mediæval town
of narrow streets huddled within ancient, often Roman
walls around a Romanesque cathedral, a true People's
House, or Duomo, with tiny parish churches ; in the
latter you find a large and usually straggling place,
occupying often quite three times the area, the new
quarters each possessing a subsidiary square and a
subsidiary Duomo in the church of one or other of
the two great Mendicant Orders, but for which there
would have been inadequate church room for these
great new populations. St Francis can hardly have
anticipated the immense part in the cities' life that his

Plate VI.

By the courtesy of Sir Joseph Duveen.

St. Francis before the Sultan.
By Sassetta (1444).

Order was destined to play, any more than to have foreseen that the accession of so many priests would necessitate large buildings for their ministrations. But we are anticipating ;—sufficient be it for the moment to remind ourselves that we should by no means overlook the conditions that the external world imposed upon the development of the Order. Whatever its ideals, a movement so penetrative and so economically dependent on the good will of the world, could only survive by adaptation, by securing not only clerical tolerance, but also civic popularity.

That the Founder did not approve of the acquisition of large houses we know from his refusal to enter the convent and hospital at Bologna and by his action in beginning to pull down the great hall of stone that the Commune of Assisi had erected at the Portiuncula. But the former he tolerated when the Protector of the Order, Cardinal Ugolino, publicly declared the building to be his and the latter as soon as it was shown to be the property of the citizens. St Francis seems to have had no objection to living in a palace, provided that he was there as a sojourner and a guest. He dreaded lest great buildings should bring worldly cares and pride. But soon the world thrust them on the Order.

It was the world that forced upon the Order the building of the great fortress-shrine to save the body of the Stigmatised from the plunder of more powerful cities or the pious fury of the relic-hunters who would have torn it limb from limb to distribute in jewelled reliquaries. Just at this time the body of St Elizabeth suffered horrid mutilations ; over the relics of St Anthony a veritable battle took place. The body of St Louis was divided ; that of St Roch stolen ; and the body of St Francis was the most precious treasure in the world. To-day the supercilious scoff, the romantic mourn for the " unfranciscan " methods of Pope Gregory and his agent Elias ; but no one has suggested what else could have been done. On an almost inaccessible crag a strong castle was built, to be at once a papal palace, a shrine for the relic, a head house for the Order and a barracks for a body-guard of friars. We do not believe that the Order was split upon this " rock of scandal." True, a hundred years later an ugly story was invented to the effect that certain dissidents, and Leo the Pecorello, in particular, threw down a bowl that Elias had set up for alms and were scourged and banished for the deed. But the Brothers must have known that the building was the Pope's and that he was promoting by Indulgences the offerings they were scattering, and that what Elias did he did as the Pope's agent. If they really committed an act of such foolish insubordination, as a protest against Elias' policy, how was it that none of the latter's enemies, such as Eccleston or Salimbene, ever recorded such a piquant story ? That St Clare was proud of the great church we know ; for to her great joy she was carried in spirit to it one Christmas night to hear the friars singing ; Thomas of Celano praises it, as also do the authors of the " Legend of the Three Companions," who speak gratefully of Gregory as its builder. Finally, all the earlier Brothers were buried in it, save Giles, who wished to be, and including Leo, who died in the great convent, bequeathing to it his most precious keepsake, the Benediction that St Francis wrote for him. We cite all this because it is most important for our subject that we should no longer antedate the division in the Order.

The church that Elias built for the Pope, though strong and stately, was very different from the glorious shrine that we admire to-day. The Upper Church was covered by a visible wooden roof, resting on round arches ; was lit by simple lancet windows without tracery, and a plain round window at its western end ; and as such became the model of most of the Franciscan Churches erected throughout Central Italy during the next half-century, a model recommended by the Chapter of Narbonne in the year 1260. The Lower Church was a mere crypt for the burial of the more saintly Brothers around their Seraphic Father, without chapels, solid, plain, dark and severe. Moreover, the Papal Basilica at Assisi was by no means the only great Franciscan church built or acquired for the Order at this period.

Almost contemporaneously a second great Franciscan church was begun by the citizens of Padua for the miracle-working relics of St Anthony. In its

sumptuous and exuberant fantasy of incongruous detail
this vast fane shows a curious contrast to the harmonious simplicity of St Francis's shrine ; but it affords
a striking example of the way in which a powerful city
would adopt an apostle of Holy Poverty and exalt him
in a gorgeous temple of civic pride. The third great
Franciscan church was the " Ara Coeli " upon the
Capitol, a magnificent ancient basilica accepted for
the Order by that champion of the " Spirituals," the
Blessed John of Parma. From the middle of the century onwards there was much rebuilding of the earliest
Franciscan churches and convents ; in Spello, Foligno,
Montefalco, Spoleto, Terni, Gualdo, Nocera, Perugia,
Cortona, Siena, Volterra, Prato, Pistoia and many
other towns are typical examples of the great aisleless,
wooden-roofed, barnlike structures, built especially
for preaching, generally upon the model of Elias's
Upper Church. Gradually these buildings became
cemeteries for the local nobility, who erected around
them their family chapels and deputed a famous artist
to decorate with frescoes.

Doubtless this was all largely the result of the policy
of Elias, that great Vicar and afterwards Minister-
General, who was most emphatically a follower of
St Francis the Apostle, rather than of St. Francis the
Hermit. In later days the hermits could never for-
give him because he organised the Order upon apostolic
lines. He tore the anchorites from their hill-tops and
compelled them to work among the poor. The old

148

monastic Orders,—Benedictines, Cistercians and so forth,—dwelt in dignified and scholarly seclusion ; Elias planted his great friaries in the mean streets of crowded cities, those *Borghi* that were soon to be enclosed within new walls. He encouraged the Brothers to follow their Founder in tending the sick and the lepers ; made hospitals and even medical schools for their greater competence in nursing. For preachers he opened schools of Theology, which soon attracted the greatest intellects ; and by his schools of music and the constant services in his churches he carried light and beauty into the darkest lives. Unfortunately, by his arrogance, his autocratic and rapacious methods and his excessive centralisation, he roused strong opposition, especially in the ultramontane—English, French and German—provinces, and he was overthrown by a powerful clique of foreign clerics, particularly Englishmen, though even these he might have worsted, had he controlled his temper. His subsequent apostasy, his joining the Emperor Frederick,—whatever may have been the motive or provocation for that lamentable act,—put him into the wrong for all posterity and gave the opportunity to the dissidents of a later generation to trace back to his slandered name their own particular quarrel with the Hierarchy.

But in the next few years his successors, Albert of Pisa and Aymon of Faversham, obtained from the Papal Curia seven times as many Bulls, dispensations and privileges as Elias in the whole period of his rule.

They decreed that official posts should be reserved for priests, which signified the exclusion of laymen from all government of the Order. The priests were given private cells or " Studies " for prayer and preparation of sermons, and thus was taken a long step in the development of the régime, against which in a later day the humble ignorant lay sons of Francis revolted in the name of Poverty. The chief point to note is that the division came gradually and that the second tradition harked back to an imaginary past to gain a holier sanction for its grievance.

For albeit there were doubtless, even during the life-time of St Francis, zealots who clung to the strictest interpretation of the clauses in the Rule relating to Holy Poverty, and ascetics who held with St Peter Damiani that " the world is so filthy with vices that any holy mind is befouled even by considering it,"— yet it is difficult to believe that more than an insignificant minority refused to follow the Founder in his apostolic work. There was as yet no division, no united opposition to St Francis's Ministers. But as time went on, the Brothers tended to fall into three classes,—dwellers in towns, inhabiting large houses, wanderers on the roads and hermits. The ideal of the first is expressed by St Bonaventure, who, like St Francis, according to Thomas of Celano, held that the Order had been raised up by God to assist the Bishops and the secular clergy, overwhelmed as these were by administrative work. Some of the Friars were to be occupied in study, to fit themselves for preaching and instructimg others ; some were to serve the Altar ; some were to nurse ; some were to visit, console and exhort the poor and ignorant ; some were to collect alms for the maintenance of the community ; while those, who had learned trades, were to work at them for the benefit of the Brethren and of strangers ; others, when directed, were to travel upon missions ;—but no one was to be idle except he were sick. That the Conventuals fell away from this high ideal in some instances is probable, though not to the extent that their jealous rivals declared. The faults of the few, says St. Bonaventure, are only too obvious, " for that which is evil floats on the surface, while true holiness is a hidden thing to be found only by certain signs."

Moreover, it was this ideal that inspired his great biography, the " Legenda Major " of the Founder. It is fashionable to-day to complain that this splendid work is little more than an " official manual, written for edification ! " Edification ? One is tempted to ask whether in the circumstances there was anything else that mattered. To this great book above all others we owe the glory of St Francis in art, in literature and missionary work. One feels that the saintly author is writing for the world at large, and not merely for the Order, or for the future historian ; in short, that, like his Master, he is above all things apostolic. For this reason, if for no other, in our humble judgement his book remains incomparably the finest general portrait of St Francis. Thus apparently thought the Chapter-General of 1266, for they ordered the destruction of all other legends,—a measure that we must regret particularly because it has created an exaggerated notion of the importance of the documents that may have been destroyed.

Most men regard the gifts of God as living principles, capable of development and self-adjustment to life around. Others, however, seem to consider inspiration as a single transcendent creative word, immutable for all eternity. They distrust and betray the law of life through a mistaken loyalty to origins. Not so St Francis, who, as we have seen, constantly read in the response of circumstance to his efforts at right service, the indications of God's Will as to what he should do next. Following his principle, we prefer to see in the immense success of the Franciscan ministry, in its missions, its great friaries and its theological schools, proof that this was its true line of development,—rather than cavil, as many critics seem to do, at modifications of the Rule that this development implied.

On the other hand, the little hermitages seem to have lost touch with life and to have fallen out of human favour. They produced no saint to be compared with St Anthony or St Bonaventure. The former is most emphatically to be placed among the Brothers of the Large Observance, not only by reason of his apostolic work, but by the fact that he formed part of the commission that was sent to Rome in the year 1230 to treat for the setting aside of certain clauses in St Francis's Will and that resulted in the Bull " Quo Elongati." The saintly lives of their few chief lights did not save the hermits from the bitter censure of our chronicler, Thomas of Celano, in his Second Life, written about the year 1245, in which he writes, " they convert the place of contemplation into a place of leisurely repose and make the anchoretic life, that was instituted for soul's perfecting, into a sewer of pleasure ! For their constitution to-day," he adds, " is to live each one according to his will." We should not forget that these strong words were published at the moment when John of Parma was elected to the Generalship and that this holy man was particularly chosen for his energy in travel and visitation. We therefore believe that there was a strong conviction in the Order that supervision was urgently required in the smaller houses.

As for the " Wanderers beyond Obedience," Minister-General Crescentius has strong words indeed for them. He accuses them of " temerariously pre-suming, like young asses' colts, to kick off the burden of Obedience," of " refusing to dwell in the convents of the Order " and of " wandering about the world at will, preaching and teaching and hearing confessions without authority, for the ruin of their own souls and the scandal of not a few."

Further, the smaller, more remote, contemplative communities were naturally more exposed to the perils

153

of contagion from the prevalent heresies. The prophecies of the Abbot Joachim now lured away many of the brightest spirits of the Order, including the saintly Minister-General, John of Parma, into a cloud of mystical fantasy, wherein they attempted to exalt St Francis, his Rule, and themselves, as his sole followers, into a shining apotheosis superior to all authority. These foolish doctrines, though denied, condemned, confuted, none the less continued to infect the writings of the section of the dissidents for over half a century, forming the chief inspiration of the extremists and stiffening opposition to the Hierarchy. By the end of the third quarter of the thirteenth century a definite division in the Order becomes visible, the minority led by Peter John Olivi, a minority ready even for secession, when twenty years later still the opportunity was given by the weakness of the hermit-pope, Celestine V. It is this section of the Order that must also take the blame for the Franciscan connection with the " Fraticelli."

Now it was in the hermitages and at a period when the extremists were being persecuted in the interests of discipline and Catholic faith, that certain new books were compiled, embodying the tradition of St Francis the Hermit, as opposed to that of St Francis the Apostle. Many of their stories were already to be found in the earlier books, especially in the Second Life by Celano ; many were, no doubt, both new and true, and to others were added a new detail. But the question is, as a whole, what is their claim upon our credence, considering their place and period of origin ?

Other papers in this volume will deal with the sources of these compilations ; it remains for us rather to point out their bias, which so often distorts a reported saying or an incident as to render the question of the mere antiquity of its tradition almost immaterial. Moreover, the very vividness of these legends makes them suspect ; first reports are usually blunt and crude, later accounts more vivid and circumstantial ; for it is far easier to write vivid fiction than vivid truth, especially when there is a spice of animus to stimulate imagination. On the other hand, a vivid touch is invariably repeated because it is particularly memorable ; wherefore it is far less likely that Thomas of Celano in his Second Life deliberately whittled down good stories, than that the Speculum repeated them from his account or from his sources together with subsequent embellishments. With regard to many of these stories in the Speculum there can be no question whatever of the bias or imagination of their editors ; wherefore we feel that we must not accept as true any statement contained in them, if we detect a secondary motive for its narration. A great many of the episodes are what is called " tendencious," that is, adapted, interpreted or distorted to prove a point or indirectly censure an opponent.

The " Speculum Perfectionis " after a positively blasphemous exordium, surely only credible by extremists, has five-and-twenty chapters on the Perfection of Poverty, containing many episodes of great beauty from St Francis' legend, many doubtless true, many already told, more simply, credibly and dispassionately in the Second Life by Thomas of Celano. They teach that a friar should have no more than habit, cord and breeches, whereas, of course, the Rule allows two habits ; no books, or only few and poor ; should beg,—a shrewd hit at the clerics,—but take no thought whatever for the morrow, not even so much as to put dried beans in water overnight ! (One wonders how, according to the " Fioretti," Juniper contrived to cook sufficient provisions for a fortnight ?) Next there follow instances of the Saint's compassion, his holy humility and obedience, although here we have bitter complaints against the prelates and wise friars who would change the Order, together with harsh predictions that learning would be its ruin. Next, attached to the seventy-first chapter, is a terrible writing, which Leo is said to have given to Conrad of Offida, purporting to be a verbatim report of a conversation that St. Francis held with Christ, full of the crudest reproaches against the world and the Order, all except those few, who would be persecuted and driven out into the desert, yet be fed with manna, for they alone were the light of the world, for whose sake the Lord would spare mankind ! The book goes on to say how St Francis railed against those friars, " puffed up with the wind of science and the vain speeches of their wisdom, who say the truth is falsehood and like blind men persecute cruelly those that walk in light ! " This is indeed a different Francis,—scolding, admonishing, denouncing, threatening, preaching by precept rather than example,—from the Poverello we have known in earlier books. Towards the end again are many chapters of great spiritual beauty, telling of the Saint's love for the creatures and giving many precious episodes of the last years of his life.

Even if we pass over certain obvious and surprising historical errors in points upon which one would have thought that every friar would have been informed,— such as, for example, the substitution of Cardinal Ugolino for Cardinal Capocci at the famous Chapter of Mats,— we feel that it is their *spirit* that condemns the authority of these writings, the same narrow and contentious spirit that animated all the chief dissidents towards the end of the thirteenth century, that caused Ubertino of Casale to leave the Order and Angelo of Clareno to seek the sympathy of a schismatic church. Doubtless before this the Conventuals had also moved a long way from the intention of their Founder and were inevitably travelling towards the day when pious laymen, such as the Blessed Paolo Trinci, should with the full approval of the Hierarchy return in their hermitages to the primitive observance, and John of Stroncone, St John of Capistrano, and, greatest of all, St Bernardino of Siena, should lead a growing band back to a stricter compromise. The point for us about the " Speculum " is that it is clearly written for the edification of the Order only as an appeal against the Hierarchy. The authors hardly seem to be aware of the existence of a world outside to be evangelised ; the characters in the book are almost exclusively friars ; St Francis in their pages is no more than a standing reproach to the worldly Brother and complacent Minister. On the other hand, one can hardly read a single page of the " Greater Legend " of St Bonaventure without realising that it is the persuasion,—if you will, the " edification " —of mankind in general that is the leading motive, both in the writing of the book and the story that it tells.

It was from the remoter hermitages that emerged a little later than the " Speculum," that most exquisite of religious romances, the " Fioretti," a poem too appealing to be trustworthy for history, yet which embodies in most perfect form the tradition that gave it birth. Its stories have a subtle fragrance, as of wild thyme or rosemary or cypresses in the sun ; they call up visions of high rocks and ilex-thickets and distant Umbrian hill-tops bathed in golden light. They transport one into a fairy-land where judgement is suspended ; one cannot accept, but one would not deny ; one resigns oneself to the charm. There is a childlike affection and admiration between the Brothers ; they speak with childlike awe of one another's exploits, recounting the most minute and intimate details and expecting one to accept the strangest miracles at their word. But the miracles in the " Fioretti " are quite unlike

those told by Thomas of Celano,—from the visit of the
Angel who carried Bernard over a broad river ; to
the demon who tore down the ruin of rocks on Mount
Subasio in rage at Rufino's constancy ; from the tale
of Brother Bentivoglia who bore a leper fifteen miles
upon his shoulder, travelling faster than an eagle, to
the marvellous prophetic dream of Brother James, who
saw all that was going to happen to the Order. The
conversion of the Wolf of Gubbio we owe to the
" Fioretti," as well as the greatest supernatural marvels
that accompanied the vision of the Seraph of the
Stigmata. The Sultan of Egypt in this romance is not
allowed to be unconverted, nor the ultimate salvation
of Brother Elias to remain in doubt.

To-day, when we visit the charming little mountain
hermitages such as the Carceri, Greccio, Poggio Bus-
tone, Fonte Colomba, Monteluco, Stroncone, Farneto,
Cettona, the Celle of Cortona, Monte Casale and many
more, we everywhere find local legends, resembling
these pretty stories, full of the same sweet natural
magic and fragrant childlike charm. At Farneto, for
instance, close beside the splendid road from Perugia
to Gubbio, you will be shown the tree that grew from
St Francis's staff, which he bade a novice plant in the
ground and water night and morning to try the youth's
obedience, and the knocker of the door with which
the Angel knocked when he came to question Elias ;
at the Carceri, on the other hand, you will see marks of
the Devil. At the Sacro Speco above Narni you will

see the well where the Saint turned water into wine,
the cavern by which he travelled to Assisi, and the
rock on which the Angel sat while playing to him
on a viol. At Citerna, on the borders of Tuscany,
you may hear of the ants that the Saint banished by a
word from the spot where he wished to preach, and of
the wicked woman whom he commended to the Powers
of Evil, and who was snatched up into the air. At
Lugnano on the border of Lazio, you will learn how
the holy man, when preaching, ordered a duck to
rescue a child that had been carried off by a wolf into
the forest ; while the boatmen who row you over to
the Isola Maggiore in Lake Trasimene, will relate how
their predecessor in St Francis's day hesitated whether
to obey him because of a raging storm, until the Saint
produced a lighted taper, which, though carried high
upon the wind as they crossed the tossing waters, for
all the efforts of the fiends could never be put out !
Often one has a sense of still stranger tales, concealed
by a local guide for fear of ridicule ; or by a friar who
feels that the sceptical world is unworthy of such
mysteries.

When we compare these disconnected and frequently purposeless wonders of local legend and
eremitic tradition with the miracles of the regular lives
of St Francis, certain distinctive qualities stand out.
They are obviously more naïve and imaginative, more
marvellous and more trivial ; above all, as one might
expect from their origin, they are not apostolic healings

or graces vouchsafed for the benefit of other men, but rather supernatural favours, rewards and consolations, given by God for his particular favourites in return for their love for Him. With all their poetry, these tales are far removed from ordinary human business ; mediæval, whereas St Francis the Apostle was the first man of our world. Their principal topics are mystical experiences, visions and dreams, ecstasies, raptures and temptations, the possession of the soul by God, or by the Devil. In our modern life, wherein charitable organisation has grown commonplace and romantic mysticism is very much in vogue, these stories are naturally popular, especially among those who do not take religion very seriously. They are the natural product of the hermit section of the Franciscan Order, and, like enough, would have been its only fruit had the answer of Silvestro and St Clare been other than it was.

Otherwise also would have run the history of our civilisation if the inspiration of St Francis had been lacking to art, literature, philosophy, in short, to all the larger world of thought. Had St Francis followed the example of St Bruno, there would have been no great friaries in populous cities, but only a host of tiny hermitages scattered over Umbrian hills. Ragged and ignorant friars might have wandered begging, or lurked in lonely cells, forgotten by the world. Who could have protected them from the prevalent mystic heresies, or saved those who were merely tramps from

schism and rebellion ?   At most, the Order could have
been no more than the last echo of an age that was
passing, picturesque, poetical, but powerless to inspire.
It was the great theological schools, attached to the
larger convents, that attracted such great masters as
Bacon, Scotus, Hales, Marsh, Middleton and Ockham,
—only to name Englishmen.   It was in illustrating
the Franciscan epic for the larger churches that Giotto
found his earliest inspiration ; it was from the larger
Franciscan tradition, and especially from St Bonaventure, that Dante learned the secret of his approach to
science.   By its ministrations and its missions this
active, apostolic Order changed the outlook of Society,
and the century of its inspiration is the period of
transition from the mediæval to the modern world.

The gestures of St Francis were too large and too
significant to be confined to the narrow stage of the
little Umbrian hermitages or even of the cities and
villages where he preached.   In an age that was arid
with effete conventions, he sowed a life-seed and a new
creative grace.   In the mirror of himself as in the
method of his teaching he showed forth the image of
a human Saviour in the living hues of sentiment and
sympathy.   For this great work he has been called
" The Fifth Evangelist," and the truth of his gospel
for mankind was Life.

THE FIRST HUNDRED YEARS OF THE FRANCISCAN SCHOOL AT OXFORD

By A. G. LITTLE, M.A., F.B.A.

THE FIRST HUNDRED YEARS OF THE FRANCISCAN SCHOOL AT OXFORD

THE Dominicans and Franciscans were sometimes classed together in the latter part of the thirteenth century as " the two student Orders." [1] That learning should become one of the leading characteristics of his Order was certainly contrary to the intention and the ideals of St. Francis. He had a humble veneration for learning and for learned men in their proper place, but their proper place was not among the Friars Minor, who had chosen " the way of simplicity." " St. Francis once said " (to quote Thomas of Celano) " that a great scholar when he joined the Order ought in some sort to resign even his learning, in order that, having stripped himself of such a possession, he might offer himself naked to the arms of the Crucified." [2] " Tantum habet homo de scientia quantum operatur " is another phrase attributed to him by his companion, Brother Leo [3] (" A man's knowledge is just what he *does* "). He foresaw also very clearly some of the changes which

---

[1] *Fr. Rogeri Bacon Opera quaedam hactenus inedita*, ed. J. S. Brewer (R.S. 1859), pp. 398, 426, 427.

[2] II Cel. ii., c. 146, § 194.

[3] *Speculum Perfectionis*, ed. Sabatier, p. 13.

165

the pursuit of knowledge would bring into the Order itself.[1] It would create an aristocracy of learning and introduce a division between the learned and the simple brethren. The possession of books was not only inconsistent with the maintenance of absolute poverty, but it would involve further changes. It would tend to the establishment of permanent houses and limit the liberty and mobility of the friars. It is noteworthy that the first permanent house for the friars was built in the university city of Bologna, and St. Francis in vain protested against it.[2]

It is easy to see why he failed to stop the new development. Learned men were attracted by the ideal of poverty and self-sacrifice no less than the simple, and why should they not use all their gifts and powers in the service of others? The determination of wise prelates —such as Cardinal Ugolino—to make full use of the Franciscan movement to evangelize the world encouraged the friars to study. And the example of the Friars Preachers must have tended to the same result. The clerkly element from the first predominated in the Franciscan Order in the countries north of the Alps, and nowhere did their message meet with more enthusiastic response than among the masters and scholars of Paris and Oxford.

Nine Franciscan friars landed at Dover on 10

[1] See esp. " Intentio Regulae," in Lemmens, *Documenta Antiqua Franciscana*, I. pp. 83–99.

[2] *Spec. Perf.* cap. 6, II Cel. i., c. 28, § 58.

September 1224. About the end of October two of them—both Englishmen—arrived at Oxford and, after staying a week with the Friars Preachers, hired a house in St. Ebbe's. Here they were soon joined by William of Ashby, the third Englishman among the original nine friars. William, though still a novice, was made the first guardian of Oxford. He seems to have been a scholar of Paris, and was a man of attractive, gentle, unassuming, and rather morbid nature, without much initiative, but able to carry out any task imposed on him. The friars quickly won recruits among the University men—many honest bachelors and many nobles entering the Order in their first house, which soon proved too small. In the summer of 1225 they moved across the road to a house belonging to Richard the Miller, who made over his house to the community of the town for the use of the friars.[1] It was situated on the south of Freren Street (now Church Street),[2] in the triangle formed by Church Street on the north, St. Ebbe's Street on the east, and the city wall on the south. This house, though very confined, had to suffice for their needs for the next four years. Agnellus, the provincial minister, always refused to allow any house of friars to accept more ground than was necessary for their immediate requirements.[3] In 1229 he permitted a

---

[1] *Tractatus fr. Thomae . . . de Eccleston De adventu Fratrum Minorum in Angliam,* ed. A. G. Little, 1909 (henceforth referred to as Eccleston), pp. 3–8, 11–13, 27.

[2] Salter, *Cartulary of the Hospital of St. John* (Oxf. Hist. Soc.), II. p. 218.

[3] Eccleston, 55.

large increase. The house of William de Wileford with all its appurtenances in the parish of St. Ebbe was purchased by public subscription and handed over to the mayor and good men of Oxford to hold for the use of the Friars Minor for ever. The price was 43 marks (28*l.* 13.4).[1] This is 3 marks more than the price for which a few years later the Dominicans sold a portion of their original site in St. Edward's parish—a more central part of the town than St. Ebbe's. This portion measured 14 × 8 perches and included the great school.[2] It is reasonable to suppose that the site of William de Wileford's house was rather larger than this, and in that case it must have occupied more than half of the triangle between Church Street, Freren Street, and the city wall.

We may connect this large increase in the area with the decision to open a school in the friary. This was the year of the dispersal of the University of Paris : masters and scholars were seeking new homes : Henry III invited them to transfer themselves to England (14 or 16 July 1229), and Oxford was crowded with immigrants, among whom were a number of Friars Minor from the schools of Paris.[3]

The time was opportune, and there was at least

---

[1] Little, *Grey Friars in Oxford*, 295–6. For date see Salter, *Cart. of Hosp. St. John*, II. 34–5. Cf. ibid. I. 23–4, II. 202.

[2] *Cartulary of St. Frideswide*, ed. Wigram (Oxf. Hist. Soc.), I. 223.

[3] Salter, *Mediaeval Archives of the University of Oxford* (O.H.S.), I. 17. Pat. 13 Hen. III. m 6 (p. 257). Shirley, *Letters Henry III* (R.S.), I. 398–9. Eccleston, 37.

one English Franciscan who seems to have been eminently qualified to act as master of the school. This was Haymo of Faversham, afterwards General Minister of the whole Order—the only Englishman to hold that office. He had entered the Order at St. Denys (for the famous convent of the Cordeliers in Paris was not yet in existence) on Good Friday, 12 April 1224, with his assistant Nicholas of Sandwich and two other masters, and came to England soon after the arrival of Agnellus. His coming added greatly to the prestige of the friars in England : " both in sermons and disputations," says the chronicler Thomas of Eccleston, " and especially in securing the favour of prelates he assisted very much the simplicity of the brethren in those early days."[1] The word " disputations " implies that he took part in university teaching, and there is other evidence of his close connexion with Oxford.[2] That he was a competent teacher is shown by the fact that he was later appointed lector at Tours, Bologna, and Padua.[3] Why not at Oxford ?

A possible and not improbable explanation is the Gospel injunction : " Neither be ye called masters " (Matt. xxiii. 10). The identification of the Rule and the Gospel was a principle among the primitive friars,

---

[1] Eccleston, 34–6.

[2] Pat. Roll, 16 Hen. III. m 7.

[3] Eccleston, 35. According to Grabmann, *Theol. Quartalschrift*, 1911, p. 544, Haymo of Faversham's *quaestiones* on the logical works of Aristotle are preserved in Bibl. Ambrosiana MS. C. 161 inf. But Callebaut (*Arch. Franc. Hist.*), XIV. 375, ascribes them to Simon of Faversham.

who held that they were bound by their Rule to observe all the precepts of the Gospel. This was the tradition in which Agnellus had lived, and, in spite of the Bull *Quo elongati* (28 September 1230), the tradition certainly persisted in some parts and may have prevented any Friar Minor from taking the degree of master for some years in the English province. At Oxford a school of theology recognized by the university could be ' ruled ' or conducted only by a master ; and at Oxford the Franciscan school was ruled for some eighteen years by a succession of secular masters. In this respect Oxford was unique among the English houses and probably in the whole Order.

The decision to entrust the post to a secular in the first instance was made easy by the fact that a man of exceptional abilities and character and position was available—namely, Robert Grosseteste. Eccleston is disappointingly brief on his appointment. " On the enlargement of the friary where the principal university flourished and where scholars were wont to congregate, brother Agnellus caused a school of fair dimensions to be built in the place of the brethren, and persuaded Master Robert Grosseteste of holy memory to lecture there to the brethren. Under him within a short time they made incalculable progress both in scholastic disputations and in the subtle moralities suitable for preaching." [1]

That Grosseteste should have accepted what must

[1] Eccleston, p. 60.

have been a comparatively obscure post is a tribute alike to his humility and to his faith in the future of the Franciscan movement. He already had a long and distinguished career behind him. By 1214 he had become the foremost teacher at Oxford and was appointed the first chancellor of the young university with the title of *Magister scholarum*. He held many preferments in the Church, all of which, except one prebend at Lincoln, he resigned for conscience' sake while he was lecturer to the friars.

He was lecturer to the friars from 1229 or 1230 till his election to the see of Lincoln on 27 March 1235.[1] Learning he regarded as essential to the life and growth of the Order : " For he said sometimes that unless the friars fostered learning and devoted themselves to the study of the divine law, of a certainty the same fate would befall us which had befallen the other religious Orders whom we see, alas ! walking in the darkness of ignorance." [2] It is at present impossible to say which of his numerous writings belong to this period. There is some reason to believe that the *De cessatione legalium*, which contains arguments for the conversion of the Jews, was written about 1232,[3] and the collection of *Dicta*,[4] consisting chiefly of lecture notes on moral

---

[1] *Chron. de Lanercost* (ed. J. Stevenson, 1839), p. 45. The author was a Franciscan, Richard of Durham ; see *Eng. Hist. Rev.* XXXI. 269-79.

[2] Eccleston, 114.

[3] F. S. Stevenson, *Robert Grosseteste*, 104.

[4] Some of these are printed in E. Brown's *Fasciculus Rerum Expetendarum* (1690), II. 274-96.

subjects and containing what Eccleston calls " subtle moralities suitable for preaching," may perhaps be ascribed to this time. But we are able to recover the chief features of Grosseteste's teaching both from his own works and from the frequent allusions to it in Roger Bacon's writings. Bacon was not yet a friar and there is no positive evidence that he attended Grosseteste's lectures. But his allusions are particularly interesting and important for our purpose, because he frequently classes together Grosseteste and two of his successors in the office of lecturer to the friars—namely, Thomas the Welshman and Adam Marsh—and establishes the fact that a special tradition of learning was founded by Grosseteste and prevailed for several generations in the Franciscan school.

The principal characteristics which distinguished Grosseteste's teaching may be summed up under three heads :

(1) The study of the Bible. " Auctoritas irrefragabilis Scripturae " is a phrase which he uses in a letter (c. 1233) to Agnellus and the convent of Oxford.[1] In a letter written some years later to the Regent Masters in Theology at Oxford, he insists that the text of the Old and New Testaments must be the basis of theological teaching : " Now the time especially appropriate to laying foundation stones . . . is the morning hour when you lecture *ordinarie* : therefore all your lectures especially at that time should be on the books of the

[1] *Robert Grosseteste Epistolae*, ed. Luard (R.S.).

New Testament or the Old."[1]   There can be no doubt
that this was the practice which he followed himself,
and we have the express statement of Roger Bacon that
Grosseteste and Adam Marsh invariably used the text
of the Scripture for the subject of their lectures in
preference to the Sentences of Peter Lombard, which
later became the favourite text-book in the schools of
theology.[2]

(2) The study of languages.   In his commentaries
on the works of the Pseudo-Dionysius, especially in the
De divinis nominibus, Grosseteste gives a kind of gram-
matical introduction to the Greek language.   It is true
that all Grosseteste's translations from the Greek were
made after he became bishop ; and Bacon says : " He
did not know languages well enough to translate except
towards the end of his life."[3]   But a letter to the Abbot
and Convent of Peterborough, written in the early
years of his episcopate, gives us a glimpse of him reading
and translating Greek as a relaxation during a few
days' respite from his official labours[4] ; and it is a fair
inference that his mind was occupied by the subject
while he was lecturing to the friars.   This inference is
confirmed by Bacon's testimony to the work of Grosseteste and his successors in the Franciscan school : " We
have seen some of the earlier generation who laboured
much at languages, such as the lord Robert the above-

[1] *Robert Grosseteste Epistolae*, 246–7.
[2] *Fr. Rog. Bacon Opera*, ed. Brewer, 328–9 (a faulty text).
[3] *Ibid.* Opus Tertium, p. 91.
[4] *R. Grosseteste Epist.* 173.

mentioned translator and bishop, and Thomas the venerable bishop of St. David's now deceased, and Friar Adam Marsh." [1]

(3) Mathematics and Physical Science. Here again the repeated conjunction of Adam Marsh's name with that of Grosseteste in Roger Bacon's writings may be taken as evidence that Grosseteste expounded his views on these subjects to the friars. " There have been found," says Bacon, " some famous men, such as Robert, Bishop of Lincoln, and friar Adam Marsh and some others, who have known how by the power of mathematics to infold the causes of all things and to give a sufficient explanation of human and divine phenomena ; and the assurance of this fact is to be found in the writings of these great men, as, for instance, in their works on the impression [of the elements], on the rainbow and the comets, on the sphere, and on other questions appertaining both to theology and to natural philosophy." [2]

Natural philosophy, Grosseteste taught, is based on mathematics. " Omnes enim causae effectuum naturalium habent dari per lineas, angulos et figuras. Aliter enim impossibile est sciri ' propter quid ' in illis." [3] He used optics as best adapted to illustrate the prevalence of mathematical law ; but the nature of

---

[1] *Op. Maj.* (ed. Bridges), III. 88. Cf. *Op. Tert.* (ed. Brewer), 88.

[2] *Opus Majus* (Bridges), I. 108. Cf. *Op. Tert.* (Brewer), 82 ; *Roger Bacon Commem. Essays*, 164, note 2 (De communibus mathematice).

[3] *Die phil. Werke Grossetestes* (Baur), 60.

light had a still wider and deeper interest for him. Light is a force or form of energy which acts by an instantaneous self-expression in all directions from a centre ; it is the simplest and most subtile body, the most akin to spirit—the type and symbol of Creative Mind.

Grosseteste was succeeded by three more secular masters in turn.[1] The first was Peter, probably Peter of Ramsey, who became Bishop of Aberdeen in 1247. He remains only a name. The second, Roger of Wesham or Weasenham, became Dean of Lincoln about 1240 and Bishop of Coventry and Lichfield 1245–56.[2] Of his scholastic work nothing is known. These two probably held the office of lector only for a short time—between 1235 and 1240. The third was Thomas the Welshman. He went to Paris about 1236 to study theology with the hope of obtaining the doctor's degree, but sacrificed this ambition at Grosseteste's request and returned to England in 1238 as Archdeacon of Lincoln.[3] He presumably became D.D. of Oxford and lectured to the friars from 1240 till his election to the see of St. David in 1247. Roger Bacon alludes several times to his knowledge of languages, but nowhere expressly states that he resembled Grosseteste

---

[1] Eccleston, 61–2.

[2] For full account of his resignation, see *William Salt Archæol. Soc.* VI. (1885), pt. ii, pp. 107 et seq.

[3] *Rob. Grosseteste Epistolae*, pp. 147–51. Cf. *Rotuli Rob. Grosseteste* (Cant. and York. Soc.), pp. 22, 31, 103, 165, 252, 306, 343, 392, 395. Mat. Paris, *Chron. Maj.* IV. 647, V.

and Adam Marsh in knowledge of mathematics and natural philosophy.[1]

All these four secular masters who ruled the Franciscan school for the first eighteen years of its existence became bishops, and, in Eccleston's words, " being always favourable to the friars in all things, they promoted their deeds and fame very greatly in diverse places. The fame of the friars of England and their progress in learning became so well known even in other provinces " that many of them were called to lecture in foreign houses—such as Lyons, Parma, Genoa, Rome.

In England itself pupils of Grosseteste and his immediate successors were sent as lecturers to the various convents. London, Canterbury, Hereford, Leicester, Bristol, Gloucester, Norwich, Northampton, are specially mentioned, besides Oxford and Cambridge. Eccleston sums up the progress made in the following statement : " The gift of wisdom so overflowed in the English province that before the deposition of Friar William of Nottingham [1254] there were in England thirty lecturers who solemnly disputed, and three or four who lectured without disputing. For Friar William had assigned in the universities for every house students who should succeed the lecturers on their death or removal." [2]

---

[1] *Fr. Rog. Bacon Opera* (ed. Brewer), 88 (for *sanctum* read *sancti*), 428 ; *Opus Majus* (ed. Bridges), III. 88.
[2] Eccleston, p. 63.

Plate VII.

St. Francis before the Pope.
By Sassetta (1444).

We thus see that the universities—Oxford and to a lesser degree Cambridge—became primarily, under the influence of William of Nottingham, the fourth provincial minister (1240–54), training colleges for teachers throughout the province. The ideal—and it was already largely realized—was that each house should have a lecturer, and that each house should have a student being prepared at one of the universities to succeed to the lectureship when it became vacant. Some light is thrown on the working of the system by a passage in a letter of Adam Marsh to William of Nottingham about 1251[1] : " Friar Hugh of Lewknor [co. Oxford], a brother of good character and laudable promise, has asked me to pray you that you will kindly command the friars, to whom he is assigned as lecturer, that they will set about making adequate provision for him, or that they do not complain at his getting released from his engagement (*assignationis*), if that be your good pleasure." The convent therefore had to provide for its *frater assignatus* during his training.

These *assignationes* were made by the provincial minister in consultation with the master of the Franciscan school in the university,[2] and probably the convent concerned had a say in the matter.[3] They were evidently made not at the beginning but fairly late in a student's academic career. Thus Adam Marsh urges that Friar Thomas of York, who had already for some

---

[1] *Monumenta Franciscana*, ed. Brewer (R.S.), I. 357.
[2] *Mon. Franc.* I. 357.   [3] Cf. ibid. 319.

years shown himself a promising student, should not be set to teaching yet, but should be *assigned* as lector to the Oxford convent : i.e. he should continue his studies with a view to becoming lector at Oxford.[1]

When a student friar first came to Oxford, he did not come as a *frater assignatus*, but was said to " stand for " such and such a convent—" *stare pro* (or *de*) *conventu*." He might afterwards, if he proved suitable, be " assigned " to some convent—probably not tha from which he originally came. But I have been able to find out very little about the system. The constitutions and decrees of the English province have all been lost, and the general constitutions only apply to students sent from other provinces. Had every convent the right or duty to send a student to a university ? Were the students chosen by the convent or the custodial chapter or the provincial chapter or the provincial minister ? How were they provided for at the university ? Was it necessary or customary for a student, before coming to the university, to study in a special school of philosophy or in the special school of theology in his custody ? For later, at any rate, if not in 1250, there was a special school of theology in each of the seven custodies into which the English province was divided.[2]

As I hope some of my hearers or readers are or will be engaged on Franciscan researches, I will give at

[1] *Mon. Franc.* I. 357.
[2] Statutes of Benedict XII, A.D. 1336 ; *Bullarium Franciscanum*, VI. 30.

some length a piece of evidence as an example of the kind of thing one should look out for.

A manuscript volume in Salisbury Cathedral Library (No. 142) containing Isidore's Etymologies has on the first flyleaf this inscription in a thirteenth-century hand : " Istum librum comodauit dominus et magister. R. Cancellarius Sar' Fratri Henrico de Wudeston' qui pro conuentu Sar' stat Oxon'. Quem qui a dominio dicti domini alienauerit anathema sit." This is crossed through and another inscription, also of the thirteenth century, substituted : " Iste liber est Ecclesie beate Marie Sar'. Quem qui alienauerit vel abstulerit anathema sit." Friar Henry returned the book when he had done with it. The initial " R " stands for Ralph of Hegham, who was Chancellor of Oxford University in 1241–2,[1] and appears as Chancellor of Salisbury at various dates between 1243 and 1270.[2] Henry of Woodstone became a person of some note : thus in 1270 he led an agitation against the Jews holding real property, which resulted in legislation.[3] What concerns us here is a reference to him at Oxford in a collection of *exempla*.[4]

[1] *Snappe's Formulary*, etc., ed. Salter (O.H.S.), 320.
[2] Le Neve, *Fasti*, II. 649 ; W. H. Jones, *Fasti Eccl. Sarisb.* (1879), p. 336. Cf. E. G. Millar, "Les Manuscrits à peintures des Bibliothèques de Londres," in *Bulletin de la Société Française de Reproductions de Manuscrits à Peintures*, 1914–20, p. 62.
[3] Brit. Soc. Franc. Studies, *Collectanea*, II. 150–6.
[4] Brit. Mus. MS. Sloane, 2478, fol. 15 b. The story comes in the *Speculum Laicorum*, ed. Welter, pp. 89–90, with the erroneous date 1356, and elsewhere. See B.S.F.S. *Collect. Franc.* II. 150.

On the day of St. James [25 July], 1256, a priest named Ralph being in mortal sin was celebrating mass for the dead in the church of St. Mary Magdalene in the suburb of Oxford. As he elevated the consecrated host and raised his eyes, he saw a man descending head downwards from a height, who with an angry look seized the body of Christ with one hand and hit the celebrant a severe blow on the jaw with the other. Ralph fainted, and, on coming to himself, he bade his server run to a priest, who was lying sick in a neighbouring house, tell him his sin, and bring back his absolution. The answer of the sick priest was that he should say the salutation of the Blessed Virgin till he could go to the bishop's penitentiary. He then finished the mass, and accepted the penance imposed by the latter, but always retained signs of his mishap. " The bishop's penitentiary at that time was Friar Henry of the Order of Friars Minor, called de Wodeston, and the said priest (Ralph) was his scholar. He asked Friar Henry to make this miracle known to all faithful Christians, out of reverence to the body of Christ, without specifying the sin."

Henry of Wodstone, a student from the convent of Salisbury, came to Oxford with books provided by friends or benefactors : he was at Oxford in 1256, and was at that time a priest, authorized by the Bishop of Lincoln to hear confessions : he was engaged in teaching, and among his pupils there was at least one secular priest.

Somewhat similar evidence exists for Cambridge ; and I may remark that the history of the Grey Friars in Cambridge still remains to be written.

Students sent from other provinces to Oxford formed another class. Every province had the right to send two students to Paris without any provision except books. There was no such rule as to Oxford till 1457,[1] but many provinces from time to time acquired the right. That there were many foreign students at Oxford at the end of the thirteenth century is clear from an injunction issued by the General Chapter of Paris in 1292 to the English minister. In order that the burden on the convent of Oxford may be somewhat lightened during the long vacation, the General Chapter ordains that foreign students in England should (during the long vacation) be divided equally among the convents of Oxford, London, and Cambridge, according to the decision of the provincial minister.[2]

There seem to be no means of knowing how many foreign friars there were at Oxford at any time or what proportion they bore to the native friars. The total number of friars in Oxford, of all the four Orders, is known at two dates in the fourteenth century. A Wardrobe Account of 10 Edward II (now in the possession of the Society of Antiquaries of London) yields the

---

[1] Sbaralea, *Supp. ad Scriptores Ord. Min.*, 717.

[2] *Archiv f. Litt. u. Kirchengeschichte d. Mittelalters*, VI. 63. On the maintenance of foreign friars at Cambridge later (1395) see *Cal. Pap. L.*, IV. 516–7 ; *Bull. Franc.* VII. p. 55.

following figures for 29 January 1317 : Friars Preachers 90, Friars Minor 84, Carmelites 45, Austin Friars 43. The first Bursar's Roll at New College yields the following figures in 1377 : Friars Preachers 70, Friars Minor 103, Carmelites 57, Austin Friars 49.

The friars' schools also supplied lecturers to bodies outside their own Order. Thus for some forty years (1275–1314) a succession of Franciscan lecturers taught theology to the monks of the cathedral church of Canterbury.[1] The Bishop of Worcester in 1285 asked that a Franciscan lecturer should be sent to the monks of his cathedral church.[2] There is other evidence of a similar kind, and no doubt more to be collected. A letter of Pope Gregory XI dated Rome 1377 throws a curious light on the subject.[3] The Friars Minor studying and lecturing on theology at Cambridge had complained to the Pope that they were unfairly treated in the matter of appointments to lectureships as compared with their brethren at Oxford. The Pope writes to the provincial minister and chapter of the English province, " to whom by ancient and hitherto peaceably observed custom the right of election belongs," ordering them to treat the friars of both universities equally, " that they may be found competent and properly equipped, and may be appointed to lecture in cathedral churches and to take the degree of master in the

---

[1] Cotton, *Grey Friars of Canterbury* (B.S.F.S.), 34–6.
[2] *Worc. Epis. Reg. Godf. Giffard* (ed. Bund), p. 263.
[3] *Bull. Franc.* VI. 584.

faculty of theology." It would appear that it was customary for friars who studied at the universities, and especially at Oxford, to be appointed lecturers on theology in cathedral schools.

Friars who were appointed to lecture on theology in houses of their Order not situated in university towns required, according to the declarations of Alexander IV in 1257 and Clement IV in 1265,[1] no licence from any authority outside the Order. Those appointed to lecture " in places where a university flourished " had also to conform to the laws and customs of the university. At Oxford, therefore, a friar, before he could teach, had to be approved by the authorities both of his Order and of the university.

At Paris the choice of friars to be presented for the degree of master rested with the General Minister, subject to the rule that out of every three thus presented one must belong to the province of France and two to other provinces.[2] No such rule prevailed at Oxford. Here the choice rested with the provincial minister and probably the provincial chapter. The General Minister[3] and the General Chapter had nothing to do with the appointments before 1336. In 1336 Benedict XII issued constitutions for the government of the Franciscan Order, and enacted " that of the friars who shall be

---

[1] *Bull. Franc.* II. 208, III. 19.

[2] *Arch. f. L. u. K. Gesch. d. Mittelalters*, VI. 107.

[3] There is one exception. Ralph of Colebruge, who took the habit while he was regent master at Paris, was transferred to Oxford by John of Parma, *c.* 1249; but the circumstances were peculiar.

appointed to read the Sentences at Oxford two shall be taken for two years from the province of England to be elected by the English Provincial Chapter ; for the third year the third shall be taken from other parts of the Order to be elected by the General Chapter in turn from the cismontane and the ultramontane parts "[1] ; and the same was enacted for Cambridge. Lecturing on the Sentences was preparatory to the master's degree, and the intention was that a fixed proportion of foreign friars should proceed to the degree of master in the English universities. There is evidence that the decree was carried out at Cambridge, very little that it was carried out at Oxford.[2] On the whole, Oxford seems to have resisted the innovation successfully and to have remained a *studium generale* under provincial administration.

---

[1] *Bull. Franc.* VI. 30.

[2] The list of masters of the Friars Minor at Cambridge, begun by Eccleston and continued till about 1360, contains several foreigners : 59 Johannes de Casale de provincia Januae, 64 Jacobus de Pennis postea episcopus [probably Jacobus de Tolomaeis, Bishop of Narni between 1348 and 1374], 66 Petrus de Arragonia, 70 Rogerus de Cicilia. The list of Oxford masters ends earlier —probably *c.* 1345 (Thomas Oterburn, the last but two, was already S.T.P. when he was licensed to hear confessions in the archdeaconry of Durham in 1343 : *Richard d'Aungerville of Bury, Fragments of his Register*, etc., ed. Kitchen, Surtees Soc., 1910, p. 28). Among the Franciscan regent masters in the latter half of the fourteenth century only one foreigner, William de Prato (before 1363), has been discovered. It may be noted that Hupert de Kalvesnaken, who was appointed before 1376 by the General Chapter to read the Sentences at Oxford to obtain the degree of master, failed to get his degree : *Bull. Franc.* VI. 578. The obstacle may of course have come from the university, not the friars : cf. *Bull. Franc.* VI. 388, 544.

I will conclude this paper with a few remarks on some of the lectors to the Friars at Oxford. Eccleston and his continuators give a list of 67 lectors covering about a century. Each of these held the office of lector or master of the Franciscan school during his period of ' necessary regency ' in the university. The university recognized only one regent at a time for each of the Mendicant Orders. Necessary regency normally lasted two years from the date of the conferment of the degree of master or doctor in theology. The rule was not very strictly enforced, and the period seems to have varied in practice from three years to a year and a half or less.

The first Franciscan to hold the office was Adam Marsh (*c.* 1247–9). As his career has formed the subject of many essays,[1] I will say nothing more about him here except that he was an ideal tutor : he had the faculty of seeing the bent of each pupil's mind and encouraging him to follow it. Before 1245 he procured a copy of the Metaphysics for Friar Thomas of York ; a little later he obtained a Bible for Friar Thomas of Docking. Thomas of York spent the rest of his life working at metaphysics ; Thomas of Docking spent the rest of his life commenting on the Bible. It is of these two I wish to speak.

Thomas of York was the fourth lector, entering on his office in the spring of 1253. The important

---

[1] The most recent is that by Father Cuthbert in *The Romanticism of St. Francis* (1924), pp. 190–235.

constitutional questions which arose and were for the time settled in connexion with his presentation for the degree of D.D. have been fully explained elsewhere, and I will draw attention here only to his scholastic work, which is less known. He wrote a great treatise on metaphysics which is preserved in three manuscripts —one in the Biblioteca Nazionale at Florence (Conv. Soppr. 437 A. 7), two in the Vatican (Lat. 4301 and 6771)—not yet edited. It was left unfinished at the author's death, but even so would fill three or four volumes. That it is worth printing may be seen from Monsignor Grabmann's description of it as being the only great presentation of the system of metaphysics produced in the best period of Scholasticism.[1] It is not a commentary on Aristotle, but an independent treatment of the subject. The contents are as follows : After an enthusiastic praise of wisdom or philosophy and its utilities, the author treats in Book I of the existence and nature of God ; in Book II of the origin of Being in general ; in Book III of Being in itself ; in Book IV of the divisions of Being—substance and accidence ; in Book V of unity and multiplicity, truth and falsehood ; in Book VI of special metaphysic " de his que subsint enti," ending in the middle of a treatise on psychology. Besides its intrinsic value, the work is

[1] "Die Metaphysik des Thomas von York," von Dr. Martin Grabmann, in *Festgabe z. 60 Geburtstag C. Baeumker* (1913), pp. 181–94. An edition was in preparation by Father P. Minges : his death (1926) may delay publication indefinitely.

important for its quotations from early translations of Aristotle and Arabic and Jewish philosophers, which are said often to furnish better readings than are hitherto available.

The only other extant work certainly by Thomas of York is a sermon on the Passion in Trinity College, Cambridge (No. 373) ; it is purely theological without a trace of philosophical learning.

Thomas of York was succeeded by another philosopher—of a more popular and less solid type—Richard Rufus of Cornwall ; and then there seems to have been a reaction against philosophy in the Franciscan school. The next two lectors were not philosophers, but theologians.

John of Wales,[1] though much interested in the lives of philosophers, was, as he admitted, quite incapable of understanding their thoughts ; and Thomas of Docking, though well able to handle philosophical problems when they arose, devoted himself to expounding the Bible.

He was regent master and lector to the friars about 1262 and was still at Oxford in 1269.[2] This was the time when Roger Bacon was pouring out his soul in his three great works to the Pope ; Docking quotes him at least once—without mentioning his name ; and there is a passage in the Opus Majus which implies, I

---

[1] For a study of him and his works, see my *Studies in English Franciscan Hist.*, 174–92.

[2] *Grey Friars in Oxford*, App. C.

think, that Bacon had attended his lectures or knew his work, and regarded him as a model commentator. Docking's fault was prolixity. His commentaries on the Epistles of St. Paul from Galatians to Hebrews (i.e. excluding Romans and Corinthians) are nearly complete, and would if quite complete have filled 1,000 pages in a manuscript which measures nearly 18 inches by 12. The commentary on Isaiah is on a similar scale ; that on Deuteronomy rather shorter. Others have been lost or exist only in fragments. His prolixity is due to a good motive—his determination to make his meaning plain to the dullest of his auditors. He is very learned. He discusses the various readings in the different versions, though he probably did not have any first-hand knowledge of either Greek or Hebrew. On the whole he is true to his principle that the historical meaning of Scripture is the solid foundation of the other meanings. He often quotes the Latin poets, and makes much use of mnemonic verses. Besides the Fathers of the Church and the recognized commentaries, he makes much use (among other writers) of the Jewish philosopher Maimonides. His favourite doctrine, perhaps, is that God is a spirit—" supersimplicissimus spirituum "— his favourite bugbear is idolatry. In one passage he enumerates seventeen main forms of idolatry. Under this heading he includes many things which we should call superstitions. Thus some people think that they will have good or bad luck according to which leg they put out of bed first ; and they give instances to prove that this really does happen. There is, says Docking, a perfectly natural explanation : people who believe rubbish of this sort are happy if they have put out the right leg first, and go about their business with a fine self-confidence ; if they have put out the wrong leg first, they are nervous and depressed and invite misfortune. Docking brings the common things of life to bear on his theological teaching. Commenting in one place on the text, " Suffer little children to come unto Me . . . for of such is the kingdom of heaven," he advises his students to study the ways of little children, and gives a description of a little boy at play which reads as though it must be based on recollections of his own early childhood in his Norfolk home.[1]

The three most famous names among the Oxford Franciscans do not appear in Eccleston's list—Roger Bacon, Duns Scotus, William of Ockam. The reason is that none of them was D.D. of Oxford. Roger Bacon probably was never Doctor of Theology, but all the most fruitful part of his philosophy he learnt at Oxford. Duns Scotus became D.D. of Paris, but his longest and perhaps most important work, the earlier commentary on the Sentences, was the result of lectures delivered at Oxford between 1300 and 1302.[2] Ockam lectured on the Sentences as B.D. at Oxford c. 1320, and had fulfilled all the conditions required for the

[1] References and a more detailed study of Docking will be given in an article on Thomas Docking in a volume of essays presented to Dr. R. L. Poole.

[2] On the life of Duns Scotus, see articles by A. Callebaut in *Arch. Franc. Hist.* X., XIII., XVII., and by F. Pelster in *Franz. Studien*, X. 1–32.

D.D. degree (as the title *inceptor* applied to him shows), when his academic career was cut short by a summons to the papal court to answer charges of heresy preferred against him owing to his Oxford lectures.[1] These charges had nothing to do with his political anti-papal teaching (that was a later development), but with purely theological and philosophical doctrines. In spite of ecclesiastical censures, the system of philosophy known as Nominalism or often as Ockamism, enunciated by a young Bachelor of Theology in the Franciscan convent at Oxford, spread to all universities and dominated European thought for the next two centuries.[2]

[1] Pelzer, " Les 51 articles de G. Occam censurés à Avignon 1326," in *Revue d'hist. ecclésiastique*, XVIII. (1922). On Ockam's early life, see J. Hofer's article in *Arch. Franc. Hist.* VI. 209–33.

[2] Cardinal Ehrle treats learnedly of the " Ausbreitung und teilweise Vorherrschaft des Nominalismus im 14 u. 15 Jht." in *Der Sentenzenkommentar Peters von Candia*, 1925.

FRANCISCAN THOUGHT AND MODERN PHILOSOPHY

By CAMILLO PELLIZZI, DR. JUR.

FRANCISCAN THOUGHT AND MODERN PHILOSOPHY

MANY of the modern prejudices against the so-called darkness of the Middle Ages are now happily disappearing : among others, the opinion that Scholasticism was a line of philosophy entirely irrelevant to the problems of modern thought. The Cartesians, and many other rationalistic philosophers who had learned the foundations of their doctrines from the Cartesian School, considered their science as essentially different from the science of the Middle Ages.

This prejudice has lingered on until quite recent times. Renan, for instance, at the beginning of his otherwise interesting study of Averroës, boldly asserts the irrelevance of his subject to the problems of modern philosophy. Still, to more recent and more painstaking students, the disregard of Rationalists for Scholasticism appears similar to the disregard, or even contempt, with which certain medieval Doctors spoke either of Plato, of Aristotle, or of both. Those Doctors pretended to object to Plato or Aristotle, but unconsciously they worked upon the foundations they had laid ; in the same way modern Rationalists object to St. Thomas,

o 193

or at least neglect him, while their doctrines are none the less largely Thomistic.

Indeed, serious thought cannot trifle away its own past, even when it criticizes it most severely. Modern and western philosophy, in particular, is connected with the medieval science of the Schools by similarities deep and essential. There is, first of all, our vocabulary. In science, the importance and " seriousness " of a word is always proportional to the amount of work that has already been done about it. Those who use an old philosophical word without any consideration for the meaning or meanings which the word took in the past, are bound to use it loosely, or even wrongly. A doctrine claiming to be entirely new may use old words irrespective of their own traditions ; but such doctrines are most probably superficial. And, real philosophy being always contemporary, the safest way to understand and to appreciate our modern writers is still to search the origins of their doctrines among the writers of the past. This is even more important when the same words are used with consciously different meanings. " *Category*," for instance, is a word that takes in Kant a meaning really different from that which it has in Aristotle ; while " *value* " does not mean at all the same for Herbart as for St. Augustine. Now, a student in Kantism or Herbartianism will always understand his own subject much better if he has a clear idea of those differences.

Scholasticism, in particular, has left us a rich vocabu-

194

lary which is by no means obsolete, and a large number of the scholastic words are still better used with their old meanings : they have traditions behind them which cannot be disregarded. A " sense datum," a " world moment," a " psychic complex," are expressions which may be applied to vague or various ideas, or to nothing but mental confusion. One could not say the same, for instance, of " form and substance," " *actum* and *potentia*," " universal and particular," " *intellectus possibilis* " and " *intellectus agens*," and so on. He who uses these latter words must either compel his mind to the discipline of their traditional meaning, or fail to be comprehensible at all.

Nor is this link of diction a merely formal one between present and past philosophy. Old and new problems are indissolubly interconnected, and from the early Greek to us, western thought proceeds on a line that has no complete discontinuities. Countries like France, England, Germany and Italy, where medieval philosophy reached greater heights and had a deeper and more lasting effect on general culture, are in fact those that have made the most important contribution to the development of our contemporary mentality.

Again, Scholasticism itself was thoroughly indebted, for its own foundations, to the Greek masters and to the Neo-platonic schools of later times. The actual links between Greeks and the Schoolmen were the Fathers of the Church. It is they who took the newly born intuition of Christianity and made of it a many-

sided doctrine not incoherent with the previous traditions of culture. The doctors of the Schools will take
from them their main inspiration and develop it in a
more critical and technical manner.

So, taken as a whole, Scholasticism is but one moment
in the eternal development of Christian consciousness ; such a moment is, somehow, eternal too, as it
embodies a form of mind which every man will have
to pass through before he reaches a higher stage. For
instance, the Scholastic axiom that *omne quod recipitur
est in recipiente secundum naturam recipientis, non secundum naturam recepti*, if timely considered, might have
saved our modern positivists and materialists several
fundamental errors. The same, and others, might also
discover with a good deal of profit, that to the Scholastic
mind the existence and the reality of matter is an
assumption far more dogmatic than the existence and
reality of God.

The assertion that Scholastics represent no more
than the childhood of modern speculation is, we think,
not entirely acceptable. Indeed, the Barbaric invasions
had lowered the standards of culture in the basin of
the Mediterranean and in western Europe as a whole ;
but classic culture was already decadent. Heresies
and schisms, which among Christians had fostered
speculation up to the fourth century, became after
the invasions more superficial and had thenceforward
less bearing on philosophy. The great Councils, from
Nicaea to Calcedon, and the works of the Fathers,

had settled the foundations of Christian faith, ethics and thought, for centuries to come. The Church was busy with the practical work of organizing its own growing body and of protecting it against external menaces. Christianity was tired of heresies ; the opinion that faith was much more a matter of direct inspiration and pious deeds than of doctrines and knowledge had spread to such an extent that, for some centuries, clerics used to read only a few books in which mystic inspiration was predominant, like the works of the Pseudo-Dionysus and a few of the works of St. Augustine.

The Church was the only organized body which was left to stand for what remained of western traditions of culture and civilization, and it had to fight a long and deadly battle against the ever irrepressible individualism of the barbaric races. But, to some extent, the Church won its battle, and from the coronation of Charlemagne to the days of the Renaissance, there happened to be a unity in western Europe, if not so much of politics, at least of matters concerning religion and culture.

Scholasticism was the philosophy of that time of unity. It was dogmatic in so far as it was based upon and implied this unity ; but it maintained this tendency even when it happened to be unorthodox, a secret that has since been lost. While the philosophy of the Fathers was a grand effort of creative thought—thought not only original, but also conscious of its own genuine creativeness—the philosophy of the Schools took for granted some results of those former efforts and worked upon them with untiring patience and, sometimes, incomparable cleverness, to solve minor difficulties and arrange the whole of science into one harmonious body. Roughly speaking, the Fathers are more concerned with metaphysics, the schools with logic and epistemology.

The Christian faith with the Fathers was not so much a received dogma, as a fresh source of spiritual life which they felt within themselves ; as witness the warning of St. Augustine : *" Noli foras ire ; in teipsum redi. In interiore homine habitat veritas."* It is the first definite assertion of humanism in a metaphysic sense : the source of truth is man. He finds the root of all that is valuable and true in that intimate share of divinity that he has in himself. Whenever he doubts Truth and Goodness, he is also doubting himself ; whatever he does against them, he does against himself.

According to Gregory of Nyssa and, to some extent, Augustine there is a creativeness in the spirit of man, that is not essentially different from the creativeness of God. Through piety and virtue, man begins to bridge the gap between God's and his own creativeness ; if Grace helps him from above, he may reach that stage of perfect internal *illumination*, which is essentially ineffable, but may be vaguely described as the most immediate experience of God within ourselves. Even more, the soul has a formative power of its own. It builds its own body and, to some extent, its own world. Everyone has, therefore, the body and the surroundings which he deserves, and in his life and experiences he will always find, so to say, as much of God as he has put in them. This also explains, in an allegoric manner, the dogmas of reincarnation and of the final judgment.

The elements of Christian faith were in themselves such as to encourage the development of this doctrine of human creativeness. God had become man to reconsecrate the divinity of man ; for this the Son of Man had bequeathed the Holy Spirit, to inspire the life of the union of redeemed mankind, the Church ; and all this was intended, finally, for the reconstruction of humanity, purified and, in its measure, divine, through the resurrection of the body and the final judgment. No doubt man had a primary part in the whole of this theogony, and the powers of initiative of the individual soul were decisive within their own borders.

As to dogmas concerning God and His operations, it is widely admitted by the Christian writers of the fourth century that they have to be interpreted allegorically and *sub specie aeternitatis* ; some go so far as to place original sin outside any determination of space and time, as an allegory of what happens eternally in the soul of man. The Trinity is also generally considered as a symbol not only of God's essence and operations, but also of the faculties of man. The Father is reflected in memory (closely connected to the " memory of pure ideas " of Plato) ; the Son, in the understanding ; the Holy Spirit in the will. The eventful disputes about the nature, or natures, of Christ, are the spontaneous outcome of such a general tendency of thought ; and the Church will solve the difficulty, *ad insipientem*, by simply stating the co-existence in Christ of the two natures, divine and human.

Neo-platonism lends itself easily to the philosophical interpretation of the new dogmas. God is the pure intelligence in which the ideas exist, and in Him alone we have a vague memory of our lost perfection ; our will aims at Him, as long as it is a real will and not a disguised *nolere*. In Him, the three faculties are perfectly equivalent and interchangeable : He gives existence to all that He thinks, and His will is both almighty and fully rational. The existence of all things consists in the fact that He has complete and harmonious knowledge of and will concerning them. We know things not because they exist, but because their essence is intelligible to us through our fundamental knowledge, which is our knowledge of God. " *Verbum sempiterne dicitur, et eo sempiterne dicuntur omnia* " (Augustine, Confessionum Lib. XI). Again, the immediate knowledge of God has been made difficult for men by original sin, that has veiled their deep divine nature even to themselves ; but through contemplation of revealed truth and active and pious life, men can arise to that state of grace, in which the essence of all things reveals itself through a higher logical medium. The *pia vetula* then, the humble and illiterate old woman, who lives in faith and hope and charity, has at least the same chances of contemplating the Word, as the subtlest and the most learned of doctors.

It is clear that these doctrines make the very existence of a knowable world dependent upon, and subservient to, some initiative of human personality. They admit that a world exists, but not knowable, or, to say the least, not intelligible ; we only understand things through God, and our similarity and proximity to God is in the proportion of our worthiness. Thus, what is dark in our intelligence will become clear to us through the action of our will, through our deeds ; what we call, with despair, the impotence of our will, will be rationally explained by our intelligence, which is, finally, our effort of contemplating God, our illumination. Sin has no positive essence of its own : it is only a shade of our human light, the *nolere* of our *volere* ; we sin in so far as we fail to *will*. God is at the beginning and at the end of all, but the soul of man is intrinsic to His operation and being, so that the *interior homo* always finds himself, so to speak, on the way between what God is and what He does, and piety and contemplation bring man ever nearer to God's cyclic perfection and plenitude.

We have now summarized these few lines of Patristic and, mostly, Augustinian philosophy, because they afford the inspiring principles of Scholasticism as a whole and, in particular, of the doctrines of the Franciscan Schools in the Middle Ages. Technically speaking, there is no such thing as a Franciscan philosophy, even as there is no Dominican philosophy. Moreover, the rivalry between the two Orders never went so far as to prevent the scholars of one Order from being influenced by masters of the other. But the Dominicans, having as their main function preaching, and therefore also disputing with infidels and heretics, were of necessity more learned about unorthodox doctrines, and their training was more in philosophy and logic than in theology and metaphysics ; whereas the Franciscans, who had to spread religion through the example of their humility and poverty, were more concerned with the principles of theology than with the " vanities " of philosophy.

It soon happened that Dominicans, in challenging the new Aristotelian tendencies that were spreading into western countries, became imbibed with the same doctrines which they set out to criticize, and often became admirers, if not followers, of Moorish commentators and Hebrew philosophers and translators, who indeed had opened a new horizon to their researches. Both Orders meant to defend the dogmas and the teachings of the Fathers ; but the Franciscans, under the inspiration of their holy Founder, had a more immediate feeling of the value of Neo-platonic and Patristic philosophy ; whereas the Dominicans felt that the old faith had, so to say, to conquer those new philosophies and make them subservient to its own truth. More than Franciscans, Dominicans felt the importance and the truth of Aristotelianism ; more than Franciscans, they realized the value of rational truth in itself. Franciscans, on the other hand, had a more intimate and lively persuasion about those truths and dogmas, which both were striving to defend.

It was an age of settlement and not of creation ; of reflection and criticism more than of original thought. The endless, overwhelming dialecticism of the Schools became a rule and a habit ; rival Orders and sects after a time got each other's defects, and developed affinities to each other's doctrines. The last in the series of the great Franciscan Doctors, Duns Scotus, unlike his earlier and greater compatriot Erigena, shows an unbounded love for subtle and often irrelevant arguments, and, though he tries to emphasize every small difference between his thought and that of St. Thomas, he is at bottom much more of a Thomist, we venture to say, than even St. Thomas himself. Indeed, Thomism is the life and soul of Scholasticism, not taken in its foundations, but in its own peculiar tendencies and work.

Thus, to understand the real meaning of the words of our title " Franciscan thought," we must go back and consider the personality of St. Francis and the work of that one Doctor who felt his personal influence, namely St. Bonaventure.

St. Francis is the dream of the Fathers that has

become ostensibly true. Being wealthy, cultured and worldly, he chose by internal illumination to become poor and humble, to think and to speak in terms plain and accessible even to the most ignorant peasants. Having many qualities and many chances of becoming one of the great of the world, he chose to be like the proverbial poor and illiterate old woman. Pious action and divine contemplation are with him so completely fused together as to produce an almost godlike perfection : and they fill the whole of his life. He preached by example ; his followers gave no special doctrine, their main ideal being the imitation of Christ through the pattern of their Master. All the highest intellectual conclusions of the Fathers appear in St. Francis under the aspect of reality, of deeds, of life : as though he had read all their writings and made it his purpose to realize them in life. His knowledge and understanding are one with his love and charity : he *understands* his corporal *sorelle*, the lower creatures of God, because he loves them in God ; and likewise his spiritual brothers, that is, men. In both cases his love and his contemplation are also *charitable*, that is active. His greed for perfection, for *ascesis*, is practical ; ideals are, with him, dominant feelings which become realities. It is like a new Incarnation.

So far as philosophy, in a technical sense, is concerned, St. Francis comes after a time in which, among Christians and Moslems as well, there had been great waves of prejudice against philosophers. The rulers of Spain had often been compelled to burn philosophers and destroy rich libraries in the open squares, in order to appease the fury of the fanatic populace. Among Christians, fanaticism had already produced public manifestations against the learned, and the growth of clandestine and sometimes monstrous doctrines and sects. The Church, in her preoccupation with worldly interests, was hardly able to resist the waves of popular zeal for asceticism and *pure* religion. St. Francis alone weathered the storm, chiefly because he represented in himself all the noblest forces that had contributed to raise that storm. He was not, as some have depicted him, an enemy of philosophy ; nor yet a philosopher. But he is a living philosophy, a *Weltanschauung*, completely expressed in terms of reality.

St. Bonaventure expresses the same reality in words borrowed from the Fathers and from the Schools. His doctrine is closely dependent upon that of St. Augustine, with the added experience that a man, Francis of Assisi, had so perfectly realized in his life the principles of illumination and piety. With Bonaventure we are still within the borders of early-Christian Neoplatonism. This world is made of *vestigia, imagines* and *similitudines* of God. There is a *vestigium* of Him in everything, an image in our human nature, a similitude in the nature of the angels. Our spiritual ascension to God (*Itinerarium mentis in Deum*) goes through six successive grades or steps : sense, imagination, reason, intellection (a primary understanding), intelligence, and the *synteresis*, the final spark in which intelligence and love combine to give our minds, not only the image, but the similitude of God. Through the lowest grade, sense, we do not come to know the substance of things, but only a *similitudo* of them ; we can penetrate the real substance of things only through our supreme assimilation with God, who is the common origin of things and minds alike.

Philosophy, ethics and the arts are thus made subservient to and dependent upon, practical mysticism ; all knowledge becomes essentially a branch of theology. Such a conclusion may at first appear paradoxical to our modern minds. Indeed, already in the most prosperous days of Scholasticism it was challenged by many. It was the tendency of the time, also under the influence of the newly discovered or newly published works of Aristotle and commentaries of Averroës and other Moorish philosophers, to widen the gulf between philosophy and theology, and to fight Averroists, sceptics and heretics on their own ground, which was the ground of pure philosophy, free from theological intrusion.

It looked as though the human mind was tired of the continuous creative effort which was forced upon it by the mystical doctrines of the past, with their strict equation between worthiness and wisdom. People really wanted the restful thought of a natural world in itself to be found there, in front of them, and to be objectively and logically studied ; they wanted to be able to develop a knowledge of things irrespective of their knowledge of themselves. The objectivism of Aristotle suited the inclinations of the new epoch and of this mental attitude : thus *modern* thought was started ! It was St. Thomas, on lines partly fixed by his master Albert of Bollstadt, who made the greatest and most successful effort to reconcile the Platonism of the Fathers with the Aristotelianism which was already spreading in the Schools. He may be said to have taken action against both tendencies, partly criticizing them, partly adding entirely new problems to the old ones.

Here we must confine outself to noting, as we said before, that the doctrine of St. Thomas was up to a point official at the end of the thirteenth century, and that the schools of Franciscans and Dominicans had interacted to such an extent, that Duns Scotus, a Franciscan who lives and works towards the end of that century, appears to be just as much of a Thomist as any average scholar of his time would be. And with all his love for scholastic subtleties and endless demonstrations, Scotus remains as one of the most conclusive minds of Scholasticism.

With St. Thomas, the problem concerning the individual subject of knowledge had entered the sphere of philosophy once and for all, and it remains one of the central problems of modern speculation. Scotus takes the individual subject for granted, but he argues that there must be an objective nature common to both the subject and the object of knowledge : a formless and senseless reality, out of which all things grow. Such reality stands like the basis of the immense cone of the universe : the vertex of the cone being the pure essence of God. Our effort of knowledge must move from intelligence, which is a reality of a superior nature, and go towards the lower grades, to understand them in their proper reality and nature, and thus to apprehend how God operates all through the universe ; the lowest type of reality presents us with the deepest scientific problems. Ethics, on the other hand, tends towards the summit of reality through action, a faculty of a kind opposite to that of knowledge, as it is free of any limitation from below and, within the limits consented by the dogma of Grace, entirely responsible to itself. The summit of reality being God, ethics and theology form one body and one soul : theology merely explains in practical terms what is known by us through revelation, authority and tradition ; action must draw inspiration from such teachings without questioning. Therefore, theology is not a real science, and the scholastic method of dialectics ought not to be applied to it. The principle that philosophy should be " *theologiae ancilla* " is thus abandoned, as theology is no longer a disputable subject, and philosophy (and therefore all sciences) is left free to its own function and its own destiny. This doctrine, which even in our days finds followers in the ecclesiastical ranks, is not thoroughly orthodox : the Church requires that a *rationabile*

Plate VIII.

St. Francis receiving the Stigmata.
By Sassetta (1444).

obsequium, not a blind one, should be paid to the revealed truths of God, and that the truths of men, *alias* philosophy, should be consistent with the former ones and, to some extent, subservient to them.

Scotus marks the end of the most interesting period of Scholasticism ; the Schools went on teaching and discussing for a long time after him, but their events would interest a history of culture in general more than the history of philosophy. The long-aged fight between nominalists and realists of different sects had already found its essential terms or extremes when the *Doctor Subtilis* published his works. The fourteenth century confronts us with the beginning of Humanism and, thus, of the Renaissance ; the Schools are played out of the main roads of western culture.

It is important to note that the mentality of Humanism is born rather under the auspices of Plato and Augustine than those of Aristotle and Thomas. Petrarch, perhaps the first Humanist in the Middle Ages, has much indeed to say against the Aristotelians ; he is a mystic and a Platonist. The same can be said, in later times, of other representatives of more modern tendencies : Marsilio Ficino, Pico, Leo the Hebrew, Erasmus, and so many others. But Pomponazzi, who held that the existence of the soul cannot be philosophically demonstrated, was originally an Aristotelian ; one century later, Telesio, who developed the embryo of a pantheistic naturalism, again sprang up of Aristotelian traditions, although he had to fight during the whole of his life against the organized Aristotelians of his days, mainly the Dominicans, who were then the guardians of philosophical orthodoxy, as the Franciscans had been three centuries earlier. After Telesio followed Campanella and Bruno, who were to a large extent his disciples. The latter, who also taught in England in the early Elizabethan days, held a pantheism of a spiritualistic kind; and human will, with him, has a higher importance than, perhaps, with any other thinker of his days. Later on we have the empiricism of Francis Bacon, till the new spirit in philosophy finds its clearest expression in the Rationalism of Descartes.

Recent researches, by Gilson and others, have shown how deeply the problems of Cartesian philosophy are connected with the mentality of the Schools, and mainly of the Dominicans, who had for centuries a stronghold of their own in the University of Paris. After Descartes, so much has been changed in the sphere of philosophy, and still the original distinction between the attitude of the Dominicans and that of the Franciscans in the Middle Ages may be traced, under different forms and new terminologies, in our contemporary philosophic thought. Monism, intuitionism, voluntarism, finalism, pragmatism, idealism, all stand on one side (to put it roughly, the Franciscans); dualism, rationalism, positivism, realism stand on the other.

On the Continent, at least, the general trend of contemporary philosophy may be said to be anti-rationalistic. The "contingentisme" of Boutroux is not altogether inconsistent with the "voluntarism" of the Fathers of the Church. The idea of *intuition* of Bergson suggests the *illuminatio* of Bonaventure, as in the "élan vital" one could trace a late development of the *synteresis*, mentioned above. Maurice Blondel, a Catholic, develops a theory of action which concludes to an "option nécessaire" : man must either nullify his own being and his own will (a thing which he cannot do) or admit the metaphysical truth of God, expressed by the simple words : "Il est." This reminds us of the onthologic proof of the existence of God by St. Anselm of Aosta ; a proof which was itself grounded on the Augustinian and, generally speaking, Patristic doctrine of illumination. Louis Rougier, if we are not mistaken in interpreting his criticism of the "paralogismes" of Kant and other writers, leads us to an original form of voluntarism and, in the field of logic, to intellectualism as opposed to rationalism.

There would be much to say as to the differences between modern tendencies to *pragmatism* (in a broad sense, including not only the doctrine of James and his school, but many others like, for instance, the so-called *humanism* of Prof. J. Schiller), and the voluntarism of the Franciscan tendency. The latter is deeply rooted in the Platonic and Neo-platonic principles that what really exists are the universals, universal ideas of things, that have no full existence but in the mind of God, who thinks and creates reality by one simple and extratemporal act of His nature. In the case of men, action and thought never melt into a such complete fusion, owing to their imperfect natures ; but, in so far as man is *illuminated*, therefore intimately connected to God through the divine element which he has in himself, his actions and his thought will harmonize too, with the result of a gradual ascension of his personality *in Deum*. Here, God stands between man on the one hand, and truth and perfection on the other ; God is thus the actual, though not the immediate, source of science and ethics. Now, with our contemporary Pragmatists, action develops itself immediately as a form of experience, and thus builds up, not perhaps the ultimate object of knowledge, but knowledge itself, with its own universals, kinds and species. God is to be found, if anywhere, at the final end of the process.

A medieval Franciscan would or might object that the modern idea places outside man the aims and motives of his action ; his mind is moved by them, and it is moved from outside : therefore, man cannot have a real *intelligentia* of what those motives are ; whereas, the Christian God is also co-natural to men, intimate to their minds and aspirations.

Modern Idealism alone, we suggest, can countenance a such criticism. With Croce, for instance, pure concept is in its own nature so indifferent and irrelevant to practice, and practice in its economic mood is so disentangled from universals of all kinds, that the problems of how we can know our aims or how the ideals of our activity can be fixed through knowledge, do not even arise. Indeed, he simply leaves such problems to be dealt with at a further stage of speculation. When he says that the unity of the life of the mind through its distinct categories is history taken in the whole and interpreted in a spiritual sense, he opens the ground for a new series of difficulties : from his one-sided *immanentism* and his all-inclusive *history* we learn too much, but practically, we learn nothing. Our active and willing *mind*, entirely merged into this history which is so much like the objective *world* of Positivists—nay, our mind being *history* itself —everything goes on as being the life of the *spirito*, but the *spirito* has no essential ideal and no final orientation.

In the doctrine of the " pure act " by Gentile we could find, perhaps, a nearer approximation to the main conception of the Franciscans. This " pure act," which is the extratemporal life, and eternal creation, of reality, is subjective but not individual. It is the act of *the* mind, and the mind lives and exists in it and for it : very much the same as the *Verbum* of the Evangelist. The *act* is thoroughly human and rational, not because it belongs to, or depends upon, humanity or intelligence, but because humanity and rationality belong to this metaphysical activity and are among the manifestations of its life. So that, pure logic and reality in itself are, for Gentile, nothing but the moment of *abstraction* in the dialectic life of the act ; indeed, its concreteness is to be found in creative action, which also is real, and not purely formal, understanding. "*Verum ipsum factum*," as runs the famous axiom of Vico. The progress of ascension of human personality lies, for this doctrine, in the effort to overcome, in every actual situation of life, the attitudes of irresponsible and, so to say, natural subjectivism, and of passive objectivism ; the *synteresis* is to be found in the third moment of the triad, when mind is no more prone to either egotism or fatalism, but realizes the unity of the two elements without destroying them.

A new Father, who would take this philosophy and develop a fresh system of theology out of it, has not yet appeared. But Gentile and most of his followers call themselves Christians, and, some of them, even Catholics. The Church itself, of course, is more suspicious of this doctrine than of any other in contemporary philosophy : as this one comes nearer the essentials of dogma, though it moves from a strictly critical basis. Indeed, ever since the thirteenth century, the Church of Rome has been suspicious of any metaphysics except that of St. Thomas ; therefore it encourages dualism in all forms, positive and mathematical researches, but no creative and original metaphysics. It thus happens that the most confirmed atheists are sometimes much nearer than mystics to the official attitude of the Church. Mr. Bertrand Russell, perhaps, would be much astonished if he were told that his mental attitude is much nearer to Roman orthodoxy than that of many other philosophers or scientists of our day.

As a matter of fact, even physics seem now to move towards a somewhat subjectivist and voluntarist vision of the world : Relativism speaks, so far, only in terms of experience and material facts ; but from the experimental admission that our experience of reality changes with the motion of the knowing subject, it will be led, gradually, to admit that reality can change according to the will of the subject. It will then understand, what scientists usually denied all through the last two centuries, that *there is* a metaphysical problem at the very origin of the physical problem. Moreover, such a metaphysical problem will be grounded, we suppose, on the admission of the original creativeness of our minds : which leads to speculative problems not un-congenial to the Augustinian and Franciscan line of thought (which is, also, the most ancient and most generally admitted foundation of Christian philosophy).

I dare hope that these remarks of mine, necessarily abridged and summary, may excite the curiosity of some student and lead him to study the many con-nections between Franciscan and modern philosophies, by accepting the main assumption : that Francis-canism, in the field of thought as in that of religious experience, ought still to be a leading force in our days.

THE LAST TWO YEARS OF THE LIFE OF ST. FRANCIS

By WALTER SETON, M.A., D.LIT.

THE LAST TWO YEARS OF THE LIFE OF ST. FRANCIS

THE Committee responsible for the celebrations in connection with the Seventh Centenary of St. Francis have largely concentrated attention upon the last two years of his life, the period lying between the great experiences on Mount Alverna in September 1224 and the Death of the Poverello at the Portiuncula in October 1226. For this reason it has seemed to me suitable to try to reconstruct as accurately as possible the events of those last years and to form—out of the somewhat scattered materials—a connected narrative. Before, however, that is attempted, there are some general considerations which must be pointed out. There is no one place or record to which the reader can go to obtain such a connected narrative of that period or indeed any other period of the Life of St. Francis. It is true that there is one section of the First Life by Thomas of Celano from Chapter 88 to the end which does claim to be devoted mainly to those years, and which does contain a good deal of material assignable to those years. But not one of those chroniclers upon whom our knowledge of S. Francis is based writes in the connected and chronological manner which is expected of a modern historical writer. Where dates are given, they are in many cases vague and sometimes inconsistent with one another. Anyone who takes the trouble to compare in detail the narratives given by typical modern writers, such as Father Cuthbert and Mr. Joergensen, will discover considerable differences between them, due no doubt to varying interpretations of the data contained in the sources. For this state of affairs it would be unreasonable to blame the chroniclers, who were primarily concerned with writing narratives of an edifying character, based of course partly on ascertained fact, but also based largely on verbal tradition. I believe, however, that by a fairly minute examination of the indications of time and place given in Thomas of Celano, in the Mirror of Perfection, and in Bonaventura, with occasional reference to the Fioretti, it is possible to reconstruct those two important and interesting years which were the closing scene in an apostolate, perhaps the most remarkable since that of Our Lord Himself. Fortunately there is an exact and undisputed date at the close of the period, viz. the death of St. Francis, which occurred at the Portiuncula at sunset on 3rd October 1226,[1] and an approximate date at its beginning, viz. the Stigmatisation of St. Francis on Mount Alverna, which occurred either on or about the Feast of Holy Cross, 14th September 1224.[2] It is the period lying between the Stigmatisation and the Death of the Saint which is to be the special subject of this study.

[1] I Cel. 88.   [2] S. Bonaventura, Leg. Maj. XIII. 3.

The Stigmatisation is so large a subject in itself that I cannot do more here than refer to it. I treated the subject as carefully as I could in the compass of one lecture which I gave in London in 1925 and which I published later in the Hibbert Journal,[1] and in spite of the vigorous reply which that article drew from Mr. G. G. Coulton,[2] I have not abandoned the position which I then took. That view was summarised as follows.

I believe that in September 1224—probably on Holy Cross Day—St. Francis, while praying and fasting on Mount Alverna, experienced a vision of a seraph; that after the vision he found that he bore in his hands and feet and side, wounds or marks which were then and remained afterwards the cause of pain; that these marks remained until his death, two years later, that he concealed them carefully during his life, but that a few intimates saw them even before his death; that after his death the Stigmata were seen by numerous credible witnesses; that the wounds were not self-inflicted; that the case of St. Francis was the first on record in which any human being experienced Stigmatisation, though there have been many cases since.

The period which St. Francis spent on Alverna before and after this supreme spiritual experience cannot be precisely defined, but he must have arrived on Alverna some time early in August, as one of his objects was to fast in honour of the Blessed Virgin Mary

[1] July 1925, pp. 633–643. [2] Hibbert Journal, January, 1926.

and the Archangel Michael from the Assumption of Our Lady (August 15th) until Michaelmas Day.[1] It is to this period on Alverna that we can safely assign the gift to Brother Leo of the piece of parchment containing on one side the Praises and on the other the Blessing of Brother Leo. Sufficient evidence for this is provided by taking together the note added by the hand of Leo on the parchment and the narrative of Celano,[2] who does not actually mention that Leo was the tempted brother, who so greatly desired some writing from the hand of the Saint.

On 30th September 1224 Francis left Alverna for the last time. The most detailed narrative of the journey from Alverna to the Portiuncula is that given by the Fioretti in the Fourth Reflection on the Stigmata, though there are accounts contained in Celano. Riding on an ass, for the wounds in his feet made it impossible for him to travel on foot, he left Alverna, taking the way through Monte Acuto, Monte Arcoppe and Foresto. Just as later he was to turn and give his memorable blessing to Assisi, so too before he lost sight of Alverna he turned to take farewell of the place which was sanctified for him by the spiritual climax of his life : " Farewell, Mount of God, Holy Mount, Mons coagulatus, Mons pinguis, Mons in quo beneplacitum est Deo habitare, Farewell, Monte Alverna ; God the Father, God the Son, God the Spirit bless thee, abide in peace, since we shall see each other nevermore."

[1] Blessing of Leo.   [2] II Cel. 49.

Francis, accompanied by Leo and a peasant, made his way down through Borgo San Sepolcro, and in spite of the fact that the townspeople were crowding around the little party, Francis was so wrapped in prayer and contemplation that he was even unaware that he was passing through the town, and after they had left the town behind he enquired when they would be getting near San Sepolcro ![1] By the first evening they arrived at Monte Casale, and, according to the Fioretti, they remained there some days. From Monte Casale Francis and his companion pushed on to Città di Castello, and there they stayed a month at the urgent prayer of the inhabitants.[2] It must have been accordingly some time in November that Francis arrived back at Santa Maria degli Angeli, the goal of his desire. We do not know very much as to the homecoming from Alverna to the Portiuncula, though if we want to know what did *not* occur we have only to study the pages of Mr. Chesterton's popular volume. " His heart rejoiced "—says Mr. Chesterton—" when they saw afar off on the Assisian hill the solemn pillars of the Portiuncula." [3] It may be observed that the Portiuncula is not on a hill, that it was then surrounded by a forest, and that it has no solemn pillars which could be seen afar off, especially by a man who was nearly blind !

At this point it is necessary to go back and to refer to an incident which must presumably be assigned to a

[1] II Cel. 98.   [2] Fioretti, 4th Reflec.   [3] P. 167.

date in 1224 previous to the visit to Alverna. Celano in his First Life tells us of an occurrence when the Saint and Brother Elias were together at Foligno. Elias had a vision in the night, in which he was bidden by a priest of venerable aspect : " Arise, brother, and tell Brother Francis . . . that two years hence, the Lord calling him, he will enter upon the way of all flesh." [1] The same incident is mentioned in the Mirror of Perfection in a conversation which Francis had with Elias in the autumn of 1226. [2]

I do not think that there is any clear indication as to where St. Francis was or what he was doing between November 1224 and the summer of 1225. It seems likely from one chapter in Celano's First Life [3] that after his return to the Portiuncula he undertook a fresh tour of evangelisation, and it is presumably about this period that Celano writes :

" He filled all the earth with Christ's Gospel, so that often in one day he would make the circuit of four or five villages or even towns, preaching to every one the Gospel of the kingdom of God . . . and though he could no longer walk he went round the country riding on an ass."

It was during the first half of 1225 that the Saint's health, which had been failing ever since his return from the East, got rapidly worse and his eye-trouble became chronic. We learn from the Mirror of Perfection [4] that the Cardinal Bishop of Ostia, becoming

[1] I Cel. 109.   [2] Spec. Perf. 121.   [3] I Cel. 97.   [4] Spec. Perf. 91, 115.

seriously anxious as to his friend's health, warned him gravely against his persistent neglect of his body, since his life was of value to the whole Church. From the same source we gather that it was the pressure from the Bishop of Ostia which led Francis to start out for Rieti to seek advice and treatment for his eye-malady from a celebrated physician there. Celano and the Mirror of Perfection are rather vague as to the departure from the Portiuncula for Rieti, but we can be fairly certain as to the date of the journey to Rieti, though Father Cuthbert has, I feel sure, gone wrong in the date. The Little Flowers and also one MS of the Mirror of Perfection[1] (viz. Vat. 4354) give us details which appear to fit in with the other facts. Apparently Francis left the Portiuncula and went first to San Damiano, to visit Clare, with the intention of staying one night only and then going on to Rieti. During that night he became so seriously ill that it was impossible for him to go on to Rieti, and he stayed at San Damiano in a wattle hut put up for him in the courtyard. It is to this stay at San Damiano that the Mirror of Perfection refers, telling us that he became completely blind for more than sixty days. The outstanding event of those sixty days of pain and darkness was the composition of the one great poem of Saint Francis, which has earned for itself a place in world literature, the poem variously known as the " Canticle of the Sun " and as the " Praises of

[1] Spec. Perf. 100.

Creatures." It is not necessary for us to examine too critically the question whether this wonderful poem was, as the Mirror of Perfection implies, the spontaneous outburst of the sick and suffering saint after a night rendered sleepless by numbers of mice running over his face and form. We may more safely accept the fact that it was composed during this sojourn at San Damiano, and we may recognise in it, whenever or wherever written, one of the most perfect expressions in words of the love of God and of all things created by God, which was the characteristic feature of Francis throughout his life. Renan speaks of the Canticle in the following words : " le plus beau morceau de poésie religieuse depuis les Évangiles, l'expression la plus complète du sentiment religieux moderne." [1] To that same period at San Damiano may be assigned the narrative [2] of the dispute between the Bishop of Assisi and the Podestà of the city, which was ended amicably by the intervention of St. Francis, who sent one of the brothers to recite to them the Canticle of the Sun with the additional verses which he had composed :

" Praise be to Thee, my Lord, for those who pardon grant for love of Thee,
And weakness bear and buffetings :
Blessed are they who in peace abide,
For by Thee, Most High, they shall be crowned."

From San Damiano St. Francis passed on to Rieti to seek some alleviation for his pain. Fortunately we can

[1] Nouvelles Études d'Histoire Religieuse, Paris, 1884, p. 331.
[2] Spec. Perf. 101.

define to some extent the date of his visit to Rieti.
Celano tells us in his First Life [1] that when he arrived
at Rieti he was honourably welcomed by the whole
Roman Curia, which was at that time staying in that
city. It is known that the Papal Court was at Rieti
from about 23rd June 1225 to 31st January 1226.
Father Cuthbert is, I feel sure, wrong in saying that
the Papal Court was in Rieti until the end of 1226, [2]
and consequently in assigning the visit of Francis to
1226. It seems to me most probable that he reached
Rieti in the late summer or early autumn of 1225 and
that his stay there was a long one. It is clear that for
some part of his stay he lived in the Palace of the
Bishop of Rieti, for Celano relates [3] the very characteristic story of how Francis, with natural sympathy for a
poor woman suffering like himself from eye-disease,
gave her his cloak and twelve loaves, an incident recorded
also in the Mirror of Perfection. In Rieti itself occurred
also the incident of Canon Gideon, [4] who was cured by
the Saint but afterwards returned to his life of sin,
that of the tempted brother who found relief from his
temptation by securing parings of the Saint's finger-
nails, [5] that of the provision of cloth for six tunics in
answer to the prayer of the Saint, [6] and the pathetic tale
of how divine music was sent to comfort Francis during
his wakeful hours at night, when his companion had

[1] I Cel. 99.
[2] P. 351, n. 3.
[3] II Cel. 92 : also Spec. Perf. 33.
[4] II Cel. 41.
[5] II Cel. 42.
[6] II Cel. 43.

felt it unfitting to bring him human music, lest he should be thought guilty of frivolity.[1]   Apart from the stay in Rieti itself, it appears that Francis spent some time in places or hermitages around Rieti, though there is no means of defining with any certainty at what period this took place.   Thus we find him at Fonte Colombo,[2] where he underwent the painful ordeal of the cauterisation of his face in the vain hope of improving his sight.   The Mirror of Perfection tells us that this took place at Fonte Colombo, though Celano describes the incident without naming the place.   To the same hermitage the Mirror of Perfection assigns the incident, also recorded by Celano without specification of place,[3] in which Francis desired that his physician should be invited to dine and in which the necessary viands were supernaturally provided to the relief of the empty larder of the Friars.   Another place near Rieti where Francis stayed was the Church of St. Fabian, and it was there that the vineyard of the poor priest who was his host was ruined by the constant visits of the faithful, but nevertheless produced more than its usual quantity of wine.[4]

From Rieti Francis made his way to Siena, accompanied by a doctor—perhaps the one who had tended him at Rieti.   As they traversed the plain by Rocca Campilii they met, according to Celano's narrative,[5]

[1] II. Cel. 126.
[2] II Cel. 166, Spec. Perf. 115.
[3] II Cel. 44, Spec. Perf. 110.
[4] Spec. Perf. 104.
[5] II Cel. 93.

the three women who greeted him with the salutation
" Welcome, Lady Poverty," and then vanished from
human sight.

We have, as far as I know, no definite means of
ascertaining the period of St. Francis' stay at Siena,
since we are not sure exactly when he went there from
Rieti.   There is, however, one indication of the date
when he left Siena for his last journey back to Assisi.
Celano tells us in his First Life[1] that it was in the sixth
month before his death, when he was at Siena for the
curing of his eye-malady, that he began to be seriously
ill, so ill as to cause Brother Elias to come to him
hurriedly from Assisi to prevent the possibility of his
dying at Siena.   This proves that he was at Siena
until about the end of April 1226.   Little is recorded
about this stay at Siena.   There is just the incident
of the brother from Breschia,[2] who succeeded in satisfying
his desire to see the Stigmata in the hands of the Saint
by a ruse to which Brother Pacificus was a party.   It
may also be during this stay at Siena that Francis
received from a Sienese nobleman a pheasant which
was sent to him to be eaten, but which became instead
a kind of pet and would not feed except in the presence
of Francis.[3]   Much more important than these stories
are two chapters in the Mirror of Perfection, which
relate to these closing months in the earthly career of
the Saint.   The first [4] of these is the conversation with

[1] I Cel. 105.
[2] II Cel. 137.
[3] II. Cel. 170.
[4] Spec. Perf. 10.

a certain Bonaventura on the subject of the method in which the Friars were to secure places in which to dwell or to build churches in cities. The whole chapter breathes the spirit of the most primitive Franciscanism, being in closest harmony with the ideals of Poverty for which Francis himself stood without wavering. They are to build poor little houses of wattle and little cells in which from time to time the brothers may pray and work; and they are to build small churches and not to make large churches. It is better for the brothers to make small and poor little buildings, observing their profession and giving a good example to their neighbours, than that they should act against their vows, giving to others an evil example.

Of a similar character was the scene[1] after Francis had had a severe hæmorrhage from the stomach, causing great alarm to his faithful companions. He called for Brother Benedict of Pirato, who acted as a chaplain and secretary to him, and dictated to him a Benediction which has been regarded by some as a kind of embryonic form of the document known as the " *Testamentum Sancti Francisci*." The Mirror of Perfection gives us only a few sentences, probably a mere summary of the document actually dictated at the time. It begins: " Write how I bless all my brethren, those who are in the order and those who are to come, until the end of the world." And he ends by bidding them ever love one another as he has loved them, and ever love and

[1] Spec. Perf. 87.

230

serve our Lady Poverty and ever be faithful and subject to the prelates and clergy of Holy Mother Church. This again is a document of the greatest interest and significance, and it belongs clearly to the last stay at Siena.

And so at Siena the decision was taken to carry the dying Francis back to Assisi. It was probably the wish of Elias, who was anxious to prevent either Siena or Perugia from gaining the advantage and glory of possessing the dead body of the Saint ; but it was assuredly equally the wish of Francis himself, who knew well that death was approaching and who desired to meet death in the place hallowed for him by so many associations, the Portiuncula. The first stage of the journey was to Celle de Cortona,[1] and there they stayed some days, probably because the invalid could not travel. In fact we are told by Celano that at that stage dropsy set in, and Francis' digestion became so bad that he could eat nothing. But ill as he was, he did not lose even then his compassion for the poor, and when a poor man came weeping about his poverty and his wife's death, he gave him his new cloak to the despair of his companions. From Celle the procession made its way to Bagni near Nocera,[2] where the dropsy became worse. The news of his grave illness reached the inhabitants of Assisi, who sent soldiers to guard the returning procession and to prevent the Perugians from

[1] I Cel. 105, II Cel. 88, Spec. Perf. 31.
[2] Spec. Perf. 22.

intercepting it. They passed on to Satriano,[1] where the escort found it impossible to persuade the inhabitants to sell them anything. The soldiers were then bidden by the Saint to go and beg for alms for the love of God, and they then obtained all they required.

It was probably Midsummer when Francis came back to Assisi for the last time. He was taken to the Palace of the Bishop of Assisi,[2] and there remained until at his own urgent desire he was borne to the Portiuncula. The stay at Assisi was of considerable length. We gather from the First Life by Celano, that he was only a few days at the Portiuncula before he died. " When he had rested for a few days in the place which he had so greatly desired "—is the phrase which Celano uses.[3] The Mirror of Perfection gives the story of his craving for a special kind of fish known as " squalus," while he was lying gravely ill in the Palace of the Bishop, and adds that it was impossible to obtain the fish at that time in Assisi, since it was winter.[4] It would thus appear that Francis remained in the Bishop's Palace until the latter days of September 1226. Nothing could be more characteristic of Francis than the incidents recorded of him during his last days in the city of his birth. There is, for example, the story of how he gave his tunic to one of his brothers, the same one to whom

---

[1] II Cel. 77.   [2] I Cel. 108.   [3] I Cel. 109.
[4] Spec. Perf. 111. This phrase is difficult to understand, as the time up to October would not be called winter. Possibly the incident occurred during some earlier period of illness.

he had earlier given the writing, whom we can thus identify as Leo.[1] There is the account given in the Mirror of Perfection [2] of how his cheerfulness and gaiety of spirit led him to cause the Lauds which he had composed to be sung at his bedside by his sorrowing companions, to the scandal of Brother Elias, who feared lest this light-heartedness would not edify the Assisians and their armed guard outside the Palace. Above all, his sense of humour did not forsake him. Just as in his young manhood he had announced that he was going to be a great prince and just as he had while in prison in Perugia told his companions : " I shall yet be worshipped as a Saint all the world over," so, as he lay sick unto death bandaged with sackcloth and wearing a garment of sackcloth, he assented to the almost playful remark of one of the brothers : " Many baldachinos and silken palls shall be placed over this little body of thine which now is clothed with sackcloth." [3]

It was a doctor from Arezzo named Buongiovanni,[4] to whom fell the duty of telling Francis that his end was drawing close. Francis insisted on being told the truth and the doctor knew that it was futile to attempt to conceal it. " Manifestly, father," replied the doctor, " according to our science of physic, thy sickness is incurable, and I believe that either at the end of September or by the fourth of the nones of October thou wilt

---

[1] II Cel. 50.
[2] Spec. Perf. 121.
[3] Spec. Perf. 109.
[4] Spec. Perf. 122.

die." The answer was no shock to Francis, who in ecstasy exclaimed : " Welcome, Sister Death."

It is, as might be expected, the Mirror of Perfection which gives us in a very scattered form the most detailed account of the last week of the life of Francis and of his triumphant death. The two narratives of Celano are briefer, and they have not got that personal touch about them which is indicative of the testimony of eye-witnesses. The complete narrative can be constructed by taking together the Mirror of Perfection and Celano. It was probably while he was still at Assisi that he sent for his two favourite companions, Leo and Angelo, bidding them sing to him of Sister Death.[1] After the two sorrowing friars had sung to him the Canticle of the Sun, he improvised for them a final verse in praise of Death :

" Praised be Thou, my Lord, for our Sister, bodily Death, from whom no man living can escape.
Woe be to them who die in mortal sin.
Blessed are they who find themselves in Thy most holy will, for the second Death shall do them no hurt."

Toward the end of September, then, Francis began his last journey, the descent from Assisi to the Portiuncula. Just as two years before he had taken farewell of Alverna and blessed the mountain which had been the scene of his spiritual exaltation, so here again he gave a farewell blessing to the city of his birth. The fact of this last blessing of Assisi as he was carried down the

[1] Spec. Perf. 123.

hill to the plain is sufficiently authenticated by the narratives, and it does not very much matter whether the form of it contained in the Mirror of Perfection [1] is adopted, or whether the much shorter form given by the Little Flowers [2] and now to be read over the Porta Nuova is accepted. That shorter form runs as follows : " Blessed be thou of the Lord, Holy City faithful to God, for through thee shall many souls be saved and in thee shall dwell many servants of the Most High, and from thee shall many be chosen for the Eternal Kingdom."

The story of the events of the last few days of the life of St. Francis, the Thursday, Friday and Saturday, 1st, 2nd and 3rd October 1226, have been told and retold and are so familiar to all who have made even the most elementary study of the Poverello that it seems useless to attempt to go afresh over them here. The story is a dramatic one, and those who want to visualise it for themselves can do so by seeing a performance of Mr. Laurence Housman's Sister Death, which preserves to a remarkable extent the historical narrative, while dramatising the theme. I know few scenes so moving as the episode in Sister Death, based upon the narrative in the Mirror of Perfection [3] and in Celano,[4] in which the dying Saint, surrounded by his most faithful companions whom he had blessed one by one, calls for bread to be brought and causes it to be broken

[1] Spec. Perf. 124.
[2] Fourth Refl. on Stigmata.
[3] Spec. Perf. 88.
[4] II Cel. 217.

into fragments and then with his own hand gives a portion to each. It was a bold action on the part of Francis to create by this act an unmistakable parallel to the Last Supper of his Lord and Master, a parallel which both Celano and the writer of the Mirror of Perfection were quick to observe ; and it was a bold action on the part of Mr. Housman to represent that episode on the stage. It can, however, be represented with complete reverence and with a restrained emotion which is irresistible.

There are a few episodes in those last few days to which I want to refer because they have a bearing upon the whole Franciscan story. One of these may be assigned either to the time when Francis was in the Episcopal Palace at Assisi or to the last days at the Portiuncula. I refer to the portrait of the ideal Minister-General given both in the Mirror of Perfection[1] and in the Second Life by Celano.[2] A brother had asked him whether he could point out one in the Order to whom the burden of the office of Minister-General could safely be committed. Sorrowfully Francis had to confess that he knew none such, and he went on to paint a picture of the ideal Minister-General, the man who would carry on the Order along the lines of simplicity and poverty, for which he personally had never ceased to strive ever since his own conversion. The portrait marked the great gulf between the ideals of the founder of the Order and those of Elias and the

---

[1] Spec. Perf. 80.   [2] II Cel. 184–186.

236

friars associated with him, who were leading the Order
to the great grief of Francis into a very different direction. It is noticeable that this portrait of the Minister-
General does not occur in Celano's First Life, presumably because it might in those early years have been
too obvious a reflection on Elias.

Another incident of significance was the blessing
of the companions. This is a rather difficult matter,
because there are differences between the story as told
in four records, the two Lives by Celano, the Mirror of
Perfection, and the Little Flowers. As regards the
place and time, it is true that Celano in his First Life
states that Francis was at Assisi when the Blessing took
place, while in his Second Life he does not specify
the place, but the context suggests that it was at the
Portiuncula. The Mirror of Perfection also does not
specify the place, but by associating the incident with
the sharing of a certain dish with Brother Bernard, it
implies that it took place at the Portiuncula. So too
does the Fioretti. The place, however, does not really
matter. There is more significance in the narrative
itself. In Celano's First Life,[1] Elias, the Vicar-General,
was on the Saint's left hand, and Francis deliberately
blessed him with his right hand, and nothing whatever is
said as to the others being blessed. Moreover, he gives
Elias a very definite and unreserved blessing, which is
recorded at some length. In the Second Life,[2] Celano
still maintains that Elias received the blessing with the

[1] I Cel. 108.   [2] II Cel. 216.

right hand of Francis, but he states that Francis laid his right hand on the head of each in turn, beginning with Elias. Celano was, however, writing after the fall of Elias, and he adds a significant sentence :

" The blessing, as is written elsewhere, had a special meaning, but rather as regards the deprivation of office."

When we come to the account given in the Mirror of Perfection,[1] we find that Francis, being blind, first puts his right hand by mistake upon the head of Brother Giles, and then discovering his mistake he places it on the head of Bernard of Quintavalle. Then he utters words of the highest praise of Bernard, ending : " Wherefore I will and command as much as I can, that whoever shall be Minister-General love and honour him as myself. Let the Ministers and all the friars of the whole order hold him as myself."

Nothing is said about the blessing of Elias or of any of the others. The narrative given in the Little Flowers [2] is again different. The brothers are standing around the dying Saint, he calls for Bernard, and Bernard bids Elias to go to the Saint's right hand to receive his blessing. Francis detects that the one on his right hand is not Bernard, and so Bernard goes to his left hand. Francis then crosses his arms, so as to bless Bernard with his right hand and Elias with his left.

I can imagine some people feeling that all this is quite trivial and unimportant detail, and so in a sense

---

[1] Spec. Perf. 107.   [2] Ch. VI.

it is. I have brought it into this narrative, chiefly in order to show the kind of problem with which we are confronted in Franciscan studies. These differences are not entirely accidental. They illustrate how the chronicles upon which we depend for our knowledge of St. Francis are — to use a modern adjective — tendencious. There are some grounds for seeing in Celano's First Life evidence of sympathy with the policy of Elias and his followers, and so it is not surprising to find that in that document it is Elias and not Bernard who secures the blessing. On the other hand, the Mirror of Perfection stands for the opposite ideal, that of the intimate companions of the Saint, who were bitterly opposed to the policy of Elias. For them Bernard was naturally a leader of the first importance, seeing that he was the first disciple of Francis. Who can say what the actual historical fact was, which underlay these divergent narratives? Probably both Elias and Bernard received the blessing of Francis, and probably he did cross his arms in giving the blessing. The crossed arms have become the symbol of the Franciscan Order. There is another incident of that last week, the record of which we find in the Mirror of Perfection,[1] and not in Celano. Saint Clare, who was also lying sick, sent a message earnestly desiring to see her friend and master. But Francis was no longer able to go to her, and he sent to her instead a message of consolation, bidding her lay aside all grief, because she and her sisters should

[1] Spec. Perf. 108.

239

before her death behold him and should be greatly consoled by that sight of him. The fulfilment of this prophecy was when the dead body of the Saint was borne from the Portiuncula to Assisi and the procession halted on the way at San Damiano, in order that Clare and the sisters might take their last farewell of their Founder and behold his body marked with the wounds of Christ.

The inclusion of this incident in the Mirror of Perfection is again characteristic, because the intimate companions whose tradition is represented in that work were in the closest sympathy with Clare in her lifelong struggle to preserve the ideals of the primitive Franciscan foundation. I said earlier in this lecture that I could not enter upon the great subject of the Stigmatisation. I cannot, however, leave this account of the last two years of the Life of St. Francis without making some mention of the public discovery of the Stigmata after his death. Celano relates in both his Lives[1] how the Stigmata were seen on the body of the dead Francis on the day after his death. The earliest narrative of the public discovery of that which had before been the secret of the few is the circular letter issued by Elias, the Vicar-General, on the day following the death of St. Francis, in which he announces the death of the Saint and at the same time categorically mentions the Stigmata. The letter is still extant in the form of a copy addressed to Gregory, the Minister of the Friars

[1] I Cel. 112–113, II Cel. 27.

Plate IX.

The Funeral of St. Francis.
By Sassetta (**1444**).

Minor in France, and it contains the following passage :

" I announce to you tidings of great joy and a new miracle. From the foundation of the world there has not been heard such a sign, save in the Son of God, who is Christ. Not long before his death our brother and father appeared crucified, bearing in his body the five wounds which are the marks of Christ, for his hands and feet had, as it were, the piercing of nails fixed on both sides, keeping the scars and showing the blackness of nails. His side appeared pierced and often gave forth blood."

With that quotation we can most suitably leave this brief review of the closing years of the wonderful servant of God who, to use the phrase of his first chronicler, Thomas of Celano, went to meet death with a song.[1]

[1] II Cel. 214.

THE REDISCOVERY OF ST. FRANCIS OF ASSISI

By WALTER SETON, M.A., D.LIT.

THE REDISCOVERY OF ST. FRANCIS OF ASSISI [1]

THE present year is the seventh centenary of St. Francis of Assisi, who died at sunset on October 3, 1226, lying naked on the ground in a small cell of wattle close to the Portiuncula outside Assisi. Centenaries, even seventh centenaries, have become frequent in the present day—perhaps too frequent. Few centenaries, however, can claim anything approaching the importance, the world-wide character, the breadth and variety of appeal, that mark the commemoration of the Poverello of Assisi. The most obvious aspect is naturally the religious aspect. It is not surprising to find the Roman Catholic Church treating the year which began on July 31, 1926, as almost equivalent in importance to the Holy Year just ended and to receive from the Pope an encyclical setting out in the most convincing terms the claim of St. Francis upon the love and devotion of the faithful. Nor is it unexpected that the Guildhouse in Eccleston Square—to mention an entirely different form of religious practice—should have organised a Franciscan celebration in October 1926. It is more striking that the Italian

---

[1] This essay appeared in October 1926 in the *Nineteenth Century and After*, and has since been revised and enlarged.

Government should, notwithstanding the Roman question, have proclaimed October 4 a national holiday, and that the head of the Italian Government, H.E. Benito Mussolini, should have issued a Message on the Franciscan centenary, in which he compares Francis with Dante, with Columbus, with Leonardo da Vinci, in the following terms :

"Il più alto genio alla poesia, con Dante ; il più audace navigatore agli oceani, con Colombo ; la mente più profonda alle arti e alla scienza, con Leonardo ; ma l'Italia, con S. Francesco, ha dato anche il più santo dei santi al Cristianesimo e all' umanità."

A special series of postage stamps has been issued in commemoration of the centenary, at least two magazines devoted specially to the same subject have appeared for more than a year before the actual year of festival begins, and in numerous centres throughout the whole world plans are on foot for the worthy remembrance of all that Francis of Assisi means to religion, to history, to art. In Assisi the celebrations will be continued until October 1927. The reason is not far to seek. There are many great saints who have shown forth in their lives the beauty of holiness. There are innumerable artists who have manifested in their work the holiness of beauty. St. Francis has earned a supreme position by his intuitive, sometimes almost unconscious, combination in the highest degree of the beauty of holiness in his character and personality and the holiness of beauty in his actions and in his outlook upon the world around him. He is, as Mussolini has indicated, a supreme saint, but he is also a supreme artist.

This article does not aim at giving a panegyric upon St. Francis of Assisi. It aims at examining a phenomenon, literary, historical, æsthetic and only incidentally religious—the rediscovery of St. Francis.

Was there a world-wide celebration of the Franciscan centenary in 1826 or in the previous centuries? There was, but only in the sense that successive Popes called the faithful in the Roman Catholic communion in each century to a distinctively religious commemoration.[1] Nor could it be otherwise, for up to the beginning of the nineteenth century St. Francis existed merely as a saint of considerable importance in the Catholic Church, and as the founder of a great and influential order in that communion. In the English Prayer-Book calendar prepared in the sixteenth century after the breach with Rome place is found for St. Benedict, but unfortunately not for St. Francis. When the sixth centenary of the death of St. Francis came round there were no world-wide celebrations, because the whole world outside the Roman Catholic communion thought of him, if it thought at all, as a dead Roman Catholic. It was inevitable that this should be the case. The

[1] "We would vie in devotion with Our predecessors, who, whenever a centenary occurred in connexion with his life, lost no opportunity of commemorating him by their apostolic authority and of decreeing festivities in his honour."—Encyclical Letter of Pope Pius XI, 1926. (Translation published by Burns & Oates and Washbourne.)

writings of St. Francis himself, the chronicles recording
his life, the exquisite legends which had been woven
around his story in the fourteenth century, were in
part lost and in the remaining part quite inaccessible
to all save the ecclesiastical specialist in the huge tomes
of the *Acta Sanctorum* or of Luke Wadding. For
example, the *Second Life of St. Francis*, by Thomas of
Celano, was practically unknown from about 1266,
when all the early legends were proscribed by the
General Chapter, until 1806, when its text was edited
by Rinaldi and published in Rome. So completely
was this important work forgotten, that doubt was
thrown upon its existence. To take another example,
the priceless *Fioretti*, which have been a joy and an
inspiration to countless readers of this generation,
were certainly never quite forgotten, but in the first
half of the nineteenth century they were known only
to the learned, who disputed whether there existed a
Latin original of the Italian text. The first English
translation of the *Little Flowers* was, as far as I have
been able to trace, one by H.E. (Cardinal) Manning,
issued in 1864.

It is difficult to define the starting-point of the
modern movement, which may be called the rediscovery
of St. Francis—by which I mean the movement through
which St. Francis has become to the world as a whole
what he was, and indeed more than what he was, to
Umbria and Italy, of the first half of the thirteenth
century ; more than what he was to them, because

248

while the devotion and love of the twentieth century cannot well exceed that of the thirteenth, the earlier century could not see him from the perspective of 700 years or realise how great a contribution his life and work were to make to humanity.

I should be inclined to take as the starting-point in that movement the work of Karl Hase, professor in the University of Jena, who published in 1856 his book, *Franz von Assisi*, at that time a notable contribution to the knowledge of the subject. An important feature of Hase's book was his treatment of the question of the Stigmatisation of St. Francis, as he was really the first modern writer to embark upon that controversial subject. More important, however, than the intrinsic value of Hase's work was the fact that its translation into French by M. Charles Berthoud attracted the attention of the great French critic Renan, who was himself a devoted admirer of St. Francis. Taking Hase's work as a text, Renan included in his *Nouvelles Études d'Histoire Religieuse* (Paris, 1884) a study entitled *François d'Assise*, which is a classic in Franciscan literature. The amazing insight of Renan is shown by the fact that while the materials for our knowledge of St. Francis have been incalculably increased since 1884, there is little in his study which would need rewriting to-day, except, of course, from the standpoint of many of us, his rather crude explanation of the Stigmatisation as the result of fraud on the part of the Vicar-General Elias. No one has ever written

more beautifully or with keener appreciation about
St. Francis, though his tone is that of the patron, not
that of the client. Some of his sayings about the saint
have become household words. I will quote just a few
to illustrate his outlook : ' On peut dire que depuis
Jésus François d'Assise a été le seul parfait Chrétien '
—an aphorism which sums up in a few words the theme
to which a volume of great length, *De Conformitate*,
was devoted by Bartholomew of Pisa. ' Ce qui dis-
tingue François d'Assise en son siècle, et dans tous les
siècles, c'est sa complète originalité.' Speaking of
the Canticle of the Sun, Renan says : ' Le plus beau
morceau de poésie religieuse depuis les Evangiles,
l'expression la plus complète du sentiment religieux
moderne.' Again, Renan summarises his inspiration
of art in these words : ' Ce sordide mendiant fut le
père de l'art italien. Cimabue et Giotto trouvèrent
leur génie en s'efforçant de peindre sa legende sur
son tombeau.' Rénan estimates thus the influence of
the Franciscan movement : ' Après le christianisme, le
mouvement franciscain est la plus grande œuvre popu-
laire dont l'histoire se souvienne.' Little wonder is
it that a Capuchin Franciscan, to Renan's great satis-
faction, said of the great liberal thinker : ' Il a écrit
sur Jésus autrement qu'on ne doit, mais il a bien parlé
de Saint François. Saint François le sauvera ! '

Renan was far too acute a critic to be led into the
mistake, which many other liberal and modernist
critics since his time have made, of failing to recognise

Francis as the humble, obedient, devout son of the Roman Catholic Church—an uncritical attitude of mind which has quite rightly been condemned by the Holy Father in his recent encyclical.[1] Renan had the ear of France, and indeed of the whole cultivated world, and so it was natural that his treatment of the life-story of St. Francis should have an immense influence in starting the examination on modern lines of the half-forgotten documents of the thirteenth and fourteenth centuries.

When speaking of the impetus given in France by Renan to the study of the Franciscan story it would not be right to pass over without mention three of the pioneers of the same study in Great Britain. The versatile pen of Mrs. Oliphant had as early as 1868 been devoted to a life of St. Francis, which had at any rate the merit of awakening wider interest in this country ; while about twenty years earlier, in 1847, F. W. Faber had produced a *Life of St. Francis of Assisi*, translated from the French of C. Chalippe. A more important name than that of either Mrs. Oliphant or Faber is that of Ruskin, who took the keenest interest in

---

[1] " How foolish they are, and how little they know the saint of Assisi, who for the purpose of their own errors invent a Francis—an incredible Francis—who is impatient of the authority of the Church, who cares nothing for the teaching of our faith, who is the herald of that false freedom which has been so much vaunted since the beginning of the present century, and is the cause of such unrest in Church and State ! Let him, the herald of the great King, teach Catholics and others by his own example how close was his attachment to the hierarchy of the Church and to the doctrine of Christ."—Encyclical Letter of Pope Pius XI, 1926.

St. Francis, so much so that he appears even to have considered the possibility of joining the Roman Catholic communion in order to be able to become a member of the third order of St. Francis. In *Deucalion* he wrote of himself as a brother of the third order, and he stayed for a long time at Assisi. Thus Ruskin had a part, and no unimportant part, in the rediscovery of St. Francis.

The outstanding name, however, in the rediscovery of St. Francis is, of course, that of Professor Paul Sabatier, whose interest in Franciscan studies was largely inspired by Renan. The publication by Sabatier in 1894 of the first edition of his *Vie de S. François d'Assise* —a book which was destined to go into forty-five editions and to be translated into many languages— was an epoch in Franciscan studies. Countless thousands of readers have derived from the writings of Sabatier, and especially from his great *Life*, their first impulse towards interest in the saint, which has frequently developed into a complete surrender to his fascination and charm. It would be idle to deny that there has not been unanimity on the subject of the work of Sabatier, either as regards his whole outlook towards St. Francis or as regards some of the critical positions which he had adopted as a result of his investigations. Sabatier's interpretation of the character and personality of Francis has sometimes not been one which can be accepted unreservedly by those whose outlook is more distinctly conservative and Catholic, but there is insufficient justification for the attitude of some, who overlook on account of theological bias the immense services rendered to Franciscan studies by the great Frenchman. Sabatier has written with exquisite beauty of style and thought about the Poverello of Assisi, and about the places which have become holy through their association with him. But Sabatier's strength has not lain solely in his command of literary style, or even in his æsthetic appreciation of St. Francis. For forty years he has laboured incessantly in the field of his choice, examining for himself the actual manuscripts, bringing to light documents of vital importance and previously unknown, developing theories as to the inter-relation of the various sources, with which many have disagreed but which none can venture to disregard.

Starting, then, from the publication of Sabatier's *Vie de S. François*, the whole movement for the accurate and scientific study of the Franciscan story has gathered momentum and has spread from one country to another. It is of course impossible to attempt here to record the detailed advances which have been made since 1890. The most that can be done is to point to some of the landmarks and to mention some of the leading investigators. The document known as the *Legend of the Three Companions* had been for a long time known to those who were investigating the sources, though it was all but unknown to any wider circle. In his search for those portions of the Legend of the saint which were believed to be lost, Sabatier made the discovery in separate form of the document, now comparatively well known, entitled the *Mirror of Perfection*. He announced that this work was written as early as 1227 by Brother Leo, one of the most intimate companions of St. Francis, and thus that it was actually earlier in date of composition than the First Life by Thomas of Celano. The large majority of Franciscan students have felt unable to accept so early a date, and have believed that the *Mirror* is a work of the fourteenth century and that the date of the manuscript used by Sabatier has been misunderstood; but Sabatier still maintains that date. It must not, however, be forgotten that it was he who discovered and published for the first time this highly important document, which now, thirty years later, is still a subject of acute controversy and much division of opinion. Sabatier's edition of the *Mirror of Perfection* was the first volume in a series of Franciscan texts, *Collection de Documents pour l'histoire religieuse et littéraire du Moyen Age*, and he followed up the *Mirror of Perfection* with other documents of vital interest to the Franciscan student, such as the *Actus Beati Francisci*, published in 1902. It must not be supposed for a moment that activity in Franciscan study was even at that stage confined to Sabatier and his collaborators, or to France. As early as 1885 the College of St. Bonaventure at Quaracchi—a house of the Order of Friars Minor specially devoted to theological and historical research—had begun the issue of the valuable series known as *Analecta Franciscana*, while in 1906 Père E. d'Alençon gave to the world a much-needed critical edition of the two Lives of St. Francis and the *Tractate on Miracles* by Thomas of Celano, a work now unfortunately out of print, and until this year the only trustworthy edition of those indispensable sources. Thus by the end of the nineteenth century widespread interest had been excited among historical writers both within and without the Order of St. Francis, among writers of the most rigid orthodoxy and those of the most liberal tendencies, and the study of St. Francis, his writings and his life, which had in earlier generations been the province of relatively few, became a field of research, and it may be added an arena of controversy, for some of the most acute mediævalists in all countries. In Great Britain the outstanding worker has been, and still is, Mr. A. G. Little, who has laboured unceasingly at the investigation of the sources for the history of St. Francis, and who among many notable contributions to Franciscan studies has given us an edition of Thomas of Eccleston's *Coming of the Friars to Britain*. Mr. Little has also made special investigations of the Friars Minor in this country, and especially at Oxford.

As might well be expected, the problems of Franciscan sources have had a remarkable fascination for German scholars, and the German universities have poured out a mass of acute and valuable work dealing with various aspects of the whole subject. Among these very numerous works two seem to me of outstanding importance and worth. One is Boehmer's *Analekten zur Geschichte des Franciscus von Assisi*,[1] which provides a critical edition of the works to be attributed to the pen of the saint. The other is Walter Goetz's *Die Quellen zur Geschichte des hl. Franz von Assisi*.[2] This latter work is one of the greatest value on account of its accurate scholarship and moderation of view, and at the time when it was written it was much the most useful statement of the findings of Franciscan research. If it could be brought up to date in the light of later discoveries and translated into English, it would be of undoubted value to British historical students.

It is not the purpose of this article to act as a kind of guide to the study of St. Francis, but rather to indicate some of the main features of the phenomenon which I have described as the rediscovery of St. Francis. The point which I want to establish is that the last seventy-five years, and especially the last half-century, have been remarkable for the creation of what may fairly be called a fresh department or province in historical research, which has engaged the attention of a by no means negligible group of workers in a number of countries, which has resulted in the publication of a mass of books and articles, and which has produced the foundation of numerous societies for the special study of the subject and of many journals devoted exclusively to the publication of the result achieved by these researches. So wide has the subject become that, while

[1] Tübingen, 1904. [2] Gotha, 1904.

a few generations ago, it would have been a possible form of specialism to take up Franciscan studies as a whole, it is no longer feasible for any one worker to attempt to keep pace with the study of the whole subject, and it has become necessary for specialism to take place within the subject itself.

Side by side with this scientific study of Franciscan sources and history has gone the constantly increasing popularisation of the story of St. Francis. Some would doubtless maintain that the whole movement is merely one phase of the outburst of interest in mediævalism. That is no doubt true as far as it goes, but it is far from being the whole truth. St. Francis makes an appeal of amazing freshness to the purely religious instinct and to the æsthetic instinct. There has been an unmistakable and regrettable tendency, especially on the part of those who have made a relatively superficial study of the actual facts of the life and writings of the saint, to go one step further than the safe and legitimate step of discovering that Francis of Assisi has a message for all time and for every generation. That step is to find in him just that message to this generation which fits in best with their own outlook on life. Thus those who stand for a Socialistic theory of life have not hesitated to claim St. Francis as an exponent of Socialism, while those who crave for extreme simplicity in religion have imagined St. Francis as a kind of predecessor of the leaders of the Reformation, or as a man whose theology bordered on Pantheism.

Here, again, the words of the recent Papal Encyclical may appropriately be quoted to traverse this unscientific and unbalanced view : ' The herald of the great King,' writes Pius XI., ' did not come to make men doting lovers of flowers, birds, lambs, fishes or hares ; he came to fashion them after the Gospel pattern, and to make them lovers of the cross.'

Such vagaries of interpretation are only to be expected when the foundation of sound and accurate study is absent. One of the most successful recent attempts to translate the message of St. Francis into the language of the twentieth century is Prebendary Mackay's *The Message of Francis of Assisi*, which has paid due regard to the actual sources, and consequently has not distorted the figure of the saint.

It is clear that it is impossible to account for this ever-widening and deepening interest in St. Francis and his story by the simple explanation that he was a great saint. There have been many other great saints, but it would be hard to point to one who has after a period of several centuries come into his own so completely as Francis. There are scholars who devote themselves to the study of Benedictine monachism or of the Dominican Order, but their work has not up to the present made the appeal either to the student of mediævalism on the one hand, or to the average person of cultivated and intelligent tastes on the other, that is made by the work, either exact or popular, of those who are devoting themselves to the Franciscan story.

It would be difficult to mention a cult in any way comparable to that of St. Francis except perhaps that of St. Teresa.

There are other aspects of the phenomenon of the rediscovery of St. Francis. One of these is the relation of Franciscanism to learning, especially to theology and to philosophy. I do not suggest that it is a modern phase that the Franciscan Order should have become a learned order. There were signs of a trend in that direction even in the time of the founder, and much more distinctly in the generation following his death. St. Bonaventure, who lived in the generation after St. Francis, and whose influence upon the development of the Order can scarcely be sufficiently emphasised, acknowledged that he found in the life of St. Francis a likeness to the origins of Christianity, in that the Church began from uneducated fishermen and later included the most famous teachers. It is the investigation of this somewhat extraordinary development which has been and still is another phase of the rediscovery of St. Francis. Increasing attention is being devoted to the philosophical and theological writings of leading Franciscans, of St. Bonaventure, of Duns Scotus, of Archbishop Peckham, of Alexander of Hales, and especially of Roger Bacon. It has been recognised as impossible to deal thoroughly with the philosophical conceptions of the Middle Ages without taking into account the work not so much of Francis himself as of some of the chief sons of Francis.

Another aspect which must be mentioned is the impact of one outstanding episode in the story of St. Francis upon psychology. I refer, of course, to the difficult problem of the Stigmatisation. This is not the place for a discussion of that question, but it has a distinct bearing upon the subject of this article. Since the time of Hase and Renan the attention of psychologists and of medical men has been given to the problem raised by the narratives of the Stigmatisation on Mount Alverna in September 1224, and, though it must be admitted that there are wide differences of opinion as to the manner and the nature of that occurrence, there has been a considerable measure of agreement that no properly authenticated case of stigmatisation occurred before the time of St. Francis, but that there have been since his time a number of cases which have been the subject of medical examination. The whole subject of the Stigmatisation of St. Francis has attracted increasing attention during the past twenty-five years, and it would be safe to assert that the last word has not yet been spoken upon it, either from the historical standpoint or from the psychological standpoint.

The question of the Stigmatisation brings us to yet another aspect of the rediscovery of St. Francis. A characteristic book appeared in 1924, namely, P. Vittorino Facchinetti's *Le Stimmate di S. Francesco d'Assisi*. After dealing with the testimony of history and the testimony of science, the author devotes a

section to the homage of literature and art to the Stigmatisation, and there follows a series of reproductions
of artistic masterpieces, carefully selected so as to illustrate the development of the Stigmatisation story in
art throughout the intervening centuries. This is
symptomatic of the interest taken in the influence of
St. Francis upon art—an influence which has by no
means ceased to operate, but which is still leading to
the publication in popular form of some of the greatest
works of art of the painters inspired by the Poverello.
For example, the Giotto frescoes in the Upper Church
of San Francesco have become among the best known
of mediæval pictures.

Is the rediscovery of St. Francis complete? Has
the present age secured, as the result of the patient
labours of the succession of investigators from Renan
until to-day, a complete picture of the saint, a sure
solution of the problem of the Franciscan sources? The
most that could be claimed is that some of the necessary
materials for an investigation of the subject have been
collected. Apart from many subsidiary problems,
there remains still one main problem to be solved.
That problem is the exact relationship between certain
primary documents—the *Second Life of St. Francis* by
Thomas of Celano, the *Mirror of Perfection*, the
Legend of the Three Companions, the *Actus Beati
Francisci et Sociorum ejus*, and the various compilations
of admittedly later date. I believe that the problem
might be solved by a group of competent mediævalists—

not committed to any solution in advance, but completely open-minded—assembling all the relevant documents and making a detailed examination of them, episode by episode, a minute textual examination as well as an examination of their contents. It is only in that way that a final decision can be reached as to whether, for example, Thomas of Celano made use for his *Second Life* of both the *Mirror of Perfection* and the *Legend of the Three Companions*, or whether all three are derived from some older common source. As in so many branches of study, the difficulty has been, and still is, that the chief investigators have yielded to the temptation of first framing a theory of the mutual relationship of the chief documents and then finding in the documents evidence in support of their theory.[1]

For nearly six centuries there was cherished a pious belief that St. Francis was standing erect in his tomb—alive and ready to issue forth therefrom to preach as before to the faithful. There was also no small element of doubt whether the reputed place of burial did actually contain the mortal remains of Francis. In 1818 permission was given by Pope Pius VII. to the Conventual Franciscans to excavate beneath the high altar in San Francesco, and their research was rewarded by the discovery of the stone coffin containing

---

[1] Since writing this paragraph, I have had the advantage as Editor of this volume of reading Professor Burkitt's article; and I should like to express my entire agreement with the results reached by him, and my conviction as to the importance of the Perugia and Rome MSS. in any investigation of this complicated problem.

a skeleton which was authoritatively declared to be that of the saint. The beautiful old tradition was of course shattered by the picks and shovels of the friars, but the story is not without an inward and spiritual significance. From the tomb thus opened in 1818 St. Francis has verily issued forth, and has become as real a figure to the men and women of the nineteenth and twentieth centuries as he was to his fellow-countrymen of the thirteenth century. His rediscovery has followed upon that exposure of his mortal remains, and he has come forth to preach not only to the Italians, but to the whole world. The public opinion of the civilised world recognises to-day in Francis of Assisi, to use the phrase of Benito Mussolini, 'il più santo fra gli Italiani ed il più Italiano fra i santi.'

ST. FRANCIS IN ROME

By Mrs. ARTHUR STRONG, LL.D., LITT.D., F.S.A.

ST. FRANCIS IN ROME

THE celebration this year of the 700th anniversary of the death of St. Francis (October 3-4, 1226—1926) carries in a very special manner the thoughts of his innumerable devotees to the exquisite sites associated with his name : to the hill-town of Assisi, seated like a queen above the valley of Spoleto, of which the Saint himself was wont to say, " Nulla io vidi piu giocondo della mia valle Spoletana " ; to the fragrant woods of Greccio with their rustic hermitages, and to the rugged steeps crowned by the *sasso crudo* of la Verna. The country-side of central Italy is rich in memories of the Saint ; a veritable network of legendary tales spreads over it, radiating from Assisi, his birthplace and special sanctuary.

Yet the very power of the association with Assisi does injustice to the Saint, and detracts from the significance of his mission. Undoubtedly, the presence of that rare personality, the inexhaustible fire of his charity, has endowed this region in particular, as to some degree the whole face of our human dwelling-place, with a glow of tender light ; undeniably also, his own heart was drawn with peculiar love to the town which was alike the birthplace of his physical and of his spiritual life, and it was to Assisi that, as his last hour drew near, he desired to be borne, thence to pass into life eternal. But St. Francis was no mere local saint, not even a saint confined to a locality and transcending it by virtue of his personality and divine power. His vocation was one which linked him with the movement of his age, placed him historically at its very centre, made him, in a word, derive, not from Assisi, but from Rome. Whatever the love he bore to his birthplace, or the associations with the little towns of the Sabina and the Casentino, the stronghold of his spirit was the city which, along with her authority, gave vitality and direction to the impulses stirring within him.

The connection of St. Francis with Rome has naturally not been ignored by his numerous biographers. Catholic and non-Catholic alike are unanimous in admitting his unswerving loyalty to Rome as seat of the Church's authority, while of recent years the dealings of the Holy See with St. Francis have been interpreted by non-Catholics in a more generous spirit than formerly. But the tendency persists to consider Rome only in her practical relation to the problems of his life, as a sort of bureau to which he came for permissions and official seals. Her whole-hearted response to his aspirations, her quickness to recognise and support her ardent servitor, are scarcely appreciated to the full, nor has the influence of the " City of the Soul " been sufficiently taken into account in the history of his spiritual develop-

ment. Yet it was in Rome that he found the answer
to his earliest difficulties, that his noblest intuitions
deepened, that he received premonition of the final
raptures. One might almost say that like other great
Italians of every age, like Virgil who was a Mantuan,
like Dante and Michelangelo who were Tuscans, or
Raphael who was an Umbrian, so Francis only found the
full fruition of his genius in the fertilising atmosphere of
the *Urbs*. In Rome also he formed numerous friendships that accompanied him through life, one of which,
with the noble matron Giacoma di Settesoli, brought
him joy and consolation in his last hours, renewing
at that supreme moment his links with the Eternal
City. It is the object of this paper to try to restore
the blurred outline of the Saint's Roman experiences.
These need to be studied afresh, with the help of the
documents as well as in the light of recent discoveries.
Fine spade-work has already been accomplished by a
number of foreign scholars : foremost among them are
the learned Franciscans, Père Édouard d'Alençon
(Capuchin), Fr. Livario Oliger (O.F.M.), Fr. Hilarin
Felder (Capuchin), Fr. Beda Kleinschmidt (O.F.M.)
and others. Of great importance also are the recent
contributions of various distinguished Italians : Dr.
Cecchelli, Prof. A. Munoz, Piero Misciattelli, and above
all the present Minister of Public Instruction, His Exc.
Pietor Fedele, whose long promised book on St. Francis
and Rome has only been delayed, we believe, by the
arduous duties of his office.

I

The recorded visits of the Saint to Rome are five in number,[1] from his first early pilgrimage in search of guidance, to the mature season when his Order is fully accepted and finally organised, and he is free to abandon himself to mystic and solitary communion with the divine.

The first visit was in 1206. Vacillating movements of repentance for an ill-spent youth and a strongly kindled desire to enter, he knew not how, into the service of Christ, were at work within him. At Spoleto he had heard a voice holding him back from joining the expedition against Markwald, but the meaning of the order given him in a dream, to realise in a spiritual sense his haunting craving for success by arms, was not yet clear.[2] Like many a troubled soul before and after him, he undertook a pilgrimage *ad limina* to pray for the solution of his difficulties. Illumination came to him in a flash. At the Tomb of the Apostle a sudden gesture of renunciation, a first embrace of his Lady Poverty, took place with all the fervour, and, as it seems to our colder times and temperament, with all the exaggeration characteristic of the Saint.[3] Flinging all the money he had with him among the pilgrims' offerings, he went out penniless from the church and

---

[1] I omit supposed visits in 1212 and 1219 for which I can find no definite evidence, though Francis very probably came to Rome seven times and even oftener.

[2] I Celano 4. [3] II Celano 8.

took his place among the beggars on the steps. He carried this symbolic renunciation so far as to exchange the clothes he wore for those of a fellow-beggar. Even the contemporary biographer who narrates the action inclines to explain it away and rationalise it, stating that the gift of all his money was actuated by disgust at the paucity of the offerings of others, and that he then joined the company of the beggars to provide for his homeward journey. The explanation is less intelligible than the deed. The act is in keeping with all we know of the Saint's personality, on a par with the later incident of the kiss to the leper or the visit to the leper-house. It is an act of folly if you will, but it is the " folly of the Cross," that sudden, violent readjustment of values which sets at naught all that the world esteems, obliterates all human respect, and shakes the very foundations of ordered social life. In the long retrospect of seven centuries, the scene in the old atrium of St. Peter stands out as typical of the whole Franciscan movement, of the intransigeance needed to restore the dying life of the spirit, a remedy, extreme but salutary, to the smothering prosperity and material concerns of the age, a supreme return to sanity in a world of craze-bewildered human beings.

On the morrow, it may be on the day itself—the exact moment is unimportant,—Francis resumed his own clothing, and, whether with money bestowed on him as he begged or with supplies more normally obtained, and certainly accessible to the son of a rich cloth merchant, returned to his native town, there to re-enact the scene of total renunciation, no longer as a stranger and a pilgrim in the Eternal City, but as a conspicuous personage in his small familiar circle, breaking from the petty restraints and ties of his past in the full face of his father's bitter indignation and in presence of the citizens and of the Bishop of Assisi. The dramatic scene in the public Piazza of the little town is well known ; as Francis flings back to an indignant father the money and the clothes he owes to him, stripping himself even to the hair-shirt which was his own, it is the Bishop who receives him to his heart and covers his nakedness in the folds of his cloak— indicating by this sacramental gesture that the Church now holds him peculiarly her own. The prologue to the missionary life thus ends, as it began, on the *leitmotif* of Rome.

II

Another three years passed before Francis found himself once more in the Eternal City. At Assisi in the little church of St. Damian, the Crucifix had spoken to him in terms less ambiguous than those of the voice heard at Spoleto. But the order given him to rebuild Christ's church [1] had been interpreted by him materially and locally, applying the labour of his hands and the alms of his friends to reconstruct Assisi's sacred edifices.

---

[1] Vocans enim ipsum ex nomine: *Francisce,* inquit, *vade, repara domum meam.* II Celano 10.

Plate X.

Mystic Marriage of St. Francis and the Lady Poverty.
By Sassetta (1444).

What was wanted of him was soon to be made clear. As followers gathered round him and the cult of poverty grew, he turned his footsteps again to Rome, in quest this time of approval for his Order and sanction for his Rule, seeking from the authority of the Church support for his own. And though he scarcely realised it as he set out, he was to find definite guidance for his missionary work.

This second visit, foreshadowed in the scene at Assisi, knits him to the very heart of Rome. Through the friendly offices of Bishop Guido and the " goodwill and charity " of Cardinal John of St. Paul [1] he obtained the interview he sought with Pope Innocent III, who in a vision, capping as it were the Saint's own earlier dream of the lofty tree which he bent to his wish, saw the Church,—imaged as St. John Lateran—*omnium urbis et orbis ecclesiarum mater et caput*—supported and upheld by this unpretentious leader of a still insignificant movement. In the Encyclical *Rite expiatis* of April 30th of this year, His Holiness Pope Pius XI compares Francis to him " who in his lifetime repaired the house again and in his days fortified the temple." [2] Innocent likewise recognised in Francis the man born of the needs of the age, the champion of the Church in her hour of peril. But the times were difficult ; everywhere movements of reform were tending to break into heresy ;

[1] Of the family of the Colonna. He was first Cardinal-Priest of Santa Prisca, and afterwards Cardinal-Bishop of Sabina. Cristofori, *St. d. Cardinali*, i, p. 33.

[2] *Ecclesiasticus*, l, 1.

professed apostles of evangelical poverty, like the curious sect of the *Poor Catholics*, were giving trouble ; and Innocent had hesitated, it is said, before admitting into his presence one who might prove to be only another Peter Valdes.[1]   But the intuition of his master-mind was unerring and his recognition of the Saint swift and generous.   The Pope's confidence was no doubt enhanced by the bearing of the man before him : no false humility or cowardice, says Dante, weighed down the son of Bernadone as he approached the Pontiff :

> " Ma regalmente sua dura intenzione
>   ad Innocenzio aperse, e da lui ebbe
>   primo sigillo a sua religione."
>
> *Paradiso,* xi, 91–93.[2]

For Francis it was an essential moment in the Life of the Spirit.   He had not only obtained the desired sanctions and permissions ; but in the presence of the Vicar of Christ that truth had become clear to him which before he could but divine as in a glass darkly. All his doubts were now resolved as to the interpretation to be put upon the words : " Francis, go and repair My

---

[1] A vivid account of the spiritual troubles of the period, and of the possible perplexities of Pope Innocent, is given by M. Beaufreton, the latest Catholic biographer of the Saint : *Saint François d'Assise,* Paris (1926), p. 130 ff.   See also Mgr. H. Mann, *Lives of the Popes,* vols. xi, xii (Innocent III), *passim.*

[2] Piero Misciattelli (*Illustrazione Italiana,* special St. Francis number, p. 34) points out that Dante is here anticipating Petrarch's saying that a man is ennobled, not by his birth, but by his life.   Hagiography has invested St. Francis with patents of nobility from which, as Beaufreton wittily remarks, no seal is absent save that of authenticity.   It is at this kind of pious snobbery that C. G. Coulton (*Mediæval Village,* p. 526) not unjustly levels the shafts of his irony.

Church." The Crucifix had spoken in Assisi, but the full meaning of the words had been disclosed in Rome.

A later story, in palliation of the Pope's supposed reluctance to see Francis and his companions, was told by Innocent's nephew, Ricardo Annibaldi, Cardinal-Deacon of S. Angelo,[1] to Jerome of Ascoli, from whom it passed into the *Legenda* of St. Bonaventura. According to this story, a first rebuff had been administered by Innocent to Francis, who in his zeal had rushed to the Lateran immediately on arrival, eluded the vigilance of the guards, and discovering the Pope walking up and down in the place called the *speculum*, had thrown himself at his feet, only to be ungraciously repulsed. In fact, according to a passage in Matthew of Paris,[2] who gives the story in a somewhat different form, the great Pope was so far startled out of his dignity by the unusual apparition as to bid Francis " go and roll himself in the mire with the pigs."

The anecdote does not seem to have found much favour with the biographers previous to St. Bonaventura, but it raises two points of great topographical interest. In the first place it represents the Pope as walking in the *speculum* of the Lateran, probably the old observatory or " spying-place " where Silvester II had studied the stars in order to pierce the mysteries of the approaching millennium, an occupation which caused the studious Pontiff to be suspected of magical practices. The story

---

[1] *I.e.* S. Angelo in Pescheria, Cristofori, *Storia dei Cardinali*, 1888, i, p. 249.

[2] On the small value of this author, see Sabatier, p. 431 ; cf. Mann, *Popes*, xi, p. 57, n. 2.

goes on to tell how on the morrow, Pope Innocent, awakening in great agitation from the Dream in which the ragged beggar whom he had repulsed was revealed as the saviour of the Church, sent messengers in hot haste to fetch him back, and how the messengers discovered Francis living in the hospice of S. Antonio near the Lateran (*juxta Lateranum*). The S. Antonio in question was long identified with the hospice of that name opposite St. Mary Major's, in the modern Via Carlo Alberto. But apart from the fact that this S. Antonio cannot possibly be described as *juxta Lateranum*, being about a mile off, an inscription on its fine Romanesque porch shows that it was only erected some thirty years after the death of Francis, with moneys left for the purpose by Cardinal Pietro Capocci, who died in 1259. The question has been recently discussed by Father Livario Oliger.[1] He comes to the conclusion, on information partly provided by Professor Huelsen, that the S. Antonio where Francis stayed is to be identified with a tiny foundation of that name situated near SS. Pietro and Marcellino and the aqueduct of Claudius, which is mentioned in a fourteenth century list of Roman churches.[2] Still more recently, the brilliant young Roman archæologist, Dr. Cecchelli,

[1] In a collection of monographs published in honour of the sixteenth centenary of the dedication of the Lateran (*Nel XVI Centenario dalla Dedicazione della Arcibasilica Lateranense del S.S. Salvatore*, Rome, 1924), p. 44. In his most important paper Fr. Oliger gives full references to the literature.

[2] G. Falco: "Il Catalogo di Torino, etc." in *Archiv. della R. Soc. Rom. di Storia Patria*, xxxii, 1909, pp. 411 ff.

in a special St. Francis number of the *Illustrazione
Italiana*,[1] has shown reason for identifying the hostelry
where Francis lodged with the old hospice of the Lateran,
the chapel of which—" a perfect jewel of thirteenth
century architecture," says Cecchelli—still exists, em-
bedded in the later hospital. This would really be
juxta Lateranum, and one hopes that Dr. Cecchelli will
soon publish his thesis in a fuller form.

It is possibly to the same Jerome of Ascoli, afterwards
Pope under the name of Nicholas IV, that we owe the
priceless record of the " Dream of Innocent III "
which is still to be seen in the Basilica of St. John
Lateran. It is from a long metrical inscription in
mosaic, the rest of which narrates the benefactions
to the Basilica of Pope Nicholas, under whose auspices
the mosaic was put up. For vividness and simplicity
the naïve hexameters are hard to beat ; one can readily
believe that they come from a pure Franciscan source.

> " Tertius Ecclesiae Pater Innocentius, hora
> Qua sese dederat somno, nutare ruinae
> Hanc videt Ecclesiam, mox vir pannosus et asper
> Despectusque humerum supponens sustinet illam,
> At pater vigilans Franciscum prospicit, atque
> Vere est (inquit) quem vidimus, iste ruentem
> Ecclesiam ; fidemque ; feret, sic ille petitis
> Cunctis concessis liber, laetusque ; recessit." [2]

---

[1] Christmas, 1925.

[2] Forcella, *Iscrizioni delle Chiese e d'altri edificii di Roma,* viii, p. 15, No. 16.
The inscription was actually in the exterior pilaster of the tribune, see Rohault
de Fleury, *Le Latran au moyen âge,* p. 180. Cf. Barbier de Montault : " La
grande pancarte de la Basilique de Latran " in *Revue d'Archéologie Chrétienne,*
1886, p. 472 (= *Œuvres Complètes,* i, p. 404) ; and Lauer, *Le Palais du Latran,*

The spirit of the passage has been well caught by Miss Janet Bacon [1] in the following English version :

" In the first hour of sleep, Pope Innocent,
    Third of the name, the Church's father, dreamed :
    He saw his Church with ruin imminent
    Shaken and falling ; but anon it seemed
    A ragged man, despised, of rude estate
    Set shoulder under her, and bore the weight.

" Waking, the Pope saw Francis.   Then he cried :
    ' The dream was true : the man I saw is here.
    'Tis he shall bear, like strong support and guide,
    The falling Church, the shaken faith.'   So fear
    Was calmed, and having nothing left to pray,
    Content and free from care he went away."

The mosaic, which is carried out in blue and gold, may be seen on the right of the Sacristy door, but originally it was near the Tribune, being actually part of the mosaics executed, though some may only have been restored,[2] by order of Nicholas—first of the Friars Minor to ascend the throne of Peter—whose authorship of the inscription is therefore very probable. This important document needs to be carefully edited. It has been transcribed times innumerable, but the copies are full of inaccuracies, the mosaic having been damaged in the course of repeated removals and much of the lettering doubtfully restored.

1911, p. 193.   On the mosaics of the tribune see Fr. Beda Kleinschmidt, O.F.M., " Die Künstlerische Kanonisation der Hl. Vaters Franzisken " in *Archiv. Franc. Hist.* iii, 1910, p. 615 f.

   [1] Director of Classical Studies at Girton Coll., Cambridge.
   [2] The latter is the more usual opinion.

Pictures of the Pope's Dream and his Sanction of the Order are fully dealt with by other contributors to this volume, in connection with the whole subject of Franciscan art.[1] Here I need only mention, because of the dependence upon Rome of their painter Camillo Rusuti, the versions of these two episodes from the Franciscan cycle in the Upper Church of Assisi. The fresco of the Pope sanctioning the Rule has been eloquently described by Paul Sabatier as: "the living symbol of the manner in which ecclesiastical authority in the time of the great pontiffs understood the Saint's mission."[2] But neither M. Sabatier nor anyone else would, I imagine, now ascribe this or its companion picture to Giotto. Modern critics confidently give them with certain others of the series to the Roman Rusuti, whose style, as known from his mosaics on the façade of St. Mary Major's in Rome, they strongly recall. The attribution, moreover, seems confirmed by the discovery, again due to Dr. Cecchelli,[3] that Rusuti was the painter of the episodes from the life of the Saint that formerly

[1] I would wish, however, to draw attention to the version by Taddio Gaddi in the Uffizi, where St. Peter appears whispering into the ear of the sleeping Pontiff, i.e. the Apostle who built the Church instructs his successor with regard to the new Apostle who is to help repair it.

[2] In *Il Rinovamento*, II, 1908, p. 425 ff., cited by Beaufreton, p. 159, n.3.

[3] See his note in *Roma*, vol. ii, 1925, p. 90, to the effect that Giulio Mancini, physician to Urban VIII, attributed to Filippo Rusuti the paintings formerly in the ancient church of S. Francesco a Ripa, and generally thought to have been by Pietro Cavallini. Many critics must re-echo Mgr. Wilpert's regret, *Mosaiken u. Malereien der Stadt Rom*, II, p. 1205, that the frescoes of S. Francesco a Ripa were not drawn before they were destroyed.

decorated San Francesco a Ripa in the Trastevere, the earliest Franciscan foundation in Rome.[1] Rusuti was probably called to Assisi because of the fame of his work in Rome, and could his frescoes in San Francesco have survived the inevitable changes and transformations that overtake the buildings of the *Urbs*, Assisi might have had a Roman rival. He belonged to that cycle of Roman painters which includes Cavallini, and which strongly influenced the young Giotto when he came to Rome in 1299, in the pontificate of Boniface VIII. I should not like to say that Rusuti has the vitality and strength of Giotto, or as fine a colouring, but he has an equal or greater power of narrative and a love of detail that derive through illuminated manuscripts from the reliefs of the Roman Empire. It is the true Roman delight in the *gesta hominum* which resisted the paralysing influence of Byzantium and never completely died out of Western art.

III

Celano records that after their reception at the Lateran, Francis and his companions went straight *ad limina Beati Petri* to render thanks to God, who " setteth the humble on high and cheereth the sorrowful with deliverance " ;[1] and Francis, as he prayed, was mindful no doubt of the earlier guidance vouchsafed

---

[1] Job v, 11. The transl. in the A.V. is " to set up on high those that be low, that those which mourn may be exalted to safety."

him at the Tomb. In the converse of the brethren, as they journeyed gaily towards Spoleto's lovely valley, the talk was largely of their " gracious reception by the vicar of Christ."

Francis was once again to derive high spiritual aid from Pope Innocent. This was in 1215, when he was present in St. John Lateran, among the crowd assembled to listen to the inaugural sermon preached by Innocent at the opening of the twelfth General and Fourth Lateran Council. The evidence for the presence of St. Francis in Rome on this occasion rests, it is true, only on somewhat uncertain testimony,[1] strongly supported, however, by evidence from passages in the Pope's sermon. As if in curious premonition of his own death not a twelve-month later, the Pontiff had chosen for his text the words : " With desire I have desired to eat this Passover with you before I suffer " (Luke xxii. 15), but turning later in his discourse to the subject of judgement and mercy, he had dwelt, with the love of symbol characteristic of mediæval thought, on the meaning of the Hebrew THAU. " THAU," he reminded his hearers,[2] " is the last letter of the Hebrew alphabet, . . . it expresses the form of the Cross such as it was before Pontius Pilate placed the title upon it. This sign he carries on his forehead who shows forth the

---

[1] See Fr. Cuthbert, *Life of St. Francis*, p. 177, n. 1, w. ref.; cf. Mann, *Lives of the Popes*, xii, p. 288.

[2] I quote from Fr. Cuthbert, *op. cit.*, p. 178. The actual text of the sermon in Migne, *P.L.*, vol. 217, col. 674 ff.

power of the Cross in his deeds, according to what the Apostle says : *They have crucified their flesh with their vices and concupiscences,* and again, *God forbid that I should glory save in the Cross of our Lord Jesus Christ, by whom the world is crucified unto me and I unto the world.*" But these words from the Epistle to the Galatians are also taken for the Introit of the Mass for the Feast of St. Francis, no doubt because those who composed the Office knew how great an impression Francis had received from the Pope's commentary, and it must be for the same reason that the words are adopted as their special motto by the Friars Minor.[1] An even stronger proof that he heard the sermon at the Lateran is afforded by the connection, so brilliantly established by Father Cuthbert, between the Saint's adoption about this time of the THAU [2] as his peculiar badge and the Pope's explanation of the sign and his promise of mercy in the judgment to come to him who should carry it on his forehead. For the third time Francis experienced in Rome a deepening of his mystical life ; the sermon of the Pope had set his feet one stage further on the road to La Verna and the final ecstasy.

If the presence of St. Francis in Rome at the time of the Council can now be looked upon as a practical certainty, there can no longer be any reason to doubt

[1] *Cf.* Sabatier, *Life of St. Francis* (E. Tr.), p. 193, n. 1, who curiously fails to note the connection of the motto with the Pope's sermon which he does not even mention. On p. 199 he throws doubts on the visit of Francis to Rome in 1215, without attempting to examine its possibilities.

[2] See Celano *de Mirac.*, 3.

the tradition which refers to this same occasion the first meeting with St. Dominic, whose attendance at the Council is an accepted fact. Wherever the meeting took place it brought St. Francis into touch with a soul akin to his own. A spiritual comradeship ensued between these two apostles of a purified Christendom, which is symbolised in those numerous pictures and reliefs that show them united in a transcendental embrace. Tradition tells of a dream in which Pope Honorius saw Dominic, like another Francis, upholding the falling Church. Whether this second dream, so beautifully represented by Fra Angelico in the predella of the great picture in the Louvre, be apocryphal or not, the story expresses, as nothing else could, the equal co-operation of Dominic and of Francis in the spiritual regeneration of the time. It is a strange perversion of historic truth to represent the Church as heaping favours upon Dominic [1] and treating him as an *enfant gâté*, while holding Francis at arm's length and only tolerating him to keep him from breaking into rebellion. Like St. Peter and St. Paul, so St. Dominic and St. Francis have never been separated in the thought of the Church. It is as Princes of a new Apostolate that they are chiefly reverenced in the churches of the *Urbs*, while in the tribune of the premier church of Christendom they are represented one on each side of the *Cathedra Petri*, captaining the noble company of

[1] Sabatier, *Life*, p. 215, represents Dominic " overwhelmed with favours by the Pope," and Francis as looked upon " with mixed sentiments."

saints that forms a guard of honour round the Tomb of the Apostle.[1]

IV

Innocent III had died in 1216 at the comparatively early age of fifty-six, worn out by his labours at the Council. Under his successor Honorius III (Cencio Savelli) it is St. Dominic who for a while takes the front of the stage, obtaining in 1218 the fuller permission for his Rule which had been partially withheld in 1215. In the previous year, 1217, Francis also returned to Rome, driven by trouble within his Order to have recourse to the Church, that the ill-disposed among his restless children might, in the strong phrase of Celano, " be smitten with the rod of her power " (*Vadam igitur et eos Sanctæ Romanæ Ecclesiæ commendabo cuius potentiæ virga percellantur malevoli* . . . II, Celano, 24). On this occasion Francis preached before Pope Honorius as recounted by Celano (II, 25) and shown in one of the Assisi frescoes. The illustrious Ugolino Conti, Cardinal-Bishop of Ostia, whose interest in Francis had gone on increasing since a first meeting between them in 1216,[2]

[1] On Francis and Dominic see especially Fr. Hilarin Felder, O.F.M. Cap. *Geschichte der Wissenschaftlichen Studien im Franziskanerorden*, 1904, p. 10 and p. 18 ff.; cf. Mann, *Popes*, xii, p. 484.

[2] The first meeting had been at Florence when Ugolino had dissuaded Francis from going to France and advised him to keep to his Italian Apostolate. The Cardinal's wise dealings with the *Clarisse* had probably influenced Francis in his desire to have him for Protector of his own Order; Beaufreton, *St. François*, p. 169 ff. According to Angelo of Clareno, Ugolino had been present among the Cardinals who advocated approval of the first rule in 1209; see the passage quoted by Sabatier, *Life*, p. 95; cf. *id.* p. 201, n. 2.

was specially anxious that the holy man should do himself credit before the Curia. But to the dismay of those present, the Saint stood silent awhile, having forgotten every word of his carefully prepared discourse ; swiftly, however, he recovered himself and yielding to inspiration spoke words of such power, says St. Bonaventura, " that it was manifestly seen that it was not himself that spake, but the Spirit of the Lord," or as Celano says—with a droll mixture of biblical metaphors—" the mountains were moved at his words, and heaving deep sighs from their profound recesses, bathed the inner man with tears."

"When the sermon was ended," goes on Celano, " after a few words of friendly discourse with the Lord Pope, Francis at length petitioned him as follows : *My lord, as you know, access to such Majesty as yours is not readily granted to men poor and despised. You hold the world in your hands, and businesses of vast moment allow you not to attend to the smallest matters. Wherefore* (he said), *I beg of your Holiness' compassion that this Lord of Ostia may be granted us for a Pope, to the end that, saving always the dignity of your pre-eminence, the brethren may resort to him in time of need and fetch from him the benefits both of protection and of governance.*"

And the Pope, much edified, set Ugolino " over the Religion." These details are of peculiar significance. In the interval of seven years since his first audience of Pope Innocent in 1210, the personal sanctity of Francis and the importance of his missionary work were so universally acknowledged, and so profoundly appreciated in Rome, that in his consciousness of growing power he felt able to present to the Pope a petition which, for all the humility of its language, is in the nature of a command. There is something whimsical, moreover, in Francis saying to the Pope, " You are much too busy, Holy Father, to attend to the affairs of poor beggars like ourselves ; just give us Cardinal Ugolino." The whole episode is typical of Italian geniality and *bonhomie*, and the Saint got, of course, exactly what he wanted. The appointment of Ugolino as Protector of the Order was a foregone conclusion. From that time the friendship between the venerable Cardinal of seventy and the young and ardent Saint, who in 1217 was only thirty-four, ripened into an intimacy of which many and charming incidents are recorded.[1] The story of Ugolino's visit to the Chapter of Mats and the Portiuncula and the humility of his deportment on the occasion are familiar episodes,[1] but we are only concerned here with what happened in Rome. Ugolino's anxiety when Francis preached before Pope Honorius has already been mentioned. On another occasion we find that in company with the Cardinal, Francis visited the *Sacro Speco* of Subiaco, laying there in the cradle of monasticism his own offering of a new flower of devotion. To this visit we owe what is probably the earliest

[1] For a good account of the relations of Francis to Ugolino as narrated by Celano see Walter Goetz: *Die Quellen zur Geschichte des heiligen Franz. von Assisi* (1904), p. 74 ff.

portrait of St. Francis, the one still to be seen at Subiaco, in which he holds the rotulus inscribed *Pax Huic Domui*, his usual salutation on entering a house.

He should also be recognised, it is thought, in the young cowled friar to the left of Ugolino, in the fresco representing the consecration of the Chapel of San Gregorio which took place on the occasion of the Cardinal's visit. Another fresco at Subiaco represents Innocent III promulgating a decree, so that in the famous Benedictine Abbey memories of St. Francis mingle with those of his two most illustrious friends and protectors. The visit to Subiaco took place during the Roman stay of 1217 more probably than in 1223, when the time and thought of Francis were entirely absorbed in the revision of the Rule, but there are technical[1] reasons for not dating the portrait earlier than 1228, the year of the canonisation. It must, however, have been executed prior to this event, which took place in July, since Francis is shown without the aureole, and without the stigmata, which only received official recognition with the act of canonisation.

The revision of the Rule, which in its final form owes so much to the care and wisdom of Ugolino, has very generally been represented as the cause of profound distress to the Saint as well as of unhappy dissension in

[1] H. Thode, *Franz von Assisi*, i, p. 72, note 1, shows from the inscription below the picture of the consecration of the chapel that this was painted in the second year of the Pontificate of Gregory IX, and the portrait of Francis is evidently of the same date. See also F. Hermanin, *I monasteri di Subiaco*, i. p. 439, and R. van Marle, *Italian Sc. of Painting*, i, 1923, p. 428 f.

the Order, and the impression still lingers that Francis accepted as his cross the submission to Rome. The question is not one that can be discussed here. We may readily believe that the work of formulating the Rule, of giving their just value to its parts, of trimming it down to the required proportions, must have been irksome in the extreme to a man of an ardent and mystical temperament, and fear lest the letter should kill the spirit must have proved a constant trial. But Rome once more lifted the burden from his shoulders, and everything that he did after the promulgation of the Rule shows how rapidly his serene and happy nature reasserted itself in his sense of a newly found freedom. Had Francis suffered from the decrees of the Holy See, Dante who—devout and convinced Catholic though he was—never hesitated to lash any Pope whose opinions conflicted with his own, would not have written the beautiful lines :

> " Di seconda corona redimita
> Fu per Onorio del Eterno Spiro
> La Santa Voglia d'esto archimandrita."
> *Paradiso*, xi, 97–99.

They show that in Dante's mind at least no injustice had been done to the Saint whom one suspects him of having loved above all others.

The Papal Bull ratifying the Rule in its revised form is dated November 29th, and not a fortnight later we find Francis, who had remained in Rome, making preparation to celebrate Christmas at Greccio in joyous and novel fashion, encouraged to this, it appears, by Pope Honorius himself. Stimulated perhaps by the sight of the beautiful *presepii* or cribs put up at Christmas time in memory of Bethlehem in the churches of Rome, and more especially in St. Mary Major's, proud guardian of the *Sancta Culla,* he seems to have determined to outdo them all. Sending messengers ahead to command the presence of a live ox and a live ass, he himself made arrangements for the episode which was to mark the climax of the scene : *In hoc sacello | Franciscus | Reclinavit Christum in praesepio,* says the inscription in the little chapel built over the sacred spot.

So far as we can tell, Francis never saw Rome again. " For him, the cult of the cradle was inseparable from that of the Cross," says Joergensen, " and Bethlehem was quite close to Golgotha." But after Golgotha and the mystic heights of La Verna, there was nothing left but to sing the hymn of praise which is the Canticle of Fra Sole, before passing to the eternal habitations.

V

In the course of his repeated sojourns in Rome definite friendships had been formed, traces of which may still be found in the actual monuments of the city, as in the tales of the chroniclers. Sponsored in the first instance by his own Bishop, he had soon become known to all the more important members of the papal court. Francis was nothing if not good company ;

his ready wit, as much as the edification of his talk and the sanctity of his example, made him a welcome guest whenever he could be induced to accept hospitality. Besides the house of his friend Cardinal Ugolino, he also stayed at that of Cardinal Leone Brancaleone, a distinguished member of the Curia, who had been Cardinal-Deacon of the little church of Santa Lucia *in Septemsolis*,[1] near the Palatine, and was later promoted to be Cardinal-Priest of Santa Croce in Gerusalemme. On one occasion, he accepted the Cardinal's invitation on condition that he should be allowed to sleep with the Brother who accompanied him, in an old tower or refuge in the garden ; but even from this modicum of shelter he was driven by the visits of " guastaldi," or " policemen " of the Lord as he called them—in other words, by demons, who so terrified the holy man that he called out loudly for his companion. In his Lives of the Cardinals, Ciaconnius says that Brancaleone lived *in muris*, that is, I take it, against or beside the old Aurelian Walls, and I have very little doubt that the chamber occupied by Francis was one of the vaults or galleries of the walls,[2] places so full of bats and other noxious creatures that the Saint's uncomfortable

[1] The little church which was on Frangipani property (see below) has long since disappeared. It will be fully discussed in Huelsen's forthcoming *Le Chiese di Roma nel medio Evo*. Cf. Bartoli in *Bulletino d'Arte*, iii, pp. 253-269 ; Lanciani *Storia d. Scavi*, iv, p. 138 f. ; Cristofori, *Storia dei Cardinali*. 1888, i, p. 230, etc.

[2] It is described by II Celano 119 as " a secluded tower with nine vaulted chambers " (transl. Ferrers-Howell).

experiences may be readily accounted for. Professor
Huelsen, the veteran leader of Roman topographical
studies whom I consulted on the point, reminds me
that a chamber in the Aurelian Wall, immediately above
the Porta San Sebastiano, is reputed to be[1] frescoed with
pictures of devils, in recollection no doubt of nocturnal
discomforts experienced by those who had tried to find
shelter in the disused galleries. Next to fixing the sites
of churches, nothing in the mediæval topography of
Rome is more important than to discover where lay the
palaces of the Cardinals. The story of the " guastaldi "
may prove to be the clue to the whereabouts of the
residence of Brancaleone, which should be looked for,
I think, near his titular church of Santa Croce, adjoining
the wall and also perhaps the old *anfiteatro castrense*.
We also hear of Francis as a guest of Nicholas Chiara-
monti, Cardinal-Bishop of Tusculum, the friend and
patron of the famous Brother Giles (Egidio). Nicholas,
indeed, though he had been a Cistercian monk, was so
devoted to the Franciscan ideal that he wished at one
time to lay aside his Cardinalate and become a Friar
Minor, but was dissuaded by the Pope. Nor must
we forget the diverting incident at the house of Cardinal Ugolino himself, when Francis, declining to
partake of the excellent fare provided by his host,
proceeded to collect from the street black crusts which

[1] Prof. Huelsen had this from Prof. Bartoli. The association of devils with
the ruins of pagan Rome was common ; see the story of Benvenuto Cellini
and the devils called up in the Coliseum, quoted by Sabatier, *Life*, p. 189, n. 1.

he set before the guests, afterwards parrying with his usual wit and charm the rebuke gently administered to him by the somewhat disconcerted Cardinal (II Celano 73).

Among others who delighted in Francis and held him in affectionate regard, were John of St. Paul, first Protector of the Order, and the learned Cardinal who plied the Saint with searching questions in Holy Scripture, declaring himself highly edified by the answers he received.[1]   These anecdotes show how frank was the intercourse between Francis and many of the most distinguished members of the Roman Curia, and how gaily he responded to the cordiality shown him. It is difficult to account for the perverse conception of a Rome in the least hostile to St. Francis, or anxious to clip his wings.   But old superstitions die hard and the notion still persists that liberty must of necessity be thwarted, where authority is upheld.

VI

We have left for the last, what was perhaps the closest, of his Roman friendships.   In the Assisi legend St. Clare, occupying with her virginal charm the whole space allotted to woman, has supplanted that exquisite flower of Roman tradition, Jacopa di Settesoli, with whom Francis was linked in bonds of the closest intimacy, and whom, in admiration of her virile character and in

---

[1] Told by Celano (II, 104), who omits the Cardinal's name.

recognition of their fraternal comradeship, he affection-
ately dubbed, not Sister, but Brother Jacopa. Père
Édouard d'Alençon, in his fascinating monograph on
Dame Jacqueline,[1] " that little jewel of learning and
grace," as Pietro Fedele calls it, has rendered familiar
the main facts of her life. Belonging by birth to the
powerful family of the Normanni, through whom she
was connected with the Anguillara, and married to a
Frangipani, Jacopa was a lady of wealth and high
position. Early left a widow, she proved herself a strong
and watchful guardian of the interests of her young
sons, prepared—though Francis, we may believe with
Père Édouard, finally dissuaded her from the suit,—
to go to law on their behalf against attempted en-
croachments on their property even by the Holy See.
For the Frangipani were great landowners, in the *Urbs*
and outside it. In Rome their far-reaching property
extended from the Arch of Titus to the Tiber, including
with the Coelian Hill and large stretches of the Palatine,
the old Septizonium or House of the Seven Planets,
erected by Septimius Severus, from which Jacopa's
husband Graziano took his title of Settesoli. Jacopa
stands out as the very impersonation of a great Roman
lady, combining with Christian saintliness the ancient
Roman virtues. Though the Frangipani lived across
the Tiber, Jacopa must often have visited her husband's

---

[1] Paris, 1899 (reprint from *Études Francisciones*, ii, 227–242). See Sabatier's
criticisms in *Opuscules de Critique Historique*, fasc. XV, Mars 1910 (" Examen
critique des récits concernant la visite de Jacqueline de Settesoli à St. François ").

Palatine property[1] and trodden its historic paths, dimly conscious perhaps of a resemblance between herself and the Imperial ladies who had walked there in the past. Like the Empress Livia she had an excellent business head, and like Julia Domna, the Syrian wife of Septimius Severus and the patron of mystics, she was filled with an ardent curiosity regarding the things of the spirit. Her friendship with Francis is often said to date from a visit of the Saint to Rome in 1212, which it is, however, difficult to establish. Or they may have met in 1215, at the time of the Council. Joergensen has charmingly described her friendship with Francis, his feeling of ease in her home. Jacopa's house, says the great Danish writer, " c'était sa Béthanie ; Jacqueline lui était tout ensemble Marthe et Marie." Few details, however, are known of the early stages of the intimacy, which by 1217 must have been considerable, if Jacopa's lawsuit, which was settled in that year, was really dropped by the advice of Francis, whose horror of litigation is well known. The coincidence of dates is remarkable. Francis was in Rome in 1217, and the act of settlement was duly signed before notaries in that same year.

---

[1] It came into his family in 1145 by purchase from the Benedictines of Camaldoli settled in San Gregorio. The whole region took its name from the Septizonium : the elections of Innocent III and of Honorius III in San Gregorio are referred to as taking place in *Septizonio*—see Lauer, *op. cit.*, p. 194. For the Frangipani property see also Fr. Ehrle, S.J., in *Mélanges Châtelain*, Paris, 1910, p. 465, and Pietro Fedele, " Sull'origine d. Frangipani " in *Archiv. d. Reale Soc. Romanane di Storia Patria*, xxxiii. 1910, p. 493.

It is often said that Jacopa was, with St. Clare, the only woman on whose face the Saint had ever looked. But Francis had a third female devotee like Jacopa, presumably a Roman, who somehow dropped out of his history. This was the strange recluse Praxedis, whose existence has been brought to our knowledge by Celano's treatise *de Miraculis*, rediscovered in 1899.[1] Praxedis, a woman famous for her sanctity throughout the whole world (*religiosarum famosissima in Urbe ac orbe Romano*), had for love of the Heavenly Spouse lived for forty years from her tenderest infancy as an anchoress within a narrow prison, when Francis granted her a special grace, being the sole woman of whom it is recorded that he received her " into obedience," himself bestowing upon her the habit and the cord.[2] After his death he delivered her by a conspicuous miracle from the terrible straits to which an accident had reduced her. The whole story suggests that Praxedis was a spiritual intimate of Francis : *cur mihi miserrimae, quae tuam dulcissimam gratiam utcumque te uiuente promerui, non succurris?* she cries to him as she lies hunched up and helpless. One wonders in what forgotten corner

[1] By Fr. van Ortroy, Bollandist, in the Franciscan Museum at Marseilles ; see *Anal. Bolland.*, xviii. 1899, pp. 81–176. The story of Praxedis is given *de Mirac.*, 181.

[2] M. Beaufreton, *St. François*, p. 227 f., believes she was a Franciscan oblate, an institution that disappeared in 1221, and was replaced by the Order of Penitence (so-called Third Order). Fr. Cuthbert (ed. 1921), p. 474, just refers to the incident of Praxedis ; otherwise Beaufreton is, I believe, the very first writer in Franciscan subjects to have given any attention to her story, cf. his *St. François*, p. 104, note 1.

of the city the Saint came across this curious personage, whether her prison-cell was in one of the poorer quarters of the Trastevere, and whether his attention had in the first instance been directed to her by the charitable Jacopa, who lived in that part of Rome.

Francis himself was connected with the Trastevere, not that he is ever likely to have been a guest of lay folk like the Frangipani, but he stayed—in 1217, it is said—in the little Benedictine convent annexed to the Church of San Biagio, which was Anguillara property. This church was later made over to the Franciscans, through the intervention possibly of Jacopa,[1] and rededicated in honour of St. Francis. Throughout every transformation[1] San Francesco a Ripa, as it is called from the vicinity of the Tiber, retains the cell said to have been inhabited by the Saint. This contains a truly imposing collection of relics of him, arranged in a wonderful seventeenth century revolving cabinet. More interesting still is the portrait of Francis to be seen there, wearing the *capuce* and holding in his hand an open book on which are inscribed the words *quis vult venire post me abneget se ipsum et tollat suam crucem*.[2] The portrait has recently been cleaned and, by the care of Monsignor Wilpert, freed of a disfiguring

[1] Panciroli, *Tesori Nascosti*, p. 573, gives the date of the gift as 1229, and names Count Rodolfo d'Anguillara as owner of the site. An idea of what the exterior of San Francesco looked like, before the disastrous modern restorations, may be obtained from Franzini's print.

[2] This is the portrait preferred to any other by H. Thode, *Franz, v. Assisi*, i, p. 73, as best answering to the description of the Saint by Celano.

modern aureole.[1] It must be left to experts to decide
what the relation is between this portrait and the one
by Margaritone of Arezzo at Castel Fiorentino, which
it is said to resemble. According to a very old
tradition it was the gift to the church of Jacopa di
Settesoli,[2] a tradition, however, that also attaches without
the shadow of a proof to the much later portrait at
Greccio. Still another portrait that once existed in
Rome is mentioned by St. Bonaventura as in the possession of a Roman lady (*matrona quaedam*), at whose
prayer the stigmata appeared in the picture which
before had lacked them, which means that the portrait
was very old and painted before the canonisation.

In the Franciscan legend Jacopa's place has been
usurped by St. Clare. Art, as well as the Fioretti, has
made Clare the prominent, indeed the only woman knit
in sympathy with St. Francis. But in the very nature
of the case, intercourse and comradeship with an independent Roman widow must have been fuller and
freer than with the cloistered mother of a contemplative
Order. We have the proof of this in the authenticated
record by his early chronicler, Thomas of Celano, of the
momentous scene at the close of his life, when, miraculously anticipating the wishes of the Saint and forestalling
his messenger to her, she presented herself with a great

---

[1] Wilpert, *Mosaiken und Malereien*, vol. ii, p. 1151, with plate; on portraits
of St. Francis see now both the smaller and the larger monographs of Padre
Vittorino Facchinetti, O.F.M. (*Iconografia Francescana*, Milan, 1924.)

[2] Wadding, *Annales*, ii, p. 228 (ann. 1212); for the portrait at Greccio
see Sabatier, *Examen Critique*, p. 301 ff.

retinue, bearing with her all that he was requesting her to bring,—by letter[1] or otherwise,—including the cloth in which to wrap his body after death. To quote from Celano : " There was heard at the door a sound of noises, the clamour of soldiers, the thronging of a great company," and Francis hearing of the arrival, and forestalling narrow-minded objections as to *clausura*, called out with eager haste, " Blessed be God, who has guided our Brother Jacopa to us ! Open the doors and lead her in thither, for the rule concerning women is not to be observed for our Brother Jacopa ! " What follows must be told in the words of Celano himself :

" There was great rejoicing between the noble host and his guest, many spiritual greetings and much shedding of tears. And to make the miracle complete, the holy woman was found to have brought whatever the letter had already requested her to bring for the Father's obsequies. For she brought a cloth of ashen hue with which to cover the body of the departing, and many candles, and fine linen to cover his face, a pillow for his head, and a certain dish for which the Saint had hungered : all that the spirit of this man had desired, God had suggested to her. I will follow this journey to its end lest I send the noble traveller away without consolation. A multitude of people was in attendance, and in particular, a large and devoted

[1] The supposed letter is presumably apocryphal ; see Goetz, *Zur Quellengeschichte*, p. 32.

company from Rome, waiting for what should shortly
become by the death of the Saint a feast day. But his
strength was so revived by this evidence of the devotion
of Rome that he predicted that he would live a little
longer. So that lady decided that the remainder of the
company should be free to go and rest, and that she
alone would stay, with her sons and a few armed retainers.
But the Saint said, " No. I shall die on Saturday, and
you shall return with them all on Sunday." Thus
it was accomplished ; at the hour foretold, he who had
fought bravely in the Church Militant, entered the
Church Triumphant. I pass over the thronging of the
people, the voices of those who gave thanks, the solemn
ringing of the bells, the sheddings of tears. I will not
dwell upon the weeping of his children, the sobs of his
dear ones, the sighing of the brethren."

This is as vivid as a page of Livy, as crowded with
life as a relief from the Trajan Column. In a quieter
vein Celano then proceeds to describe the mourning
of Jacopa over the dead.

" She, therefore, all drenched in tears, was led
secretly apart and the body of her friend was placed in
her arms. ' Here,' said the vicar,[1] ' hold even in death
the man whom you cherished living.' She bedewed the
body with warmer tears, redoubled her mournful cries
and sobs, and renewing her embraces and caresses of the
lifeless body lifted the veil that she might see him revealed.

[1] I.e. Brother Elias of Cortona.

What more shall I say? She beheld that precious vessel in which a not less precious treasure had lain hid, adorned with its five pearls of great price."[1]

Jacopa, having penetrated the ineffable mystery of the Stigmata, ordered that it should be made manifest, and the body shown to the whole company of the devout throng without. One of those present, a young boy, afterwards a high official of the Papal court, is called by the chronicler to witness of the truth and accuracy of the recital.

One cannot but wish that Giotto, who has given the dramatic form we all know to the *Pianto delle Clarisse*, had also painted the Lament of Brother Jacopa. But by the time Giotto was working at Assisi, the story of Jacopa had been almost totally suppressed. A tamer version of it is reproduced in the *Mirror of Perfection*.[2] In St. Bonaventura's *Legenda* it is whittled down to the pious anecdote, on the level of the Fioretti, of the little lamb which the Saint gave to Jacopa, and which used to butt its mistress with its tiny horns to wake her up in the morning. Most modern biographers are agreed in supposing that the friendship was too intense, the language in which Celano tells it too direct and passionate to suit the hagiographers, who feared

[1] These translations are likewise by Miss Janet Bacon, to whom I wish to express my gratitude for the trouble she has taken to weigh the exact meaning of the mediæval Latin.

[2] The two versions of the story of Jacopa, given in *Speculum* (cap. 112) and Celano *de Mirac.* (37–39) respectively, have been critically analysed by Beaufreton, *St. François*, p. 288 ff.

it might prove a cause of scandal to the pious. Little by little, Jacopa, Praxedis, one Colomba,[1] and possibly other devoted lay-women disappeared from the Franciscan legend, where Clare the nun was left to reign supreme. But the noble episode of the friendship of Jacopa and Francis was not forgotten, and Bernard of Bessa, the secretary and successor of Bonaventura, gives us an impressive though epitomised version of the death scene,[2] and there is an allusion to it in the life of Bernard of Quintavalle in the *Annals of the Twenty-four Generals*, with the new detail of the blessing to Brother Bernard.[3] Wadding likewise preserves the story, though in an incomplete and unsatisfactory version.[4]

Since Père Édouard d'Alençon published his *Dame Jacqueline*, Jacopa has to a certain extent been reinstated in the Franciscan legend. In his edition of the *Speculum* Sabatier had perceived her importance ; [5] Father Cuthbert and M. Joergensen describe the scene at the Saint's death-bed ; M. Beaufreton dwells eloquently on Jacopa's magnificent outburst of grief over the dead body of the Saint ; and most of the popular biographies

[1] A woman of this name is said to have given to St. Francis the hermitage of Fonte Colombo ; but see Fr. Cuthbert, ed. 1921, p. 381, n. 2.

[2] *Archivio della R. Soc. Romana di Storia Patria* for 1903, pp. 207–217.

[3] *Anal. Franc.* iii, p. 42. *Cum vero beatus Franciscus gravissime infirmaretur, et domina Jacoba de Septemsoliis, nobilissima Romana quae ad eum de urbe uenerat quandam comestionem cum magna deuotione paratam Sancto Patri sedule obtulisset* (follows the blessing to Bro. Bernard).

[4] *Annales*, ii, p. 132 (ann. 1212).

[5] See his ed. of *Speculum*, p. 273 ff., w. ref. to an earlier note on Jacopa by P. Éd. d'Alençon in *Miscell. Francisc.*, iv, p. 168.

and articles brought out for the Franciscan Jubilee make sympathetic mention of her. Mr. Laurence Housman brings her into several of his delightful Franciscan plays, though he makes her almost into an Assisiate, and alas, substitutes an unfamiliar Sister Giacomina for the beloved Brother Jacopa.[1]

The charming article, contributed to the history of the Frangipani family by Pietro Fedele, under the name of "*Leopardo e Agnello di Casa Frangipani*,"[2] shows how much concerning the circles to which Jacopa belonged is still hidden in Roman archives. The story of her life and its circumstances throws light, not only on one of the most poignant episodes in the life of St. Francis, but also on the Roman society of the time, on its habits, its pleasures and pursuits, its houses, its servants, and even the things they ate,—the cakes of almond paste made in Casa Frangipani, for instance, being specially celebrated.[3] St. Francis himself partook of them with relish and asked for some as he lay sick.

After the death of Francis Jacopa apparently devoted the rest of a long life to furthering the ideals of her friend and ministering to his brethren. It is said that she resided mainly in Assisi, where one likes to think of her as being present at the canonisation of July 26, 1228, and at the laying of the foundation-stone

[1] See further Sabatier, *Life*, p. 340; Mrs. R. Goff, *Assisi of St. Francis*, pp. 36, 146, 216, 218, 242 f.

[2] In *Archivio, della R. Soc. R. di St. Patria*, xxviii. 1905, p. 207 ff.

[3] They still survive under the Italian name of *frangipane* or *marzapane*, French *massepain*, English *marzipan*.

of the great basilica which took place on the following day. She was probably in Assisi when the translation of the Saint's body from its first resting-place in S. Giorgio to the Lower Church in 1230 was accomplished in the sensational manner we all know. She may also have witnessed the ceremony of consecration by Innocent IV in 1245,[1] when by the Bull *Is qui ecclesiam* the basilica was declared *mater et caput* of the Order. And here, in the Lower Church, not far from the Tomb of the illustrious Saint who had been her loyal friend and companion, Jacopa herself was laid to rest, as recorded in the inscription :

HIC REQUIESCIT JACOPA, SANCTA
NOBILISQUE ROMANA

words of a grand simplicity that call up in Assisi those far-away days in Rome when Francis had first met his Brother Jacopa. They are permanent evidence of that " devotion of Rome " which had afforded Francis supreme and longed for consolation as he lay dying.

The very basilica built in the Saint's honour links him in quite peculiar manner to the Eternal City. To pious but narrow-minded souls its splendour has seemed alien to Franciscan ideals of humility and poverty— an insult almost to him who had wished to be known as the " little poor man." But to the more generous-minded it appears as the due of the Saint in glory.

[1] She seems to have been still alive in 1273 ; Sabatier, *Speculum*, p. 276.

It rises above the Tomb, enshrining in its triple majesty memories of the Poverello of Assisi, even as in the distant *Urbs* another and greater basilica, it, too, built over a Tomb, enshrines in yet more dazzling splendour the memory of him who had been the Fisherman of Galilee.

ADDENDA

P. 275. *speculum*, presumably the same as the classical *specula*, a sort of watch-tower.

P. 282. Fine examples of the Franciscan THAU cross at the end of the MS. with the *De reverentia Corporis Domini* in Rome (*Bibl. Valicell.* B. 24, fol. 117 v) ; another at the end of the MS. with the Blessing to Bro. Leo at the Sacro Convento in Assisi.

P. 289. *presepii* : it was long believed that St. Francis had instituted the custom ; but see Dom Leclercq in *Dict. d'Arch. Chrét.*, art. *crèche*, and for the antiquity of the " Crib " at St. Mary Major's, see Mgr. G. Biasiotti, " Riprod. della Grotta . . . di Betlem nella bas. di S.M.M." in *Dissert. Pont. Acad. Rom di Archeol.* 1920, p. 97 ff.

P. 296. *S. Francesco a Ripa* : from notes on the old foundation of S. Biagio kindly sent me by Prof. Hülsen it appears that S. Biagio still existed in 1420 by the side of the newer Franciscan foundation, and that " like many other small churches " it was only destroyed at the beginning of the sixteenth century. I omit transcribing here all the proofs accumulated by Hülsen, as his book will be out at Christmas.

Bibliography. When not otherwise stated, the ed. of Fr. Cuthbert's *St. Francis* is the first (1912). For the Latin text of Celano's three treatises I have used the ed. of P. Éd. d'Alençon (Rome, Desclée, 1906), and for English transl. of Celano I and II A. G. Ferrers-Howell's " The Lives of St. Francis of Assisi, etc.," 1908.

TWO FRANCISCAN MYSTICS: JACOPONE DA TODI AND ANGELA OF FOLIGNO

By EVELYN UNDERHILL.

TWO FRANCISCAN MYSTICS : JACOPONE DA TODI AND ANGELA OF FOLIGNO

A GREAT movement, whether religious or secular, only begins to show its full quality and power when it spreads from the founder and his first nucleus of disciples, and begins to draw in and transmute men and women of many different temperaments. It is then that we see what elements are indeed essential to it ; what new things of permanent value it has to give the race. This is supremely true of Christianity, which first shows its world-changing power when it captures St. Paul, and through him the Gentile world. It is also true of the Christian revival initiated by St. Francis. Thus, in studying the later developments of the Franciscan spirit, in observing the many types it was able to attract and transform, we are in the truest sense learning more about St. Francis himself.

There was developed among these disciples and spiritual descendants of Francis a particular and recognizable type of spiritual feeling and experience. We need not say that this sort of feeling and attitude—this special way of loving and realizing God—came into existence as the result of the Franciscan movement. There are clear traces of it in religious literature before his day. But in the souls which were formed by Francis and which tried to live by his example, it seems to have found a peculiarly favourable soil. It appears very clearly in the work of the great poet of the movement, Jacopone da Todi ; and in the mystical experiences and recorded teachings of one of the most remarkable of those women who capitulated to the Franciscan demand and kept the spirit of the Founder alive—the Blessed Angela of Foligno.

Now this special spiritual outlook embraced in its span the most transcendental and most homely aspects of religion. It included both the awestruck sense of the majesty of God and the most fervent and intimate love of Christ. Both are clearly present in Francis himself. We see him repeating all night in the house of Bernardo Quintavalle the great, unanswerable question of the adoring soul—" My God and All ! What art Thou and what am I ? " We see him before the crib at Greccio in an ecstasy of tender devotion ; or again " singing in French speech " romantic songs to his Love, or on La Verna entering with such ardent realism into the sorrow and meaning of the Passion that he bore upon his limbs the very marks of Christ. We see the same extremes in a more acute form in the poems of the far more sophisticated and learned Jacopone ; who was able to draw, as Francis could not, on all the resources of Christian philosophy. At one moment he carries us so far into the most abstract conceptions of Deity, that the mind is dazzled and we feel

the poet himself has almost exceeded the proper bounds
of speech :

O infigurabil luce,	O Inconceivable Light !
chi te può figurare,	Who can Thy secrets tell ?
ché volesti abitare	Thou Who wast fain to dwell
en la scura tenebría ?	In darkness deep and obscure !
Tuo lume non conduce	No more is Thy lantern bright
chi te veder gli pare	To guide the soul who would
potere mesurare	spell,
de te quel che sia.	Measure and mark Thee well,
Notte veggio ch'è dia,	And seize on Thine Essence pure.
virtute non se trova,	Virtue nor strength is sure ;
non sa de te dar prova	The night is turned to the day,
chi vede quel splendore.	No words, no language have they
	Thy splendour and light that
	see.[1]

At another moment we seem to be before the crib with
Francis, and hear again in Jacopone's carol the accent
of his delighted love :

Ben so che, garzoncello,	Ah, little boy, full well I know
hai perfetto sapere,	Thy wisdom is a perfect thing,
e tutto quel potere	Thy power hath as strong a wing
c'ha la perfetta etade ;	As ever rounded years possessed.
donqua, co picciolello	Ah, little one, and is it so
poteve contenere	That Thou canst hold unfaltering
tutto lo tuo volere	The will and nature of a king
en tanta vilitade ?	In such a little lowly nest ?

Or again it is the romantic aspect of Franciscan feeling
that he gives us : and we hear once more the " French-
like rejoicings " with which Francis praised the name
of Christ :

[1] This and the following quotations from Jacopone's *laude* are taken by
kind permission from the translations of Mrs. Theodore Beck.

Tal amador è fior de puritade,
nato nel campo de verginitade,
egli è lo giglio de l'umanitade,
de suavitate
e de perfetto odore.

That Lover is the flower of purity,
Born in the garden of virginity ;
He is the Lily of Humanity
Perfect of fragrance and of loveliness.

Still more in the great lyric *Amor de Caritate*, once attributed to St. Francis himself and possibly inspired by one of his songs, does Jacopone give supreme poetic form to that ardent passion of the soul for Christ which is the very heart of Franciscan spirituality :

Giá non posso vedere creatura,
al Creatore grida tutta mente ;
cielo né terra non me dá dolzura,
per Cristo amore tutto m'è fetente ;
luce de sole sí me pare oscura,
vedendo quella faccia resplendente,
cherubin son niente,
belli per ensengare,
serafin per amare,
chi vede lo Signore.

Now on no creature can I turn my
sight,
But on my Maker all my mind is set ;
Earth, sea, and sky are emptied of
delight,
For Christ's dear love all else I clean
forget :
All else seems vile, day seems as dark
as night ;
Cherubim, seraphim, in whom are
met
Wisdom and Love, must yet
Give place, give place,
To that One Face
To my dear Lord of Love.

Ché cielo e terra grida e sempre
chiama,
e tutte cose ch'io sí deggia amare ;
ciascuna dice con tutto cuor :—Ama
l'amor c'ha fatto briga d'abracciare ;
ché quello amore, però che te abrama,
tutti noi ha fatti per ad sé trare ;
veggio tanto arversare

For heaven and earth and all things
else do cry,
That Love is all my task, my life,
my place ;
Their heartfelt voices cry aloud—
" Draw nigh !
The Love that made thee, hasten
to embrace !

bontade e cortesia
de quella luce pia
che se spande de fuore.

That Love that thirsts for thee
  eternally,
  Commands us, to His arms thy soul
    to chase;
  He pours His light and grace,
      And courtesy,
      All, all on thee,
    In spreading streams of Love!"

En Cristo è nata nova creatura,
spogliato lo vechio, om fatto novello;
ma tanto l'amor monta con ardura,
lo cor par che se fenda con coltello,
mente con senno tolle tal calura,
Cristo me tra' tutto, tanto è bello!
Abracciome con ello
e per amor sí chiamo:
—Amor, cui tanto bramo,
famme morir d'amore!

Now, a new creature, I in Christ am
  born,
  The old man stripped away;—I am
  new-made;
And mounting in me, like the sun at
  morn
  Love breaks my heart, even as a
  broken blade:
Christ, First and Only Fair, from me
  hath shorn
  My will, my wits, and all that in
  me stayed,
  I in His arms am laid,
    I cry and call,—
    "O Thou my All,
  O let me die of Love!"

We may agree that the man who wrote this was indeed a true Franciscan poet; revealing in his work the breadth and depth, richness and intensity of the new spirit brought by Francis into the Christian world. We need not suppose that he experienced all that he sang; for the one hundred poems, amongst the many attributed to him, which criticism allows to be authentic, range over the whole field of spiritual experience— from the extremes of penitence to the loftiest reaches of the contemplative soul—and weave together the simplest and most philosophic aspects of religion.

Jacopone, like his younger contemporary, Angela of Foligno, was a convert ; an example of that absolute break with the past in middle age, and heroic dedication to new and difficult ideals, which sometimes occurs in the history of great souls and is seen in its most impressive form in the early Franciscan movement. He was, according to tradition, a successful and avaricious lawyer ; fond of luxury and pleasure, and hostile to religious ideas. His poetry further reveals him as a person of great artistic and literary sensibilities, and a lover of music. He possessed an active and flexible mind, capable of a wide range of interests, from political controversy to transcendental contemplation. He had the artist's power of absorbing and making his own material drawn from many different sources ; and also the vigorous and combative temper which afterwards showed itself in that passion for reform which brought him into collision with the official Church.

About the year 1268, when he would be forty years old, this prosperous worldling was abruptly converted ; joined the Third Order of St. Francis, conformed to its most severe demands, distributed all his property to the poor, and adopted the career of a wandering preacher and " minstrel of God." The well-known and dramatic story, which ascribes his conversion to the sudden death of his beautiful young wife, and the discovery that she wore under her magnificent clothes the penitent's

Plate XI.

Bassano, Museo Civico.

St. Francis receiving the Stigmata
By Benedetto Montagna.
(First half of Sixteenth Century)

hair-shirt, may well be true : but it only comes to us in a late and legendary form. What *is* true, is the thorough-going character of the conversion, however brought about : the startling completeness with which Jacopone broke with the past. Tales are told of the almost insane antics whereby he demonstrated his new contempt for the wisdom and conventions of the world, and the " folly of love " by which he was now possessed : and many of his poems express the horror and distrust of learning which was a convention among the Spiritual friars. Nevertheless, those poems themselves prove to us that he brought to the service of God, not the holy ignorance and mental destitution which he praises so highly, but an extremely well-furnished and efficient intellect. He gave to the Franciscan spirit the literary expression it required ; and gave it in the form of songs which conceal in the simple metres of vernacular hymns or *laude* the most profound religious and mystical ideas.

Poetry is a powerful missionary agent. There can be little doubt that it was through the songs of Jacopone and his many imitators that these spiritual ideas spread so quickly through Italy and beyond it, raised the level of religious thought and feeling, and disclosed a new vision of reality to countless souls. Jacopone was a highly educated man. He was able to absorb both the secular and the religious culture of his world. We find in his poems, mingled with the simplest expressions of intimate Christian feeling, and with reminiscences of

those Italian love poets who influenced Dante's youthful
work, many lofty Platonic conceptions directly derived
from St. Augustine and Dionysius the Areopagite—
two writers who seem to have been specially congenial
to him. In thus widening the area over which the
exquisite spirit bequeathed by St. Francis could find
nourishment and literary material, whilst himself remaining loyal to the principle of poverty in its most
rigid form—for he was a great leader among the Spiritual
friars—he performed a great and most necessary task.
For no religious movement arising out of the special
and intense experiences of an individual can produce
its full effect, until it thus brings in and transforms
material from outside the first circle of enthusiasm. A
simple instance among many of Jacopone's power in
this direction is seen at the end of his great poem on
Holy Poverty ; where the profound spiritual results
of that perfect destitution from possessions, external
and internal, material and mental alike, which St. Francis
held to be the secret of freedom and joy, are gathered
up and expressed :

Da onne ben sí t'ha spogliato
e de virtute spropriato,
tesaurizi el tuo mercato
en tua propria vilitate.

Emptied when thou art of Good and
Right,
Dispossest of Virtue and Delight,
Prize that bargain, clasp thy treasure
tight,
In thy lowness and humility :

Questo cielo è fabricato,
en un nihil è fondato,

—For this Heaven is built and
'stablished fast,
In the Nothingness where First is Last,

o'l'amor purificato
vive nella veritate. . . .

Where Pure Love, whence all alloy
    hath past,
    Dwelleth with Eternal Verity. . . .

Viver io e non io,
e l'esser mio non esser mio,
questo è un tal trasversío,
che non so diffinitate.

Lo, I live ! yet not my self alone ;
I am I, yet am I not mine own ;
And this change, cross-wise, obscure,
    unknown,
    —Language cannot tell its mystery.

Povertate è nulla avere
e nulla cosa poi volere ;
ed omne cosa possedere
en spirito de libertate.

Poverty has nothing in her hand,
Nothing craves, in sea, or sky, or land :
Hath the Universe at her command !
Dwelling in the heart of Liberty.

I can only speak shortly of the political and controversial side of Jacopone's varied career. We are thinking of him now as the great poet who first gave the Franciscan spirit artistic form ; and his conflicts with the ecclesiastical authorities represent that aspect of his nature which was furthest removed from St. Francis' ideals. Still, we should have no truthful picture of the real man if we ignored these episodes in his life. In his old age he became one of the leaders among the Spiritual Franciscans—the band of enthusiasts who struggled, sometimes with more fervour than common sense, to keep alive the literal observance of St. Francis' ideals. An early document calls him " one of those friars in whom Christ and His Spirit were most firmly believed to dwell," and no doubt his powerful mind and early training in the legal world, as well as his spiritual elevation, would tend to bring him into a position of dominance. His vigorous and naturally combative nature threw itself with eagerness first into the struggle between the observant and mitigated friars, and next into the degrading conflicts which raged round the election and resignation of Pope Celestine IV and the papacy of Boniface VIII.

All real mystics long to make the externals of religious life match their interior vision of the loveliness of God ; and many, like Jacopone, are forced by that vision to attack the faulty human institutions which seem to hide it from the world. Francis was himself one of the greatest and most impassioned of all reformers ; but his method was the Christ-like and pacific method of persuasive love, and he worked with the stuff of common life. Jacopone, too, was filled with a reforming zeal ; but it fed the hidden fire of his old vehement nature, and his method was the militant, uncompromising method of direct attack. Thus we are conscious in him of a discord between the active and poetic sides of his nature ; a cleavage between the poet of the love of Christ and the bitter satirist whose attacks upon Boniface VIII earned him three years of terrible imprisonment in the dungeons of Palestrina. The expert pen he had dedicated to the service of poverty was capable of a wide range of literary expression, gentle and savage, lofty and scurrilous. On one hand, it could produce the lovely Platonic hymn to Divine Love as the Wisdom and Measure of the Universe :

Amor, divino fuoco,
amor de riso e gioco,
amor non dái a poco,
ché se' ricco smesurato. . . .

O Love, Thou fire divine, of laughter
  spun ;
  Love that art smile and jest,
  Thou giv'st us of Thy best,
Thy wealth unmeasured that is never
  done. . . .

Amor dolce e suave,
de cielo, amor se'chiave ;
a porto meni nave
e campa el tempestato.

O sweet and gentle Love, Thou art
  the key
  Of heaven's city and fort :
  Steer Thou my ship to port,
And from the tempest's fury shelter
  me.

Amor che dái luce
ad omnia che luce,
la luce non è luce,
lume corporeato. . . .

Love, Giver of Light to all that fain
  would shine.
  Thy light alone is bright,
  There beams none other light,
Save with a sullen glow that is not
  Thine. . . .

Amor che dái forma
ad omnia c'ha forma,
la forma tua reforma
l'omo ch'è deformato.

Love, all things that have form are
  formed by Thee ;
  And man, whose form is bent
  In vile disfigurement,
Thou dost re-form in Thine own
  majesty.

That same pen could also lash without mercy the
corruption of the Church, and the sins, real or supposed,
of its ruler. Reading the terrible verses Jacopone
addressed to the Pope, we can hardly be surprised that
they were rewarded by imprisonment and the more
dreadful penalty of excommunication. He was released
from his dungeon in 1303, when the French troops
entered Alagna. He was an old man, and had only

three years to live ; but tradition ascribes to those three years some of the greatest of his mystical songs. His vehement spirit, which threw itself with such violence first into the quest of God and then into conflict with man, seems to have been subdued and purified in suffering : and he came out, perhaps, to a vision of life nearer to that of St. Francis, than any that his earlier years had known. The dating of his poems is conjectural, but I think these verses well represent his last phase :

—O alma nobilissima,
dinne que cose vide !
—Veggo un tal non veggio
che onne cosa me ride ;
la lengua m'è mozata
e lo pensier m'ascide,
miracolosa side
vive nel suo adorato.

(*The Auditor questions*) " Most noble
    and majestic Soul,
O tell me, tell me, what you see ? "
(*Soul*) " I see such Dark, so deep so
    blind,
That all things, ever, smile on me.
My tongue may stammer and may fail,
    My thought may stark and lifeless
      be,
      Yet Faith, that wondrous mystery,
      Can live in the Adored alone."

—Que frutti reducene
de esta tua visione ?
—Vita ordinata
en onne nazione ;
lo cor ch'era immondissimo,
enferno inferione,
de trinitá magione
letto santificato.

(*Auditor*) " And what the fruits that
    thou shalt pluck
Of this thy vision sweet and fair ? "
(*Soul*) " The fruit shall be an ordered
    life,
Redeemed and lovely everywhere.
The heart that was impure and vile,
    More deep than Hell in its despair,
    Shall be a home for love and
      prayer,—
    A mansion for the Three in One."

Se creatura pete
per lo mio amor avere,
vadane a la bontade
che l'ha distribuire,
ch'io non aggio que fare,
ella ha lo possedere,
può far lo suo piacere,
ché lo s'ha comparato.

O Creatures, if ye now should come
For my affection clamouring,
Go to that Goodness, Whose it is,
Who holds it for distributing.
He all my being doth possess,
I am not lord of anything;
For He may do His pleasuring
With what He bought to be His
own.

Now we come to our second great example of the transforming and life-giving power of the Franciscan spirit. If in Jacopone it made from what seems unpromising material a great poet of the Love of God, in his younger contemporary, Angela of Foligno, it made from still more unpromising material a supreme mystic and mother of souls. Angela was a woman who belonged like Jacopone to the prosperous middle class; who lived like Jacopone till early middle age in apparent contentment with the ideals and satisfactions of her world; who like Jacopone was seized and transmuted by the mysterious alchemy of the Cross, and became one of the great creative spirits of the Franciscan revival. Until the last few years, Angela of Foligno was little more than a name to us; perhaps not even that, except to specialists in religious history. Even now, she is only beginning to be appreciated at her full worth by the small circle of readers which is interested in the literature of mystical experience, or finds its own spiritual nourishment in the teachings of the saints. Yet this woman, the contemporary of Dante, had visions not unworthy of the attention of

that supreme poet ; she developed to a high degree
the mystic's power of spiritual creativeness ; her friends
and pupils called her a Mistress of Theologians, and she
exercised at the height of her development a formative
influence on some of the most spiritual personalities of
her day. The still unfinished researches of the Franciscan scholar, Père Ferré, to whose published results
I am greatly indebted, are doing much to help us to
realize Angela as a vivid and most human personality :
the critical edition of her works now being prepared
will restore her to her rightful place among the great
Catholic mystics.

If we are short of authentic material for the reconstruction of Jacopone's life, and do not really know
much save by inference of his personality, or the inner
and outer events which turned a successful lawyer into
a troubadour of God, this complaint cannot be made
in Angela's case. Born about 1248, she died in 1309.
Nine years later, the narrative of her revelations and
teaching was seen and approved by Cardinal Jacopo
Colonna. Few converts have given a more detailed
and coherent account of their own development, and
few records of religious experience have come down to
us in a more authentic form. There still exists in the
Communal Library at Assisi a little MS which was
certainly written in the first half of the 14th century,
and contains a full account of her life, visions, and
doctrine, with many realistic details that the printed
editions of her works suppress. It is called " The Book

of Sister Lella of Foligno of the 3rd Order of St. Francis "; a title which seems to carry with it a homely and reassuring sense of reality. The Blessed Angela in her great moments, when she is struggling to tell us of her apprehensions of God, may seem a remote and awe-inspiring figure. But the Sister Lella of this document is some one whom we can all understand. She is just one of the countless men and women who have fallen under the spell of the Franciscan spirit, and achieved in its strength a new and life-giving life. We identify her without difficulty with the tiny, fragile creature whose body in its little grey silk dress and white veil still lies in a glass sarcophagus above her altar in the church of Foligno.

The spiritual history of Sister Lella falls into three distinct divisions; which it is tempting to identify with the three stages of the traditional Mystic Way—Purgation, Illumination, and Union. The first stage began with her conversion, about the year 1285, when she was 37 years old. It lasted six years. The next, which opens with her celebrated vision on the road between Spello and Assisi in 1291, lasted about four or five years; and to this most of her great ecstatic experiences belong. During her last period, from about the year 1297—when she was approaching 50 years of age—till her death, we see her in her creative aspect; turning away from her own subjective experiences, which have now performed their educative office and prepared her for the work of a mother of souls.

We begin then, as she begins her own story, with a picture of the unregenerate Angela, between 35 and 40 years old. She was then a prosperous married woman, living in the little town of Foligno with her husband and sons. There was nothing about her to suggest that she was destined to be one of the greatest followers of Francis. She was fond of comfort, fine clothes, good food and pleasure. Her vanity was not satisfied by social success. She also desired a reputation for piety, without paying the price ; and confesses it with disarming candour. It seems likely that she was already in name but not in fact a Franciscan Tertiary ; and made an elaborate pretence of living up to her obligations.

" I caused it to be told to those whom I had bidden to my house that I ate neither fish nor meat. . . . I diligently made an outward show of being poor, but caused many sheets and coverlets to be put where I lay down to sleep and taken up in the morning so that none might see them. . . . During the whole of my life I have studied how I might obtain the fame of sanctity."

We must agree that the outlook for Sister Lella's soul at this stage was not promising. Yet not much more than ten years separated this masterpiece of self-indulgent insincerity from the great saint and mystic who was the mother of many spiritual sons, and who worked in the tempestuous soul of Ubertino da Casale a complete spiritual renovation. We have in her a wonderful example of the re-making of human personality, the liberation of its hidden greatness, achieved through the literal pursuit of Franciscan poverty.

Angela ascribes the beginning of her conversion to her growing uneasiness over certain grave sins which she had never confessed ; although, as part of her general religious pretence, she continued to go to the sacraments. We do not know what these sins were ; but as she afterwards enumerated frivolous running and walking, smelling flowers and wearing fancy shoes, amongst her crimes, we need not suppose anything of a very dreadful nature. She prayed to St. Francis, the natural friend of all uneasy spirits, begging him to send her a confessor to whom she could dare to speak ; and that same night he appeared in a dream—significant dreams played a large part in Angela's spiritual life— and said to her, " Sister, had you asked me sooner, I had sooner granted your request ! " The next morning, returning from Mass at the Franciscan Church, she went into the Cathedral ; and there, seeing in the pulpit her cousin, or perhaps uncle, Arnaldo, a friar minor and chaplain to the Bishop of Foligno, she at once recognized in him the confessor by whom she was to be absolved. After this she tried, in spite of family opposition, to live in a more Christian way ; and at least to fulfil the bare obligations of a Franciscan Tertiary as regards simplicity of life, renouncing her magnificent clothes and delicate food. Few mystics

Y*

have exhibited to us as clearly as she does that gradual and difficult re-making of human personality, that solid unsensational process of self-conquest, which forms the first stage in every real and enduring spiritual life. She tells us how it was forced upon her, in spite of her natural reluctances, that she must " choose the thorny path " of absolute detachment from possessions and desires ; and how, bit by bit, with many hesitations, she gave up all that she most loved, till at last she achieved that perfect Franciscan poverty which was the ideal of the Spiritual Friars.

It took five years for this stage to be reached ; by which time Angela was living in great retirement with one companion near the Franciscan church at Foligno. Her husband, children, and mother had all died within three years of her conversion, swept away perhaps by the pestilence which visited from time to time the Umbrian towns : and she no doubt appeared to her neighbours to be merely one of those middle-aged widows who had repented of a worldly past and given the rest of their lives to the service of God. There was nothing to distinguish her from the numerous Franciscan tertiaries who formed the backbone of the religious laity in Umbria at this time. Inwardly she says that she had now trodden twenty of those thirty steps on the Way of the Cross which lay between her conversion and her full mystical development. This characteristically Franciscan conception is obviously derived from the 30 hidden years of the Life of

Christ ; and we notice here the intensely Evangelical and Christocentric character of Franciscan mysticism, how close it keeps to the symbolism of the New Testament.

I emphasize this long quiet time of inward travail, because it is something which we can all understand, and which shows us how homely and how human is the material out of which a mystical saint is made : how the Franciscan spirit works in, and gradually transforms, the common faulty stuff of human nature, and makes of it a new thing. Jacopone da Todi was one instance of this : Angela is another. Her account is full of little revealing glimpses of the struggle between the ingrained love of comfort and the nascent love of God—the natural and the supernatural self—which remind us that the real life of the Spirit has at least as much to do with will as with feeling and belief.

"I reflected and *obliged* myself to wish to do penance . . . I *determined* to forsake everything . . . all my friends dissuaded me from this thing. But at last the Divine Mercy sent a great illumination into my heart. . . . So then I resolved in good earnest."

That resolution, and the distribution of her property which put it into effect, mark the close of Angela's first phase. The second opens with the great vision on the road to Assisi, which is the most celebrated of her experiences. She tells us how, having almost finished the giving of her goods to the poor, she said to God, " Lord, that which I do, I do only that I may find Thee ; wherefore, having done it, grant me the grace that I may find Thee "—and to this prayer she seemed to herself to receive the amazing answer, " When thou hast accomplished that which thou art doing, the whole Trinity will descend unto thee."

The fulfilment of this promise came abruptly, as she walked with a number of pious women going on pilgrimage to the shrine of St. Francis at Assisi. She had just renewed her vows as a Franciscan Tertiary, and was praying to St. Francis that she might serve his order well. The result is told best in her own words :

" Now when I was come to that place which lieth between Spello and the narrow road which leadeth upward unto Assisi, and is beyond Spello, it was said unto me :

" ' Thou hast prayed unto My servant Francis, and I have not willed to send thee another messenger. I am the Holy Spirit, who am come unto thee to bring thee such consolation as thou hast never before tasted. And I will go with thee even unto Saint Francis. I shall be within thee, and but few of those who are with thee will perceive it. I will bear thee company and will speak with thee all the way ; I will make no end to my speaking. And thou wilt not be able to attend unto any save unto Me, for I have bound thee and will not depart from thee until thou comest for the second time unto Saint Francis. Then will I depart from thee in so far as this present consolation is concerned, but in no other manner will I ever leave thee, and thou shalt love Me.' "

" I can never describe," says Angela, " the joy and sweetness I felt, especially when He said, ' I am the Holy Spirit who am entering into thee.' "

Absorbed in this secret conversation, she came to Assisi, made her first station in the Church, and dined with her fellow-pilgrims, without betraying anything of the overwhelming experiences which were taking place in her soul. Going back into the Church for the second time, however, she felt the sense of the Divine Presence gradually passing from her : leaving her in such grief and desolation, that she fell upon the ground uttering loud inarticulate cries. All her fellow-pilgrims and the friars ran to her in alarm ; and among them her cousin Arnaldo, now a friar of the Convent of St. Francis. Horrified to discover in a member of his respectable family the cause of this disgraceful scene, he told his relative, with some sharpness, to return home and refrain from disturbances in church.

But meeting Angela a little later in Foligno, and questioning her as to the cause of her strange conduct, Arnaldo discovered with amazement that he had to do, not with a hysterical woman, but with a great ecstatic. Then began a collaboration to which we owe one of the masterpieces of Christian mysticism. Between 1291 and 1296—the period of her mystical formation—

Arnaldo wrote at his cousin's dictation all that she was able to tell or he to understand of her great visions and experiences of God ; visions which seem to owe nothing to reading or theological instruction, and yet show an amazing intuitive grasp of religious and philosophical truth. I do not think Père Ferré goes too far when he compares these revelations with those of St. Teresa herself. No doubt both these mystics owed much—more than they knew—to their religious background, and to such theological ideas as inevitably reached them through sermons, conversations, and similar channels. Angela, as a member of a religious corporation saturated in mystical ideas, can hardly fail to have absorbed to some extent the colour of her environment. But even so, the ten great visions of the Being of God which she poured into Arnaldo's astonished ears must be given a high place in the literature of direct religious experience.

" The eyes of my soul were opened and I beheld the plenitude of God, whereby I did comprehend the whole world, both here and beyond the sea, and the abyss and all things else ; and therein I beheld naught save the divine power in a manner assuredly indescribable, so that through excess of marvelling the soul cried with a loud voice, saying, ' This whole world is full of God ! ' Wherefore I now comprehended that the world is but a small thing ; I saw, moreover, that the power of God was above all things, and that the whole world was filled with it."

" There was a time when my soul was exalted to behold God with so much clearness that never before had I beheld Him so distinctly. But love did I not see here so fully ; rather I lost that which I had before and was left without love. Afterwards I saw Him darkly ; and this darkness was the greatest blessing that could be imagined, and no thought could conceive aught that would equal this."

" Then was there given unto the soul an assured faith, a firm and certain hope, wherein I felt so sure of God that all fear left me. For by that blessing which came with the darkness I did collect my thoughts and was made so sure of God that I can never again doubt but that I do of a certainty possess Him."

" Here, likewise, do I see all Good ; and seeing it, the soul cannot think that it will depart from it or it from the Good, or that in future it must ever leave the Good. The soul delighteth unspeakably therein, yet it beholdeth naught which can be related by the tongue or imagined in the heart. It seeth nothing, yet seeth all things, because it beholdeth this Good darkly—and the more darkly and secretly the Good is seen, the more certain is it, and excellent above all things."

" Unto this most high power of beholding God ineffably through such great darkness was my spirit uplifted but three times only and no more ; and although I beheld Him countless times, and always darkly, yet never in such an high manner and through such great darkness."

" All that I say of this seemeth unto me to be nothing, I even feel as though I offended in speaking of it ; for so greatly doth that Good exceed all my

words that my speech doth appear to blaspheme
against it."

We can still share the bewilderment of Fra Arnaldo,
when an elderly widow as yet unsuspected of an excessive spirituality, poured forth these amazing experiences ;
with their apparent reminiscences of Christian Platonism,
their exalted theological outlook, and complete aloofness
from the commonplaces of popular devotion. Even
though we accept the substance of Angela's revelations
as inspired, we have still to account for the philosophic
aptness of the language with which she tries to clothe
them—language which takes us direct to the sources
of mystical theology in St. Augustine and Dionysius
the Areopagite, and which we cannot, without straining
probability, suppose her to have invented for herself.

Now here, I believe, is the point of contact between
our two mystics. Jacopone da Todi, 20 years Angela's
senior, and having his headquarters at Todi but a
few miles from Foligno, was already famous as a poet
and leader of the Spiritual Franciscans at the time when
her revelations began. Many of his *laude* were used
as hymns at gatherings of the Tertiaries and other
religious confraternities. We may be sure that they
were familiar to all fervent Franciscans of the Umbrian
plain ; and that Angela, who may well have known him
at first-hand, is certain to have received the influence of
his works. When we reflect on the amount of potted
theology, as well as less desirable matter, which the

persevering use even of " Hymns Ancient and Modern " can instil into the mind, we find here at least a plausible explanation for the startlingly metaphysical—and, if I may so put it, extremely unfeminine—character of Angela's conception of God. Jacopone, we know, with the poet's instinct for suggestive image, seized and wove into his poetry many of the paradoxical ideas of Dionysius and Augustine. Angela, quick to recognize anything that would express the inexpressible, would find in his *laude* the language she required.

And if this be so, we have here a very interesting example of the way in which religious truth is spread ; the completing parts which can be played in this process by literature and by vision—by the interaction of various temperaments and gifts. St. Francis, that exquisitely sensitive instrument for the revelation of the love of God—the adoring poet and humble penitent, the bridegroom of Lady Poverty, Brother of the Birds, and devoted servant of the Cross—brings to the world and leaves in the world a new spirit. That spirit first touches and transforms a hard-headed and combative lawyer, worldly and self-indulgent ; turning him from unreal to real interests, making of him the supreme singer of the heights and depths of mystical love. Then it seizes upon a very ordinary, self-regarding, vain and comfort-loving woman ; pressing her to walk in the way of the Cross, and making her first a deep gazer into the secrets of the Divine Nature, and then a great and self-forgetful mother and teacher of souls. And just because the poet and scholar followed his special vocation, the mystic and spiritual shepherdess was the better able to follow hers. For it is one of the great discoveries of Christianity—and a discovery which the Franciscan movement demonstrates with a special vividness and power—that no saint ever stands alone ; and no fruitful knowledge of God is ever won or imparted in isolation from other men.